D0148019

In the
Field

Guided Field Assignments
and Readings
in Early Childhood Education

Join us on the web at

EarlyChildEd.delmar.com

In the
Field

Guided Field Assignments
and Readings
in Early Childhood Education

Kent Chrisman & Donna Couchenour

THOMSON

DELMAR LEARNING ™ Australia Canada Mexico Singapore Spain United Kingdom United States

THOMSON

DELMAR LEARNING

In the Field: Guided Field Assignments and Readings
in Early Childhood Education
Kent Chrisman and Donna Couchenour

Vice President, Career Education Strategic Business Unit:
Dawn Gerrain

Director of Learning Solutions:
John Fedor

Managing Editor:
Robert L. Serenka, Jr.

Acquisitions Editor:
Christopher Shortt

Product Manager:
Philip Mandl

Editorial Assistant:
Alison Archambault

Director of Production:
Wendy A. Troeger

Production Manager:
Mark Bernard

Content Project Manager:
Angela Iula

Technology Project Manager:
Sandy Charette

Director of Marketing:
Wendy E. Mapstone

Channel Manager:
Kristin McNary

Channel Manager:
Scott Chrysler

Art Director:
Joy Kocsis

© 2008 Thomson Delmar Learning, a part of the Thomson Corporation. Thomson, the Star logo and Delmar Learning are trademarks used herein under license.

Printed in the United States

1 2 3 4 5 XXX 11 10 09 08 07

For more information contact Delmar Learning,
5 Maxwell Drive, PO Box 8007, Clifton Park, NY 12065-2919.

Or you can visit our Internet site at http://www.delmarlearning.com.

ALL RIGHTS RESERVED. No part of this work covered by the copyright hereon may be reproduced or used in any form or by any means—graphic, electronic, or mechanical, including photocopying, recording, taping, Web distribution or information storage and retrieval systems—without written permission of the publisher.

For permission to use material from this text or product, submit a request online at http://www.thomsonrights.com
Any additional questions about permissions can be submitted by email to thomson rights@thomson.com

Library of Congress Cataloging-in-Publication Data
Chrisman, Kent.
In the field : guided field assignments and readings in early childhood education / Kent Chrisman & Donna Couchenour.
  p. cm.
Includes bibliographical references and index.
ISBN-13: 978-1-4180-5371-0
ISBN-10: 1-4180-5371-6
1. Student teaching—United States. 2. Early childhood education—United States. I. Couchenour, Donna L. (Donna Lee), 1950- II. Title.
LB2157.U5C47 2008
372.21--dc22
                                          2007026609

NOTICE TO THE READER

Publisher does not warrant or guarantee any of the products described herein or perform any independent analysis in connection with any of the product information contained herein. Publisher does not assume, and expressly disclaims, any obligation to obtain and include information other than that provided to it by the manufacturer.

The reader is expressly warned to consider and adopt all safety precautions that might be indicated by the activities herein and to avoid all potential hazards. By following the instructions contained herein, the reader willingly assumes all risks in connection with such instructions.

The Publisher makes no representation or warranties of any kind, including but not limited to, the warranties of fitness for particular purpose or merchantability, nor are any such representations implied with respect to the material set forth herein, and the publisher takes no responsibility with respect to such material. The Publisher shall not be liable for any special, consequential, or exemplary damages resulting, in whole or part, from the readers' use of, or reliance upon, this material.

The authors and Thomson Delmar Learning affirm that the Web site URLs referenced herein were accurate at the time of printing. However, due to the fluid nature of the Internet, we cannot guarantee their accuracy for the life of this edition.

Contents

Chapter 3

PROFESSIONAL BEHAVIORS IN FIELD SETTINGS   75

Chapter 4

THE SCIENCE OF TEACHING AND LEARNING   89

Chapter 5

THE ART OF TEACHING 129

Chapter 6

TEACHING CONTENT IN EARLY CHILDHOOD EDUCATION 153

Chapter 7

PARTNERSHIPS WITH FAMILIES AND COMMUNITIES   173

Chapter 8

UNDERSTANDING THE GOALS AND ROLES OF SUPERVISION IN FIELD PLACEMENTS AND STUDENT TEACHING   191

List of Field Assignments

Preface

The purposes for writing *In the Field: Guided Field Assignments and Readings in Early Childhood Education* include the following: (1) to provide published information especially designed for high-quality field placement experiences in early childhood settings, (2) to recognize the importance of field experiences in the preparation of early childhood teachers, and (3) to assist students in reflecting on observations, classroom participation, and teaching experiences during field work in early childhood settings.

The authors of this text have written chapters that discuss a range of professional preparation topics for early childhood settings, including best teaching practices in content areas, working with families, and responding to supervision. Each chapter is written to be useful in a variety of two- and four-year preparation programs. Those who will find the this textbook helpful include the following:

- students in associate degree programs that have field assignments in child care and school age programs
- students enrolled in baccalaureate degree programs that have field assignments in child care, prekindergarten, kindergarten, and primary grades
- graduate students who are in initial certification programs
- mentors of early childhood education students
- university faculty serving as field supervisors
- administrators
- professional development coordinators

It is the hope of the authors that this book travels with students from semester to semester as they observe, participate, and teach in a variety of field experiences. Faculty may find that *In the Field* is useful as a stand-alone text for some courses or as a companion book in other early childhood courses. The format includes sections of content for reading and activities for writing that are designed to be adaptable in many kinds of field assignments. Each chapter includes objectives, resources, references to current literature, and field assignments. The text also includes a CD resource, an instructor's manual, and a student online companion guide.

ANCILLARIES

CD-ROM

The CD-ROM that accompanies *In the Field* contains editable versions of every field assignment contained in the text. Users of *In the Field* can complete the field assignments electronically or print each field assignment as needed.

Instructor's Manual

The instructor's manual that accompanies *In the Field* has the following sections:

■ alignment of the Interstate New Teacher Assessment and Support Consortium (INTASC) principles with the National Association for the Education of Young Children (NAEYC) standards for early childhood teacher preparation and professional development

■ alignment of National Board for Professional Teaching Standards (NBPTS) with NAEYC advanced standards and essential tools

■ field assignments from *In the Field*, classified by NAEYC standards

■ rubrics (based on NAEYC standards for professional preparation) for use with each field assignment

■ a list of related readings

Student Online Companion

The student online companion provides web sites that are additional to those listed in the textbook for students to use as they complete field experiences in early childhood education settings. The authors have also provided guides for selecting and using sources from the web.

The student online companion can be accessed at http://www.earlychilded.delmar.com.

Acknowledgments

The authors gratefully acknowledge the work of the following reviewers in the preparation of this text. Without their efforts, the text would have undoubtedly been less useful to readers.

Linda Anderson Welsh, MA,
Austin Community College,
Texas

Georgianna Duarte, PhD,
University of Texas
at Brownsville

Amy Huffman, MA,
Guilford Technical Community College,
North Carolina

Ron Wahlen, MEd,
Shaw University,
North Carolina

Elizabeth A. Jenkins, MEd,
Orlando Tech, Orange County Public Schools,
Florida

Gail Goldstein, MEd,
Central New Mexico Community College

Linda Gamble, MEd,
University of Maine
at Farmington

Lois Wachtel, BA,
Director, Temple Sinai Pre-School,
Florida

We also readily acknowledge the support and assistance of the editorial staff at Thomson Delmar Learning, especially Erin O'Connor and Philip Mandl.

Chapter 1

Early Childhood Education and Field Experiences

Objectives

After reading and reflecting on this chapter, early childhood students will be able to:

- Explain the purpose for field work in early childhood teacher preparation
- Discuss the characteristics of effective field assignments
- Understand the need for participating in field assignments in various high-quality field sites
- Participate in methods for including field experience discussion and assessment in academic coursework

Introduction

For decades, teacher educators have specified the importance of both strong academic preparation and exemplary clinical field experiences to effectively prepare teachers. However, in contemporary early childhood teacher preparation, multiple challenges exist in relation to connecting what we know to be best practice with young children, to teaching about best practice in college classrooms and professional development venues, and to providing candidates with examples of such practice in the field. Therefore, it is essential that such teacher preparation programs include field assignments that require deep knowledge and critical reflection by interns or student teachers. In addition, such assignments must be integral to academic course discussions and assessment procedures.

WHAT ARE THE PURPOSES
OF FIELD EXPERIENCES?

Early childhood teacher preparation programs, almost universally, are planned to provide future, or pre-service, teachers with a knowledge base, skills, and dispositions that are acquired from both college courses and field experiences in a variety of early childhood settings. College courses are sometimes referred to as *academic preparation,* and field experiences are described as *practical preparation.* The reality is that the integration of *both* the theoretical and the practical is vital to all aspects of teacher preparation. For example, in early childhood education settings, observers may express concern that children are playing or that the teacher does not frequently use direct whole-group teaching methods. Many Child Development or Introduction to Early Childhood Education courses provide information to knowledgeable pre-service teachers about what and how children learn through play, such as mathematical concepts as they build with blocks, scientific concepts in a discovery center, and literacy skills in pretend play areas. Also, curriculum courses in the early childhood teacher preparation program are likely to point out the need for teachers to use a variety of active learning strategies with young children to best meet all of their needs. Thus, the well-informed early childhood education student interprets his or her observation differently than one who sees *children who are just playing* and *teachers who aren't teaching.* A primary purpose of field experience for early childhood teacher preparation is to provide a context for connecting theoretical understanding and practical experiences.

WHAT DO WE MEAN BY "FIELD
EXPERIENCES" OR "FIELD WORK"?

Most field experience is assigned as a part of coursework or through a pre-service teacher's professional preparation program. Although volunteer (that is, not assigned or required) service is extremely valuable, such experiences are typically helpful to the school or other educational setting, but they are not designed around either standards for best practice with young children or standards that guide early childhood teacher preparation. When students independently seek volunteer experiences related to early childhood education, the following guidelines for selecting sites may be useful to ensure that such volunteer experience helps to enhance their professional development:

■   If you are considering volunteer work in child care, look for a center that is accredited by the National Association for the Education of Young Children (NAEYC) or a family center that is accredited by the National Association for Family Child Care (NAFCC). Although accreditation does not guarantee that best practices are always in place, teachers and care-givers typically have knowledge of child development and high-quality early education as well as a sense of professionalism. Also, pre-service teachers could search for teachers and caregivers who have formal prep-aration in early childhood education; such educators are likely to have a Child Development Associate (CDA) credential, an associate degree in early childhood education or child development, or a bachelor's degree in early childhood education or child development.

- If you are considering volunteer work in kindergarten or a primary grade, look for a teacher who has specialized early childhood education certification—not only elementary education credentials. Early child-hood certification does not guarantee that you will exclusively observe best practices, but early childhood teachers typically understand child development and high-quality kindergarten and primary teaching as well as the profession of early childhood education.

- If you are considering volunteer work in an agency or faith-based set-ting, interview the director or supervisor about goals for children and families. Listen for responses that demonstrate an understanding of the importance of families in children's lives as well as a sensitivity to diverse families.

When field assignments are made as a requirement of your teacher preparation program, your course instructor might have a specific field site or some available choices of field sites for you. Types of field work that are assigned by early childhood teacher educators include the following:

- conducting guided observations of children, families, teachers, and class-room activities
- assisting teachers in various settings with children, families, or both
- attending family meetings, such as Parent-Teacher Association (PTA), Parent-Teacher Organization (PTO), or policy council meetings
- attending local school board meetings or center advisory board meetings
- attending Individualized Education Plan (IEP) meetings or other meet-ings in which families and professional staff collaborate to meet a child's needs
- tutoring individual or small groups of children
- teaching a small group of children with a teacher-planned lesson (may be child-directed, such as in a learning center, or teacher-directed)
- planning a lesson and teaching a small group of children (may be child-directed, such as in a learning center, or teacher directed)
- participating in an agency that provides services for children and fami-lies, such as a family resource center or parent-to-parent groups
- conducting supervised applied research

■ intensive experiences such as practica or student teaching that require multiple levels of observation and participation whereby pre-service teachers are immersed in an early education setting

In order to be effective learning situations, field experiences that are required for course or training credit are typically structured to provide pre-service teachers support in their observation or participation. Such assignments often include a written report that will be submitted to the college course instructor so that students are required to demonstrate their understanding of the experience through reflective self-evaluation. These reports are then assessed based on the objectives or goals for the course. The goals are often related to national standards for early childhood teacher preparation programs such as those designated by the NAEYC and the National Council for Accreditation of Teacher Education (NCATE). The NAEYC standards, applicable to two-year, four-year and graduate programs, are briefly described in Figure 1–1. See Appendix A for NAEYC's detailed statements regarding Associate (2-year), Initial (4-year), and Advanced (graduate) Standards. Figure 1–2 contains a form to be used for recording your various field experiences. On this form, record the type of field experience, the time and date, the name and location of the field site, a description of your observation or participation, and the NAEYC program standard to which each field experience relates. If more information than is available in Figure 1–1 is needed about the standards, see Appendix A (NAEYC Standards for Initial Licensure, Advanced, and Associate Degree Programs).

Field experiences support observation and participation

Standard 1: *Promoting Child Development and Learning*
Pre-service teachers use their understanding of young children's characteristics and needs, and of multiple interacting influences on children's development and learning, to create environments that are healthy, respectful, supportive, and challenging for all children.

Standard 2: *Building Family and Community Relationships*
Pre-service teachers know about, understand, and value the importance and complex characteristics of children's families and communities. They use this understanding to create respectful, reciprocal relationships that support and empower families and to involve all families in their children's development and learning.

Standard 3: *Observing, Documenting, and Assessing to Support Young Children and Families*
Pre-service teachers know about and understand the goals, benefits, and uses of assessment. They know about and use systematic observations, documentation, and other effective assessment strategies in a responsible way, in partnership with families and other professionals, to positively influence children's development and learning.

Standard 4: *Teaching and Learning*
Pre-service teachers integrate their understanding of and relationships with children and families, their understanding of developmentally effective approaches to teaching and learning, and their knowledge of academic disciplines to design, implement, and evaluate experiences that promote positive development and learning for all children.

4a: *Connecting with Children and Families. Pre-service teachers know, understand, and use positive relationships and supportive interactions as the foundation for their work with young children.*

4b: *Using Developmentally Effective Approaches. Pre-service teachers know, understand, and use a wide array of effective approaches, strategies, and tools to positively influence children's development and learning.*

4c: *Understanding Content Knowledge in Early Education. Pre-service teachers understand the importance of each content area in young children's learning. They know the essential concepts, inquiry tools, and structure of content areas, including academic subjects, and can identify resources to deepen their understanding.*

4d: *Building Meaningful Curriculum. Pre-service teachers use their own knowledge and other resources to design, implement, and evaluate meaningful, challenging curriculum that promotes comprehensive developmental and learning outcomes for all young children.*

Standard 5: *Becoming a Professional*
Pre-service teachers identify and conduct themselves as members of the early childhood profession. They know and use ethical guidelines and other professional standards related to early childhood practice. They are continuous, collaborative learners who demonstrate knowledgeable, reflective, and critical perspectives on their work making informed decisions that integrate knowledge from a variety of sources. They are informed advocates for sound educational practices and policies.

Figure 1–1 National Standards for Early Childhood Education Teacher Preparation Programs (Source: National Association for the Education of Young Children)

Field Assignment 1–1 Record of Various Field Experiences

Type	Date(s) and times	Location of field site (include name of school or center)	Description of activity completed at the field site	NAEYC standard number addressed
Conduct guided observation of child				
Conduct guided observation of family				
Conduct guided observation of teacher				
Conduct guided observation of classroom				
Assist teacher with children				
Assist teacher with families				
Attend family meeting				
Attend school board meeting				
Attend advisory board meeting				
Attend IEP meeting				
Attend collaboration meeting				
Tutor				
Teach small group				

(continues)

Field Assignment 1–1 (continued)

Type	Date(s) and times	Location of field site (include name of school or center)	Description of activity completed at the field site	NAEYC standard number addressed
Plan and teach small group				
Participate in agency activities				
Conduct supervised applied research				
Complete a practicum or internship				
Perform student teaching				
Other				

An electronic version of each field assignment is available on the CD-ROM that accompanies this text.

The NCATE provides standards and evaluates teacher preparation programs that lead to state licensure. This Council has provided specifics related to quality field experiences and clinical practice for teacher preparation programs. Some of these guidelines include the following:

■ The participating early childhood program, school, or center collaborates with the institution providing teacher preparation to provide resources and expertise in implementing positive learning experiences for pre-service teachers.

■ Early childhood professionals in both settings (university and early childhood program, school, or center) share professional development activities and educational programs for children and for pre-service teachers.

■ Specific placements for pre-service teachers are decided jointly by professionals in field sites and those in the teacher preparation program.

■ Field site professionals and teacher preparation faculty are accomplished early childhood professionals who continue in their own professional development as they mentor and supervise pre-service teachers.

■ Field experiences must be designed and sequenced in order to best support the pre-service teacher's professional development.

- All field experiences will encourage pre-service teachers to apply and reflect on their knowledge, skills, and dispositions as they become teachers.

- Pre-service teachers both observe and are observed by others.

- Pre-service teachers interact with field site and teacher preparation personnel as well as with their peers. Such interactions focus on their knowledge, skills, and dispositions as they become teachers.

- Pre-service teachers engage in a variety of activities that lead to furthering their professional development in early childhood education.

- Pre-service teachers collect data from children's learning, analyze the data, reflect on their own teaching, and make decisions to improve children's learning.

- Multiple forms of assessment are used to evaluate pre-service teacher learning.

- Pre-service teachers participate in a variety of early childhood settings with opportunities to explore and expand their own knowledge, skills, and dispositions.

- Pre-service teachers gain experience with diverse groups of children and families.

- Pre-service teachers participate in field experiences that provide the following types of experiences:
  - Children with identified exceptionalities
  - Children of different ages (birth to eight years)
  - Children from various locales (rural, urban, suburban)
  - Children from families of varying economic levels

Field Assignments 1–2 and 1–3 provide lists for you to consider and complete in relation to your early childhood teacher preparation field experiences.

Field Assignment 1–2 NCATE Guidelines for Collaboration with Field Placements

For each item, enter an example that provides evidence that the guideline has been met.

- Personnel from the teacher preparation institution and the field site collaborate in the operation of the field experience for pre-service teachers. Early childhood professionals in both settings ensure that pre-service teachers observe and participate in developmentally effective instruction and assessment with young children.

Example(s):

- Early childhood professionals in both settings share professional development activities and educational programming for children and for pre-service teachers. Engaging in ongoing professional development through conference attendance, coursework, research, presenta-

(*continues*)

Field Assignment 1–2 (continued)

tion, and publication is essential for professionals who are responsible for working with early childhood pre-service teachers in the field.

Example(s):

• Placements are specifically selected and decided jointly by early childhood professionals on campus and at the field site. Collaborative efforts to provide high-quality field experience for pre-service teachers is essential.

Example(s):

• Personnel on campus and in the field site are accomplished early childhood professionals who continue their ongoing professional development. Credentials include state teaching certification in early childhood education and advanced degrees in early childhood education, child development, or a related field. Experience in teaching young children in high-quality early education settings is also expected.

Example(s):

• Field experiences are designed and sequenced in collaboration to best support pre-service early childhood teachers' professional development. Field experiences are designed to provide guidance to early childhood students in order to make each assignment meaningful. Sequencing of field experiences typically moves pre-service teachers from less interaction with children (observation or participant observation) to more interaction that is planned and assessed.

Example(s):

An electronic version of each field assignment is available on the CD-ROM that accompanies this text.

Field Assignment 1–3 NCATE Guidelines for Pre-service Teachers and Field Experiences

In early childhood education field experiences, pre-service teachers:
• apply knowledge, skills, and dispositions

• reflect on their ability to apply knowledge, skills, and dispositions

• are observed by others (experienced teachers, pre-service teachers, personnel from collaborating institutions)

• observe others (both in-service and pre-service teachers)

• interact with
  – field site professionals

(continues)

Field Assignment 1–3 (continued)

- teacher preparation institution professionals
- peers
• engage in a variety of professional development activities
List _____

_____
_____

• collect data about children's learning

• analyze data about children's learning

• use data about children's learning to plan and teach

• reflect on your own teaching and make decisions for change or follow-up

• observe and use multiple forms of assessment
List _____

_____
_____

• observe and participate in a variety of early childhood education settings (for children from birth through third grade)
List _____

_____
_____

• gain experience with diverse groups of children and families
List _____

_____
_____

• gain the following types of experiences
  - children with identified disabilities
      Describe experience

      _____
      _____
      _____

  - children of different ages (birth to two years, three to five years, and six to eight years)
      Describe experience

      _____
      _____
      _____

  - children from different locales
      Describe experience

      _____
      _____
      _____

(continues)

Field Assignment 1–3 (continued)

– children from different economic levels
    Describe experience

_____

_____

_____

_____

An electronic version of each field assignment is available on the CD-ROM that accompanies this text.

HOW IS EARLY CHILDHOOD EDUCATION DEFINED?

The professionally agreed-upon definition of *early childhood education* refers to educational programs for children from birth through eight years of age. Typically two-year early childhood programs prepare early childhood practitioners to work in child care with infants, toddlers, or preschoolers. At this time, Alaska is the only state to certify associate degree professionals as assistant teachers for preschool classrooms. The Alaska Department of Education explicitly states that assistant teachers may not be hired as the only teacher in any public school classroom. Other states do not provide any form of state teaching certification at this level. Many two-year early childhood preparation programs have articulated agreements with nearby four-year early childhood teacher certification programs so that those receiving an Associate of Arts (AA), an Associate of Science (AS), or an Associate of Applied Science (AAS) degree can move to a state teacher certification program without the loss of a large number of credits.

The early childhood profession generally advocates for the existence of articulation agreements between or among teacher preparation venues. Articulation indicates that there is an agreed-upon plan for courses or competencies that will routinely be accepted so that teacher candidates can plan a program beginning with an AA, AS, or AAS degree and move seamlessly into a program for early childhood teacher licensing. The existence of NAEYC's common standards for two-year and four-year preparation programs is a useful support mechanism for programs who are working toward this goal.

The most common configuration for early childhood teaching certification is preschool to third grade. Figure 1–2 shows that eighteen states certify early childhood teachers in this range. An additional eleven states define early childhood teacher certification from birth through third grade, and one state (Idaho) provides both early childhood education and early childhood special education certification to those who complete a blended teacher preparation program. *Blended programs,* by definition, are those that prepare early

State	*ECE Certification*	*Web Site*
Alabama	$P\text{-}3^{rd}$	*http://www.alsde.edu/*
Alaska	$P\text{-}3^{rd}$; Assistant teacher certification through CDA or AA	*http://www.eed.state.ak.us*
Arkansas	$P\text{-}4^{th}$	*http://www.arkansased.edu*
Arizona	*Birth-8 years*	*http://www.ade.state.az.us*
California	$N\text{-}3^{rd}$	*http://www.cde.ca.gov/*
Colorado	$K\text{-}2^{nd}$	*http://www.cde.state.co.us*
Connecticut	$P\text{-}3^{rd}$	*http://www.state.ct.us/sde/*
Delaware	$Birth\text{-}2^{nd}$	*http://www.doe.state.de.us/*
Florida	*Preschool (Birth-4 years); PreK/ Primary (3 years-3rd)*	*http://www.fldoe.org/*
Georgia	$K\text{-}3^{rd}$	*http://www.doe.k12.ga.us*
Hawai'i	$P\text{-}2^{nd}$	*http://www.doe.k12.hi.us/*
Idaho	*Blended ECE/ECSE for Birth-3rd*	*http://www.sde.state.id.us/; click Department of Education; on Programs pulldown menu, select Certification (Teacher)*
Illinois	$Birth\text{-}3^{rd}$	*http://www.isbe.state.il.us*
Indiana	$K\text{-}3^{rd}$	*http://www.doe.state.in.us*
Iowa	*Pre-K-K; $P\text{-}3^{rd}$*	*http://www.iowa.gov; click Education*
Kansas	$Birth\text{-}3^{rd}$	*http://www.ksbe.state.ks.us/*
Kentucky	*Interdisciplinary ECE— Birth-Primary (incl. K)*	*http://www.education.ky.gov/*
Louisiana	$P\text{-}3^{rd}$	*http://www.state.la.us/; click Education in Louisiana*
Maine	$K\text{-}3^{rd}$	*http://www.state.me.us/; click Education*
Maryland	$P\text{-}3^{rd}$	*http://www.maryland publicschools.org/*
Massachusetts	$P\text{-}3^{rd}$; $K\text{-}3^{rd}$	*http://www.doe.mass.edu/*
Michigan	*P-K*	*http://www.michigan.gov*
Minnesota	$K\text{-}3^{rd}$	*http://www.education.state.mn.us*
Mississippi	$K\text{-}3^{rd}$; $K\text{-}4^{th}$; P-K; P-1 (endorsement: added to above configurations)	*http://www.mde.k12.ms.us*

(continues)

Figure 1–2 Configurations of Various States for Certifying Early Childhood Teachers*

State	ECE Certification	Web Site
Missouri	Birth-3rd	http://www.dese.mo.gov/
Montana	8 years and younger endorsed to elementary certification only	http://www.bpe.mt.gov/
Nebraska	Preprimary-3rd	http://www.nde.state.ne.us
Nevada	Birth-2nd; Birth-K	http://www.doe.nv.gov/
New Hampshire	N-3rd	http://www.ed.state.nh.us
New Jersey	P-3rd	http://www.state.nj.us/; click Education
New Mexico	B-3rd	http://www.sde.state.nm.us
New York	B-2nd	http://www.nysed.gov
North Carolina	Birth-K	http://www.dpi.state.nc.us/
North Dakota	Birth-3rd; K endorsement	http://www.dpi.state.nd.us
Ohio	P-3rd	http://www.ode.state.oh.us
Oklahoma	P-3rd	http://www.sde.state.ok.us/
Oregon	3 years-4th	http://www.ode.state.or.us/
Pennsylvania	N-3rd	http://www.ode.state.oh.us
Rhode Island	Birth-2nd	http://www.ridoe.net
South Carolina	P-3rd (9/2005) from P-4th	http://www.ed.sc.gov
South Dakota	Birth-P; Birth-8 years; K endorsement	http://www.doe.sd.gov/
Tennessee	P-3rd	http://www.state.tn.us/; click Education
Texas	EC-4th	http://www.tea.state.tx.us/
Utah	K-3rd	http://www.usoe.k12.ut.us
Virginia	Early primary; P-3rd	http://www.pen.k12.va.us/
Vermont	Birth-3rd	http://www.vermont.gov/; click Education
Washington	B-3rd	http://www.k12.wa.us/
West Virginia	P-K	http://wvde.state.wv.us/
Wisconsin	Birth-8 years Early childhood-Middle childhood Birth-11 years	http://www.dpi.state.wi.us
Wyoming	Birth-3rd	http://www.k12.wy.us

Figure 1–2 Configurations of Various States for Certifying Early Childhood Teachers* *(continued)*

*Abbreviations in Figure 1–2 are the same as those used by the particular state: B=birth, P=preschool, PK or PreK or Pre-K=pre-kindergarten, K=kindergarten, 1 or 1st=first grade, 2nd=second grade, 3rd=third grade, 4th=fourth grade, EC or ECE=early childhood education, ECSE=early childhood special education, primary=kindergarten through third grade, preprimary=preschool and kindergarten.

childhood professionals to teach in both early childhood education and early childhood special education (birth to third grade). Consider Figure 1–2 to examine the various configurations that states have put into place for certifying or licensing early childhood educators.

Early childhood professionals work in many types of educational programs for children from birth through eight years of age. Some of these programs include child care, preschool, Head Start, Even Start, family literacy, family support centers, kindergarten, and first, second, and third grades.

HOW IS QUALITY DEFINED IN EARLY CHILDHOOD TEACHER PREPARATION PROGRAMS?

In the past decade, many states have created high-quality training programs for early childhood professionals who are employed in child-care centers, family child care, and preschool settings. Some two-year early childhood education programs now articulate with training or professional development programs so that certain types of training might be converted into college credit and be applied toward a CDA or an AA, AS, or AAS.

For example, Pennsylvania has instituted PA Pathways as a professional development program for child care providers and administrators (Pennsylvania pathways, n.d.). In order to maintain a common overall career development system, Pennsylvania child caregivers receive information about content required for their ongoing professional development in the form of the Core Body of Knowledge (CBK). Items included in the CBK are shown in Figure 1–3. In addition to the CBK, PA Pathways has created systems for managing information about training offerings and for assessing training needs. Trainers are screened to be certain that they are well qualified to provide professional development related to topics in early childhood education. Check to see whether your state has an early childhood professional development program in place. You should be able to find this by linking to your state Department of Human Services, Department of Public Welfare, or child care licensing offices. Research your state's program and provide a brief summary of it in the space below.

Field Assignment 1–4 Researching Your State's Early Childhood Professional Development System

Research your state's program and provide a brief summary of it in the space below.

An electronic version of each field assignment is available on the CD-ROM that accompanies this text.

Knowledge Area 1: Child Growth and Development

Knowledge Area 2: The Environment, Curriculum, and Content

Knowledge Area 3: Families in Society

Knowledge Area 4: Child Assessment

Knowledge Area 5: Communication

Knowledge Area 6: Professionalism and Leadership

Knowledge Area 7: Health, Safety, and Nutrition

Director's Knowledge Area 8: Program Organization and Administration

Home-Based Provider's Knowledge Area 8: Program Organization and Administration

Figure 1–3 PA Pathways Core Body of Knowledge

A recent advance in the field of measuring quality in early childhood professional preparation is the NAEYC associate degree program accreditation. With the existing four-year teacher preparation program accreditation designed by NCATE and NAEYC as a model, the associate degree program accreditation is centered on the five standards described in Figure 1–1. Beyond several campuses that were involved in piloting the program, the first associate degree programs in early childhood education have applied in spring of 2006. The primary goal of this teacher preparation accreditation system is to ensure that programs are implementing characteristics known to provide high-quality preparation for early childhood teachers. The assessed work of associate degree candidates provides the essential information for a campus self-study. A team of reviewers from similar types of programs will travel and conduct the review on-site. The major implication from an accreditation program such as this is to provide outstanding associate degree programs in early childhood education and ultimately to have that translate to teaching of young children and working with their families. More information can be found at http://www.naeyc.org.

Early childhood initial (those that provide certification or licensing for teachers) and advanced (graduate education for certified early childhood educators) teacher preparation programs have the opportunity to have their degree requirements reviewed by NAEYC and NCATE. Early childhood programs that are housed in institutions of higher education that are accredited by NCATE may submit a report, following specific guidelines to present information about their programs. The focus of these program reports is on demonstrating that the program meets all of the NAEYC standards (as shown in Figure 1–1) through assessment of pre-service teacher work. This process is relevant to pre-service teachers in that NCATE accreditation and recognition are related to the quality and relevance of your professional preparation.

As its mission, NCATE "works to make a difference in the quality of teaching, teachers, school specialists and administrators. NCATE believes every student deserves a caring, competent and highly qualified teacher" (About NCATE, n.d.).

HOW IS QUALITY MEASURED IN EARLY CHILDHOOD EDUCATION PROGRAMS FOR CHILDREN FROM BIRTH THROUGH EIGHT YEARS?

In addition to having high-quality teacher preparation programs, it is imperative that early childhood teacher educators have access to high-quality programs that serve children and families. Placing pre-service teachers in the field is a tremendous responsibility in that the quality of children's education must be ensured. States, national associations, and experts in program evaluation are currently providing various ways to assess the quality of programs for educating young children. Pennsylvania has instituted the Keystone STARS program with the primary goal of improving the quality of child care in the state (Pennsylvania Department of Public Welfare, 2006) STARS is an acronym for

Standards
Training
Assistance
Resources
Support

The program has the dual goals of facilitating improvement in the quality of child care and recognizing the achievements of child care providers. Although training of child care providers and early childhood professionals is a critical component of this program, STARS are awarded to licensed providers or centers who have exceeded the basic regulations for child care that exist through legislation. Pennsylvania has three categories of providers: child care centers, group day homes that have seven or more children, and family day care homes providing care for four to six children. See Figure 1–4 for the research-based performance criteria for child care centers. In order to progress through the STARS system, child care centers must provide evidence to support their practices in each of the criteria listed.

Oklahoma has also created a program to recognize quality child care. In the Reaching for the Stars initiative, child care programs are eligible to achieve One Star, One Star Plus, Two Star, or Three Star levels of recognition (Oklahoma Dept. of Human Services, n.d.). Quality standards in the Oklahoma system include staff education and training, compensation, learning environments, parental involvement, and program evaluation. Staff from

Director Qualifications

Director Professional Development

Staff Qualifications

Staff Professional Development

Staff Compensation

Child Observation/Assessment

Program Learning Environment

Community Resources

Parent Involvement

Transitioning of Children

Business Practices

Staff Communication and Support

Continuous Quality Improvement

Figure 1–4 Pennsylvania STARS Center Performance Criteria

the Early Childhood Collaborative of Oklahoma (ECCO) found that positive outcomes have been associated with the Reaching for the Stars program in that the quality of care for all preschool children in Oklahoma had increased, that 80% of preschool classrooms were providing good or excellent care, and that most caregivers interacted sensitively with young children (Dunn, Dykstra, & Norris, 2003). This evaluation of the state initiative to improve the quality of child care demonstrates that such programs can be effective in achieving that goal and also that progress can be effectively measured.

On a national level, NAEYC has had an early childhood program accreditation system in place since 1985. Recently "reinvented," this voluntary accreditation, available to education programs for infants through kindergarten, is widely known and highly regarded. In 2006, "there are more than 10,000 NAEYC-accredited programs, serving nearly one million children and their families" (NAEYC, n.d.).

Central to the newly revised NAEYC accreditation system are (1) the quality of children's daily experiences in early childhood programs and (2) promoting positive outcomes for all areas of a child's development. Four areas of focus have been generated as the basis for the entirely evidence-based accreditation criteria and program standards: children, teaching staff, partnerships with families and communities, and administration. The entire accreditation system is grounded in six evidence-based values. See Figure 1–5 for the six values.

Other highly regarded tools that early childhood professionals may use to ensure quality in early childhood programming include those that have

---

- *The uniqueness of childhood as a developmental phase*
- *The essential contribution to optimal child learning and development of reciprocal, respectful relationships with children and their families*
- *The distinctive opportunity from birth through kindergarten to support children's intellectual, language, and social-emotional development*
- *The essential role of partnerships with families and communities*
- *The significance of a strong program infrastructure in providing high-quality care and education*
- *The importance of the quality of children's lives in the present, not only as preparation for the future*

Figure 1–5 Six Values from NAEYC Early Childhood Program Accreditation

been developed by early childhood researchers Thelma Harms, Richard M. Clifford, and Debby Cryer (2004) at the University of North Carolina's Frank Porter Graham Child Development Institute. A collection of five Environmental Rating Scales have been created through research conducted at this Institute regarding best practices in early education. These rating scales are designated as follows:

■ *Early Childhood Environment Rating Scale (ECERS)* to assess early education programs of children from two-and-one-half through five years (including kindergarten). See Figure 1–6 for 7 subscales and 43 items (Harms et al., 2004).

■ *Infant/Toddler Environment Rating Scale (ITERS)* to assess early education programs of children from birth through two-and-one-half years. See Figure 1–7 for 7 subscales and 39 items (Harmset al., 2004).

■ *Family Day Care Rating Scale (FDCRS)* to assess family child care programs that are implemented in a provider's home. See Figure 1–8 for 7 subscales and 40 items (Harms et al., 2004).

■ *School-age Care Environment Rating Scale (SACERS)* to assess child care programs for children from 5-12 years of age. See Figure 1–9 for 7 scales and 49 items (Harms et al., 2004).

■ Hemmeter, Maxwell, Ault, and Schuster (2001) produced the *Assessment of Practices in Early Elementary Classrooms (APEEC)* with the specific goal of creating an observational tool to provide information about the quality of education in first-, second-, and third-grade classrooms. See Figure 1–10 for a checklist based on the APEEC.

The Division for Early Childhood (DEC) of the Council for Exceptional Children (CEC) has created a set of "Recommended Practices" for use in early intervention and early childhood special education programs (Sandall, McLean, & Smith, 2000). These practices include child-focused interventions, family-based practices, interdisciplinary models, technology applications, assessment, and cultural and linguistic sensitivity. DEC uses the term *child-*

focused interventions to refer to "the decisions and practices used to structure and provide learning opportunities for children" (Wolery, 2000, p. 29). Related propositions are organized into three "take-home messages" (Wolery, 2000, p. 31) and 27 recommendations. See Figure 1–11 for these messages and recommendations.

Field Assignment 1–5 Observation of Early Childhood Environments

Schedule a time to observe in one of the environments for which the environment rating scales are specifically designed. Obtain a copy of the appropriate rating scale book and complete the rating. Describe the environment that you observed and write a summary of what you found in relation to the rating scale that you selected. Discuss results in class.
Rating scale selected:

Description of environment:

Summary of results related to rating scale:

An electronic version of each field assignment is available on the CD-ROM that accompanies this text.

Field Assignment 1–6 Observation of Examples of Values in Early Education

Provide at least two examples from your field experiences that relate to each of these values:

▪ The uniqueness of childhood as a developmental phase
   Examples:

▪ The essential contribution to optimal child learning and development of reciprocal, respectful relationships with children and their families
   Examples:

▪ The distinctive opportunity from birth through kindergarten to support children's intellectual, language, and social-emotional development
   Examples:

▪ The essential role of partnerships with families and communities
   Examples:

▪ The significance of a strong program infrastructure in providing high-quality care and education
   Examples:

(continues)

Field Assignment 1–6 (continued)

■ The importance of the quality of children's lives in the present, not only as preparation for the future
Examples:

An electronic version of each field assignment is available on the CD - ROM that accompanies this text.

A. *Space and furnishings*
   indoor space
   furniture for routine care, play, and learning
   room arrangement for play
   space for privacy
   child-related display
   space for gross motor play
   gross motor equipment

B. *Personal care routines*
   greeting/departing
   meals/snacks
   nap/rest
   toileting/diapering
   health practices
   safety practices

C. *Language-reasoning*
   books and pictures
   encouraging children to communicate
   using language to develop reasoning skills
   informal use of language

D. *Activities*
   fine motor
   art
   music/movement
   blocks
   sand/water
   dramatic play
   nature/science
   math/number
   use of TV, video, and/or computers
   promoting acceptance of diversity

(continues)

Figure 1–6 ECERS-R Subscales and Items

E. Interaction
   supervision of gross motor activities
   general supervision of children
   discipline
   staff-child interactions
   interactions among children

F. Program structure
   schedule
   free play
   group time
   provisions for children with disabilities

G. Parents and staff
   provisions for parents
   provisions for personal needs of staff
   provisions for professional needs of staff
   staff interaction and cooperation

Figure 1–6 ECERS-R Subscales and Items *(continued)*

A. Space and furnishings
   indoor space
   furniture for routine care and play
   provision for relaxation and comfort
   room arrangement
   display for children

B. Personal care routines
   greeting/departing
   meals/snacks
   nap
   diapering/toileting
   health practices
   safety practices

C. Listening and talking
   helping children understand language
   helping children use language
   using books

D. Activities
   fine motor
   active physical play
   art
   music and movement
   blocks   *(continues)*

Figure 1–7 ITERS-R Subscales and Items

> dramatic play
> sand and water play
> nature/science
> math/number
> use of TV, video, and/or computers
> promoting acceptance of diversity
>
> E. Interaction
>   supervision of play and learning
>   peer interaction
>   staff-child interaction
>   discipline
>
> F. Program structure
>   schedule
>   free play
>   group play activities
>   provisions for children with disabilities
>
> G. Parents and staff
>   provisions for parents
>   provisions for personal needs of staff
>   provisions for professional needs of staff
>   staff interaction and cooperation
>   staff continuity
>   supervision and evaluation of staff
>   opportunities for professional growth

Figure 1–7 ITERS-R Subscales and Items *(continued)*

> A. Space and furnishings for care and learning
>   furniture for routine care and learning
>   furnishings for relaxation and comfort
>   child-related display
>   indoor space arrangement
>   active physical play
>   space to be alone
>
> B. Basic care
>   arriving/leaving
>   meals/snacks
>   nap/rest
>   diapering/toileting
>   personal grooming
>   health
>   safety
>
> C. Language and reasoning
>   informal use of language

(continues)

Figure 1–8 FDCRS Subscales and Items

helping children understand language
helping children use language
helping children reason
D. *Learning activities*
   eye-hand coordination
   art
   music and movement
   sand and water play
   dramatic play
   blocks
   use of TV
   schedule of daily activities
   supervision of play indoors and outdoors
E. *Social development*
   tone
   discipline
   cultural awareness
F. *Adult needs*
   relationship with parents
   balancing personal and caregiving responsibilities
   opportunities for professional growth
G. *Supplementary items: Provisions for exceptional children*
   adaptations for basic care (physically handicapped)
   adaptations for other special needs
   communication
   language/reasoning
   learning and play activities
   social development
   caregiver preparation

Figure 1–8 FDCRS Subscales and Items *(continued)*

A. *Space and furnishings*
   indoor space
   space for gross motor activities
   space for privacy
   room arrangement
   furnishings for routine care
   furnishings for learning and recreational activities
   furnishings for relaxation and comfort
   furnishings for gross motor activities
   access to host facilities
   space to meet personal needs of staff
   space to meet professional needs of staff
B. *Health and safety*
   health policy

(continues)

Figure 1–9 SACERS Subscales and Items

health practices
emergency and safety policy
safety practice
attendance
departure
meals/snacks
personal hygiene

C. *Activities*
arts and crafts
music and movement
blocks and construction
drama/theater
language/reading activities
math/reasoning activities
science/nature activities
cultural awareness

D. *Interactions*
greeting/departing
staff-child interactions
staff-child communication
staff supervision of children
discipline
peer interactions
interactions between staff and parents
staff interaction
relationship between program staff and classroom teachers

E. *Program structure*
schedule
free choice
relationship between program staff and program host
use of community resources

F. *Staff development*
opportunities for professional growth
staff meetings
supervision and evaluation of staff

G. *Special needs supplementary items*
provisions for exceptional children
individualization
multiple opportunities for learning and practicing skills
engagement
peer interactions
promoting communication

Figure 1–9 SACERS Subscales and Items *(continued)*

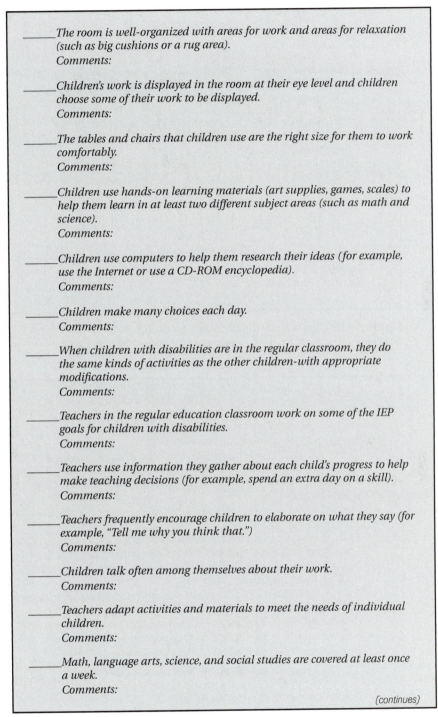

_____The room is well-organized with areas for work and areas for relaxation (such as big cushions or a rug area).
Comments:

_____Children's work is displayed in the room at their eye level and children choose some of their work to be displayed.
Comments:

_____The tables and chairs that children use are the right size for them to work comfortably.
Comments:

_____Children use hands-on learning materials (art supplies, games, scales) to help them learn in at least two different subject areas (such as math and science).
Comments:

_____Children use computers to help them research their ideas (for example, use the Internet or use a CD-ROM encyclopedia).
Comments:

_____Children make many choices each day.
Comments:

_____When children with disabilities are in the regular classroom, they do the same kinds of activities as the other children-with appropriate modifications.
Comments:

_____Teachers in the regular education classroom work on some of the IEP goals for children with disabilities.
Comments:

_____Teachers use information they gather about each child's progress to help make teaching decisions (for example, spend an extra day on a skill).
Comments:

_____Teachers frequently encourage children to elaborate on what they say (for example, "Tell me why you think that.")
Comments:

_____Children talk often among themselves about their work.
Comments:

_____Teachers adapt activities and materials to meet the needs of individual children.
Comments:

_____Math, language arts, science, and social studies are covered at least once a week.
Comments:

(continues)

Figure 1–10 Observation Checklist Based on the APEEC. Hemmeter, M. L., Maxwell, K. L., Ault, M. J., & Schuster, J. W. (2001)

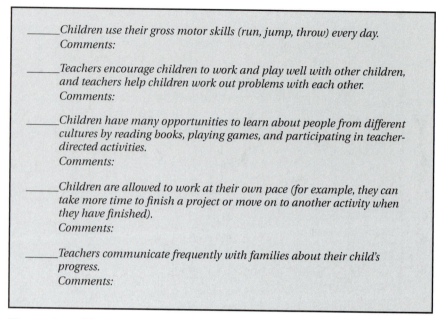

_____*Children use their gross motor skills (run, jump, throw) every day.*
Comments:

_____*Teachers encourage children to work and play well with other children, and teachers help children work out problems with each other.*
Comments:

_____*Children have many opportunities to learn about people from different cultures by reading books, playing games, and participating in teacher-directed activities.*
Comments:

_____*Children are allowed to work at their own pace (for example, they can take more time to finish a project or move on to another activity when they have finished).*
Comments:

_____*Teachers communicate frequently with families about their child's progress.*
Comments:

Figure 1–10 Observation Checklist Based on the APEEC. Hemmeter, M. L., Maxwell, K. L., Ault, M. J., & Schuster, J. W. (2001) *(continued)*

A. *Adults design environments to promote children's safety, active engagement, learning, participation, and membership.*
  • *Physical space and materials are structured and adapted to promote engagement, play, interaction, and learning.*
  • *The social dimension of the environment is structured and adapted to promote engagement, interaction, communication, and learning.*
  • *Routines and transitions are structured to promote interaction, communication, and learning.*
  • *Play routines are structured to promote interaction, communication, and learning.*
  • *Environments are designed and activities are conducted so that children learn or are exposed to multiple cultures and languages.*
  • *Learning environments meet accepted standards of quality including curriculum, child-staff ratios, group size, and physical design of classroom.*
  • *A variety of appropriate settings and naturally occurring activities are used to facilitate children's learning and development.*
  • *Services are provided in natural learning environments as appropriate.*
  • *Interventionists facilitate children's engagement with their environment.*
  • *Environments are provided that foster positive relationships.*
B. *Adults individualize and adapt practices for each child based on ongoing data to meet children's changing needs.*
  • *Practices are individualized for each child.*
  • *Practices target meaningful outcomes for the child.*

(continues)

Figure 1–11 DEC Take-Home Messages and Recommendations

- *Data-based decisions are used to make modifications in the practices.*
- *Recommended practices are used to teach and promote whatever skills are necessary for children to function more completely, competently, adaptively, and independently.*
- *Children's behavior is recognized, interpreted in context, and responded to contingently.*

C. *Adults use systematic procedures within and across environments, activities, and routines to promote children's learning and participation.*
- *Interventionists are agents of change to promote and accelerate learning.*
- *Practices are used systematically, frequently, and consistently within and across environments.*
- *Planning occurs prior to implementation.*
- *Practices are used that are validated, normalized, useful across environments, respectful, and not stigmatizing.*
- *Consequences for children's behavior are structured to increase the complexity and duration of children's play, engagement, appropriate behavior, and learning.*
- *Systematic naturalistic teaching procedures such as models, expansions, incidental teaching, mand-model procedures, and naturalistic time delay are used.*
- *Peer-mediated strategies are used to promote social and communicative behavior.*
- *Prompting and prompt fading procedures (modeling, graduated guidance, increasing assistance, time delay) are used.*
- *Specialized procedures are embedded and distributed within and across activities.*
- *Recommended instructional strategies are used with sufficient fidelity, consistency, frequency, and intensity.*
- *For problem behaviors, interventionists assess the behavior in context to identify its function and then devise comprehensive interventions.*

Figure 1–11 DEC Take-Home Messages and Recommendations *(continued)*

Conclusion

This chapter presented information about the foundation of high-quality early childhood education and teacher preparation programs that serve as guides to helping pre-service teachers understand the importance of quality in all of their field work. High-quality programming and implementation of accepted professional standards will translate into providing positive outcomes for teacher candidates as they integrate knowledge from their academic coursework and skills gained from guided field experiences. An important corollary to this premise is that when field experiences are not focused on creditable exercises, standards, or programs, pre-service teachers are not receiving the necessary preparation that is based on current evidence in the profession.

Field experiences Guide pre-service teachers in understanding the importance of high-quality early childhood programs

References

Dunn, L., Dykstra, S., & Norris, D. (November 2003). *"Reaching for the stars" center validation study executive summary.* Norman, OK: Early Childhood Collaborative of Oklahoma.

Harms, T., & Clifford, R. M. (1989). *Family day care rating scale (FDCRS).* New York: Teachers College Press.

Harms, T., Clifford, R. M., & Cryer, D. (2004). *Early childhood environment rating scale, revised edition, updated (ECERS-R).* New York: Teachers College Press.

Harms, T., Cryer, D., & Clifford, R. M. (2003). *Infant toddler environment rating scale-revised (ITERS-R).* New York: Teachers College Press.

Harms, T., Jacobs, E. V., & Romano, D. (1995). *The school age care environment (SACERS).* New York: Teachers College Press.

Hemmeter, M. L., Maxwell, K., Ault, M., & Schuster, J. (2001). *Practices in early elementary classrooms: An observational instrument.* New York: Teachers College Press.

National Association for the Education of Young Children. (n.d.). *Introduction to NAEYC Accreditation.* Retrieved April 27, 2007, from http://www.naeyc.org/academy/web_ready/HistoryNAEYCAccreditation.asp.

National Council for Accreditation of Teacher Education. (n.d.). *About NCATE.* Retrieved April 27, 2007, from http://www.ncate.org/public/aboutNCATE.asp.

Oklahoma Department of Human Services. *Oklahoma Child Care Services: Reaching for the Stars.* Retrieved April 27, 2007, from http://www.okdhs.org/programsandservices/cc/stars/.

Pennsylvania Department of Public Welfare. *Keystone stars child care quality initiative*. Retrieved February 12, 2006, from http://www.dpw.state.pa.us/child/childcare/keystonestarchildcare/default.htm.

Pennsylvania Early Learning Keys to Quality. *Keystone Stars Core Professional Development*. Retrieved April 27, 2007, from http://www.pakeys.org/profdev/KeystoneSTARS.aspx.

Sandall, S., McLean, M. E., & Smith, B. J. (2000). *DEC recommended practices in early intervention/early childhood special education*. Longmont, CO: Sopris West.

Wolery, M. (2000). Recommended practices in child-focused interventions. In S. Sandall, M. E. McLean, & B. J. Smith (Eds.), *DEC recommended practices in early intervention/early childhood special education*. Longmont, CO: Sopris West.

Chapter 2

Becoming An Early Childhood Professional

Objectives:

After reading and reflecting on this chapter, early childhood students will be able to:

- Explain the varied roles involved in teaching young children.
- Discuss the meaning of professionalism for early childhood educators.
- Describe the stages of professional development for early childhood educators.
- Differentiate among generic, technical, practical, and critical reflections on teaching

Introduction

Although the routes that individuals take in their journeys toward professionalism often vary, a common goal must be to increase understanding about the meaning of professional knowledge and practice in early education. This chapter provides elements from applications of research and professional standards that are commonly accepted as hallmarks of the early childhood profession.

THE MEANING OF PROFESSIONALISM FOR EARLY CHILDHOOD EDUCATORS

Attending to early childhood professionals' voices about the meaning of professionalism is one way to understand what it means to become a professional in this field.

31

"Early childhood education provides the first of many steps in the journey of lifelong learning. Therefore, as an early childhood professional, I have an awesome responsibility to provide a warm, nurturing environment that encourages cognitive, emotional, social, and physical development in young children, while supporting the needs of their families."
—**Cheryl Burt, Kindergarten Teacher**

"All my life I have enjoyed working with children. My professional career started when I was hired as a special needs assistant for a child with a brain injury. At that time, I began to be his advocate and his teacher. During those five years, I was encouraged by the elementary teachers to go on to college to earn my teaching degree. I wanted this so badly I enrolled in a college 65 miles from my home and drove three hours a day to class."
—**June Blades, University Child Development Center Director**

"I believe the early years (birth to age eight) are the most important years, as they provide the foundation for later learning to build upon.
I have personally worked with children in infancy to third grade. . . .
The importance of a positive, nurturing environment through these formative years is undeniable. Caregivers and professionals help our youngest children learn how our world works. It is through these experiences that they learn to talk, read, write, and understand numbers. Proficiency in each subject area is vital to successful learning in the later elementary years and beyond as they are exposed to more complex ideas and expectations. Early childhood professionals and other adults play a critical role in creating environments where children thrive. Strong early childhood programs will help all children have the foundation they need to build a bright future."
—**Marsha Erisman, Preschool Teacher**

"I am an advocate for children, providing a safe, nurturing, and developmentally appropriate environment in which to grow. I realize that I have a small window of opportunity to be present in the life of each child and to support that child's development. This opportunity I am given to touch the life of a child may impact that child in ways that will have a long-term effect. I believe that through my intervention in and support of this child's development, I am able to make a small contribution to society. As a caregiver, I am a small but integral member of a lifelong teaching team that will have a lasting impact on a child and a family, on that child's overall well-being, and on that child's ability to go on and construct a meaningful life. My hope is that the child will learn to trust his world as a safe place, a place where the child feels confident enough to continue his exploration and his learning. It is a very small but important contribution to the future. For me, it is a daily thrill to observe a child interacting with the environment and knowing that a seemingly insignificant experience is an important building block toward greater learning. Because I come from a science background, I love how neuroscience and the discoveries made in brain development support everything we are doing. I recognize that the family is a vital unit in society, and that I have an important responsibility to support that family. I strive to provide these children with opportunities that will allow them to discover themselves and their environment; guiding them as they grow emotionally, socially, physically, and cognitively in all directions, so that as they begin to move away from us, they are ready to take on the next level of developmental challenges. What could be more important and more meaningful (and more fun!)?

"From the children, I remember how to laugh and how to see the world with their fresh eyes again, renewing my own love for life and for learning. I am relatively new to the field of early childhood education, but this is what it means to me."
—Sandra Bennett, Infant Teacher

These quotes are related to perceptions that early childhood teachers have regarding professionalism in the field. Note that the meaning of professionalism is often related to the specific position held by an early childhood professional. Attention is given to a professional's dedication and sense of responsibility. Also, it is clear that sometimes early childhood professionals sacrifice a great deal of time from their personal lives in order to engage children's families as well as to participate in continuing professional development.

Early childhood teacher preparation draws from current research and best practice in order to best understand the meaning of professionalism. Initial teacher preparation guidelines from the National Association for the Education of Young Children (NAEYC) (Hyson, 2003) include a standard about becoming a professional. Facets of this standard include the following:

- identifying and conducting oneself as a member of the early childhood profession
- knowing and using ethical guidelines and other professional standards related to early childhood practice
- acting as continuing, collaborative learners
- thinking reflectively and critically
- advocating for children, families, and the profession

The following sections provide some detail about each of these five areas.

Field Assignment 2–1 Voices of Early Childhood Professionals

Interview at least five early childhood professionals who hold various positions in the field about their understanding of the meaning of professionalism. Using the five concepts related to the NAEYC standard on professionalism, identify the concepts that you garnered from each of the five voices for early childhood.

An electronic version of each field assignment is available on the CD-ROM that accompanies this text.

IDENTIFYING AND CONDUCTING ONESELF AS A MEMBER OF THE EARLY CHILDHOOD PROFESSION

In order to achieve this aspect of professionalism, a candidate for becoming an early childhood teacher must understand what makes up the field of early childhood education. Often, students in early education consider the field to be only that segment to which they aspire; for example, a student who wants to become a Head Start teacher sees early childhood education as teaching preschool age children, a student who wishes to work in infant child care settings sees that as the early childhood profession, a student who plans to work in early intervention believes that is the primary focus of the field, one who sets out to teach kindergarten or first grade believes that is the essence of the field of early childhood. The truth is that early childhood education is a broad and varied profession. Therefore, it is essential that developing early childhood professionals understand the entirety of the field. With this understanding must come advocacy for all early childhood venues and personnel. Unifying all of early education is required in order to be sure that all young children and their families receive the highest quality of educational services. In addition, early childhood educators from varied settings must collaborate with one another in order to provide the best possible education for all young children. See Figure 2–1 for a comprehensive, but not exhaustive, list of early childhood roles and settings.

Roles

Child caregiver
Child care provider
Child care administrator
Resource and referral staff member
Preschool teacher
Preschool administrator
Kindergarten teacher
Primary grade (first-third) teacher
Assistant teacher
Early intervention teacher or team member
Head Start teacher or staff member
Parenting coordinator
Laboratory school staff member
Community college faculty member
University faculty member

Settings

Child care center
Home care
Agency
Faith-based institution
Public school
Private school
Community center
College or university

Figure 2–1 Early Childhood Roles and Settings

Plan lessons
Arrange environments
Teach content through a variety of strategies
Assess children's learning
Organize materials
Incorporate local, state, and federal regulations
Interact frequently with individual and small groups of children
Communicate with families
Support all children's learning
Collaborate with colleagues and administrators
Advocate for children, families, and early childhood education
Evaluate the existing program
Reflect critically on practice and changes
Engage in ongoing professional development (informal and formal)
Attend school, district, and community meetings

Figure 2–2 What Do Early Childhood Teachers Do All Day (and Evening)?

Field Assignment 2–2   Observation of Tasks of Various Early Education Staff Members

Using information from Figures 2–1 and 2–2, visit at least three types of early childhood settings. Note tasks that you observed various staff members performing.

Date: Time: Location:
Early childhood setting type:
Name of site:
Title of staff member:
Tasks performed:

An electronic version of each field assignment is available on the CD-ROM that accompanies this text.

In addition to knowing about professional roles and settings in which early childhood educators practice, those preparing to become early childhood professionals will be

- knowledgeable about the unique history of the field
- familiar with the accepted universal values
- able to understand and apply child development theory and research
- aware of the specific mission of the profession
- cognizant of the connections between early childhood and related disciplines
- prepared to collaborate with a variety of professionals (Hyson, 2003).

Unique History of Early Childhood Education

As one views the historical roots of the profession of early childhood education, as shown in Table 2–1, it becomes clear that multiple strands have influenced current knowledge, beliefs, and practice. These strands include philosophies about children and parenting, the kindergarten movement, nursery schools, child care, child development theory, scientific advances, and early intervention.

Table 2–1 The Historical Roots of Early Childhood Education

1592–1670	John Amos Comenius	education begins on a mother's lap
1712–1778	Jean Jacques Rousseau	education begins at birth
1746–1827	Johann Pestalozzi	education begins in the home
1782–1852	Friedrich Froebel	coined *kindergarten* for children younger than six years (1837)
1832–1876	Mrs. Carl Schurz	established first kindergarten in U.S. (1856)
1804–1894	Elizabeth Peabody	founded kindergartens around the U.S.
late 1800s		many organized group child care centers and tenement house nurseries
1843–1916	Susan Blow	opened the first public school kindergarten in St. Louis (1873)
1907	G. Stanley Hall	advocated for scientific study of children to be applied in kindergartens
1907	Maria Montessori	opened Casi dei Bambini in Rome
1910	McMillan sisters	began nursery schools in England
1916	John Dewey	viewed teachers as active scientists, assessing children's learning and preparing them to be citizens in a democratic society
1919	Harriet Johnson	Bank Street (teacher preparation)
1921	Patty Smith Hill	Teachers College (teacher preparation)
1922	Edna White	Merrill-Palmer Institute (teacher preparation)
1920s	Abigail Eliot	operated a nursery school in Boston
1930s	Works Progress Administration (WPA)	nursery schools to provide employment for teachers and to help unemployed families with children
1940s	Lanham Act	federal funds for child care in factories

(continues)

Table 2–1 (continued)

1957	Sputnik	call to prepare children for competitive world
1960s	Jean Piaget	research about children's cognitive development, influencing thought in American education
1965	Project Head Start	comprehensive early education program focused on preschoolers
1967	Project Follow Through	expanded Head Start to kindergarten and primary grades
1975	PL 94–142 Education for All Handicapped Children Act	first federal legislation requiring public education for all children with disabilities
1983	National Council for Accreditation of Teacher Education (NCATE)	notes early childhood education as a unique discipline for children from birth through age eight
1986	Individuals with Disabilities Education Act (IDEA)	funding included for early intervention programs for children (birth to three years)
1987	National Academy of Early Childhood Programs	national voluntary accreditation system for early childhood programs
1989	United Nations	Convention on the Rights of the Child
1990	ABC Child Care legislation	first federal legislation for child care funding, including caregiver training
2005	Society for Research in Child Development (SRCD)	advocacy for preschool to third-grade teacher certification
2007	NAEYC launches Office of Applied Research	to enhance the impact of current research on early education practice

Accepted Universal Values

NAEYC, the largest early childhood education professional association in the country, has created a Code of Ethical Conduct and Statement of Commitment for Early Childhood Professionals. The core values espoused in this document "are deeply rooted in the history of the field of early childhood care and education" (NAEYC, April 2005).

■ *Appreciate childhood as a unique and valuable stage of the human life cycle.* Understanding of childhood as unique and valuable supports the notion that young children learn differently from older children and adults. As we value the importance of early learning, we must also value the unique ways in which children learn best—through experience and activity.

■ *Base our work on knowledge of how children develop and learn.* The essence of effective teaching in early childhood education is based on knowledge of child development. Education of young children looks very different from education of older children. Effective classroom environments are created to support and challenge children as they learn.

■ *Appreciate and support the bond between the child and family.* An important component of successful early education is family involvement. Strong early childhood teachers involve families in a variety of ways, most importantly including *all* families. Some family members may volunteer at school or to do tasks at home, some may lead in parent associations, some may participate in parenting workshops, and many will support their children's learning at home. Early childhood teachers serve as a conduit for building and maintaining positive parent-child relationships as well as family, school, and community partnerships.

■ *Recognize that children are best understood and supported in the context of family, culture, community, and society.* (Culture includes ethnicity, racial identity, economic level, family structure, language, and religious and political beliefs, which profoundly influence each child's development and relationship to the world.) It is imperative that early childhood professionals understand and support children in relation to (rather than in opposition to) their families, cultures, and communities. Successful transitions from home or community education programs to school depend in large part on continuity for children. Continuity is considered through practices such as having translators available, welcoming all families to all school events, reaching out to reticent families, and including various cultural experiences into the life of the educational program.

■ *Respect the dignity, worth, and uniqueness of each individual (child, family member, and colleague).* Creating an atmosphere of respect begins with each early childhood professional. Conflicts in social settings are inevitable. Use of effective conflict resolution strategies and providing a climate so that all individuals have a voice are ways to demonstrate respect for all.

■ *Respect diversity in children, families, and colleagues.* Celebrations of human differences can lead to greater understanding among various groups. Making authentic efforts to learn about cultures that are different from your own typically leads to appreciation of those differences. Teaching young children how to interact with one another in respectful ways begins with good modeling by early childhood professionals.

■ *Recognize that children and adults achieve their full potential in the context of relationships that are based on trust and respect.* Historically, an important aspect of early childhood education has focused on the whole child, including not only cognition and academic achievement but also the social and emotional foundations for learning. Contemporary research does not dispute this perspective. Learning really does encompass the whole child so that social and emotional development is clearly related to children's academic success. The key to healthy development is centered in positive relationships. Educational strategies must be selected for their effectiveness in light of their impact on the whole child and not test scores alone.

Understanding and demonstrating the NAEYC Code of Ethics is essential in your growth as a professional

---

- *Appreciate childhood as a unique and valuable stage of the human life cycle.*
- *Base our work on knowledge of how children develop and learn.*
- *Appreciate and support the bond between the child and family.*
- *Recognize that children are best understood and supported in the context of family, culture, community, and society.*
- *Respect the dignity, worth, and uniqueness of each individual.*
- *Respect diversity in children, families, and colleagues.*
- *Recognize that children and adults achieve their full potential in the context of relationships that are based on trust and respect.*

Figure 2–3 Universal Values for Early Childhood Education Professionals

Field Assignment 2–3 Observation of Early Childhood Professionals' Universal Values

1. Observe in a variety of early childhood settings and describe examples that demonstrate each of the universal values for early childhood professionals.

   Appreciate childhood as a unique and valuable stage of the human life cycle.
   Time: Date: Location:
   Example of this value in action:

   Base our work on knowledge of how children develop and learn.
   Time: Date: Location:
   Example of this value in action:

   Appreciate and support the bond between the child and family.
   Time: Date: Location:
   Example of this value in action:

   Recognize that children are best understood and supported in the context of family, culture, community, and society.
   Time: Date: Location:
   Example of this value in action:

   Respect the dignity, worth, and uniqueness of each individual.
   Time: Date: Location:
   Example of this value in action:

   Respect diversity in children, families, and colleagues.
   Time: Date: Location:
   Example of this value in action:

   Recognize that children and adults achieve their full potential in the context of relationships that are based on trust and respect.
   Time: Date: Location:
   Example of this value in action:

2. Interview at least two early childhood professionals about the seven universal values and ask what each value means to their work in early education. Summarize their responses.

   Appreciate childhood as a unique and valuable stage of the human life cycle.
   Professional response #1:

   Professional response #2:

   Professional response #3:

   Base our work on knowledge of how children develop and learn.
   Professional response #1:

   Professional response #2:

(continues)

Field Assignment 2–3 (continued)

Professional response #3:

Appreciate and support the bond between the child and family.
Professional response #1:

Professional response #2:

Professional response #3:

Recognize that children are best understood and supported in the context of family, culture, community, and society.
Professional response #1:

Professional response #2:

Professional response #3:

Respect the dignity, worth, and uniqueness of each individual.
Professional response #1:

Professional response #2:

Professional response #3:

Respect diversity in children, families, and colleagues.
Professional response #1:

Professional response #2:

Professional response #3:

Recognize that children and adults achieve their full potential in the context of relationships that are based on trust and respect.
Professional response #1:

Professional response #2:

Professional response #3:

3. As you plan and implement an activity or lesson in an early childhood setting, reflect about how you have considered each of the seven universal values.

Summary of activity or lesson planned and implemented:

Appreciate childhood as a unique and valuable stage of the human life cycle.
Time: Date: Location:
Reflection about application of this universal value:

(continues)

Field Assignment 2–3 (continued)

Base our work on knowledge of how children develop and learn.
Time: Date: Location:
Reflection about application of this universal value:

Appreciate and support the bond between the child and family.
Time: Date: Location:
Reflection about application of this universal value:

Recognize that children are best understood and supported in the context of family, culture, community, and society.
Time: Date: Location:
Reflection about application of this universal value:

Respect the dignity, worth, and uniqueness of each individual.
Time: Date: Location:
Reflection about application of this universal value:

Respect diversity in children, families, and colleagues.
Time: Date: Location:
Reflection about application of this universal value:

Recognize that children and adults achieve their full potential in the context of relationships that are based on trust and respect.
Time: Date: Location:
Reflection about application of this universal value:

An electronic version of each field assignment is available on the CD-ROM that accompanies this text.

Understanding and Applying Child Development Theory and Research

Early childhood education is based on an understanding and philosophy of the whole child. The theoretical and research basis for knowing how children change over time is seen as essential for effective teaching of young children. All of the developmental processes must be considered in planning, implementing, and assessing high-quality educational programs for young children: physical and biological development; cognitive and language development; and social and emotional development.

Current theories that are held in esteem by a majority of those in the early childhood profession include Bronfenbrenner's bioecological theory, Erikson's psychosocial theory, Piaget's cognitive developmental theory, and Vygotsky's sociocultural theory. Additional theories about perceptual motor development and sociomoral development are viewed as essential to the knowledge base of early childhood educators. Details about all of these theories are found in Chapter 4.

Leaders in the profession of early childhood education have long held the perspective that "research gives early childhood practitioners and policymakers essential knowledge to use in making decisions on behalf of young children and families. The goals are to integrate the best available research evidence with the wisdom and values of professionals and families" (Buysse &

Child and Youth Care Quarterly	Kluwer Academic Publishers	http://www.ovid.com
Child Development	Society for Research in Child Development	http://www.srcd.org
Child Study Journal	State University of New York, College at Buffalo	http://www.buffalo.edu
Childhood Education	Association for Childhood Education International	http://www.acei.org
Contemporary Issues in Early Childhood	Symposium Journals	http://www.symposium -journals.co.uk
Developmental Psychology	American Psychological Association	http://www.apa.org
Dimensions of Early Childhood Education	Southern Early Childhood Association	http://www. southernearlychildhood .org
Early Child Development and Care	Taylor and Francis Group	http://www. taylorandfrancisgroup .com
Early Childhood Education Journal	Kluwer Academic Publishers	http://www.ovid.com
Early Childhood Research and Practice	University of Illinois at Urbana–Champaign	http://www.ecrp.uiuc .edu
Early Childhood Research Quarterly	National Association for the Education of Young Children	http://www.naeyc.org
Educational Leadership	Association for Supervision and Curriculum Development	http://www.ascd.org
Exceptional Children	Council for Exceptional Children	http://www.cec.sped .org
Family Relations	National Council on Family Relations	http://www.ncfr.org
Infancy	International Society on Infant Studies	http://www.isisweb.org
Infant Behavior and Development	Elsevier	http://www.elsevier .com

(continues)

Figure 2–4 Peer Reviewed Professional Journals for Early Childhood Professionals

Infant Mental Health Journal	Wiley	http://www.wiley.com
Infants and Young Children	Wolters Kluwer Health	http://www.iycjournal.com
Journal of Applied Developmental Psychology	Elsevier	http://www.elsevier.com
Journal of Child and Family Studies	Kluwer Academic Publishers	http://www.ovid.com
Journal of Early Childhood Literacy	Sage	http://www.sagepub.com
Journal of Early Childhood Research	Sage	http://www.sagepub.com
Journal of Early Intervention	The Division for Early Childhood of the Council for Exceptional Children	http://www.dec-sped.org
Journal of Marriage and the Family	National Council on Family Relations	http://www.ncfr.org
Journal of Research in Childhood Education	Association for Childhood Education International	http://www.acei.org
Reading Research Quarterly	International Reading Association	http://www.reading.org
Reading Teacher	International Reading Association	http://www.reading.org
Teaching Exceptional Children	Council for Exceptional Children	http://www.cec.sped.org
Young Exceptional Children	The Division for Early Childhood of the Council for Exceptional Children	http://www.dec-sped.org
Young Children	National Association for the Education of Young Children	http://www.naeyc.org
Zero to Three	Zero to Three	http://www.zerotothree.org

Figure 2–4 Peer Reviewed Professional Journals for Early Childhood Professionals *(continued)*

Wesley, in press, as cited in Using Research, n.d.). Part of the process of becoming an early childhood professional, then, is to acquire information about child development and teaching practices that is based on current evidence. One important way to achieve this goal is to read peer reviewed professional journals. Some journals provide primary research reports and others are composed of articles that may be more practical but are evidence based. Figure 2–4 provides a list of some of these journals.

Field Assignment 2–4 Reading and Reflecting on Peer Reviewed Journal Articles

1. Peruse at least two of the journals listed in Figure 2–4.
2. Select one article in each journal to read and provide a reflection.
3. Write the bibliographic information, summary, and reflection on this form.
4. Observe in a high-quality early childhood field site specifically to relate information from the articles that you read to teaching and learning.
5. Summarize your experience of linking the theory or research to practice in early education.

Reading #1
Author:
Year:
Title:
Journal name:
Volume, number:
Page numbers:
Summary of article:

Your reflection:

Discussion of linking theory to practice related to an observation from a field site:

Reading #2
Author:
Year:
Title:
Journal name:
Volume, number:
Page numbers:
Summary of article:

Your reflection:

Discussion of linking theory to practice related to an observation from a field site:

Reading #3
Author:
Year:
Title:
Journal name:
Volume, number:
Page numbers:
Summary of article:

(continues)

Field Assignment 2–4 (continued)

Your reflection:

Discussion of linking theory to practice related to an observation from a field site:

An electronic version of each field assignment is available on the CD-ROM that accompanies this text.

The Mission of the Early Childhood Education Profession

Based on the mission of the NAEYC, the mission for the profession in general terms "is to serve and act on behalf of the needs, rights and well-being of all young children with primary focus on the provision of educational and developmental services and resources" (NAEYC Mission, n.d.). Interpreting this broad statement to teaching young children, one must begin with the "to serve and act on behalf . . ." segment. By its nature, the early childhood profession is one of service and advocacy. Service professions include those that are health related, social work and social services, and counseling—all intended to provide help, support, and services for individuals and families. It is typical for service professionals to have a mission related to advocating for clients or consumers who are in positions where it is difficult for them to advocate for themselves. Since young children cannot have voting privileges, it is imperative that others advocate for their needs in the public policy arena.

The next segment of the mission statement refers to "the needs, rights and well-being of all young children." Considering each of these separately, children have basic needs for optimal development that have been termed irreducible by Brazelton and Greenspan (2000). These include the following:

■ ongoing, nurturing relationships

■ physical protection, safety, and regulation

■ experiences that consider individual differences of children

■ experiences that are developmentally appropriate

■ appropriate limits, predictable structure, and reasonable expectations

■ a stable, supportive community

■ cultural continuity.

Early childhood professionals are thus obligated to understand and apply consideration of these basic needs in their programs for young children and their families.

Field Assignment 2–5 Interviewing Early Childhood Professionals about the Mission of Early Childhood Education

Create a list of four or five interview questions from the information in this chapter about the mission of the early childhood profession. Be sure to include some content in your questions that relates to *service orientation* and *advocacy*. List the interview questions that you have developed here.

1.

2.

3.

4.

5.

Interview at least the early childhood professionals who have different roles (for example, toddler teacher, first grade teacher, center director). Summarize their responses and then compare and contrast the responses.

Early childhood professional: _____ Role: _____
Summary of responses:

Early childhood professional: _____ Role: _____
Summary of responses:

Early childhood professional: _____ Role: _____
Summary of responses:

Compare and contrast responses:

An electronic version of each field assignment is available on the CD-ROM that accompanies this text.

The rights of children are often undervalued in our society. Some incorrectly assume that when children have rights, the adults—including parents and teachers—have their rights denied. This is a fallacy. Attending to the rights of all individuals in a system is an important aspect of service professions. In the best of all worlds, rights are balanced with responsibilities.

However, responsibilities must be taught, and children must receive nurturing and support as they learn how to fulfill responsibilities that are reasonable for their developmental levels. The United Nations conducted a Convention on the Rights of the Child in 1989 and listed 41 rights of children and youth. In order to grasp the meaning of this entire list, the Children's Rights Alliance (n.d.) categorized these rights into nine themes:

1. **A child is** . . . anyone under 18 years of age

2. **You all have rights** . . . regardless of gender, skin color, language, ability or disability, economic status

3. **Being you** . . . a right to a name, to know your name and heritage, to think and believe what you like, to privacy, to specialized care and education to meet your needs

4. **Family and being cared for** . . . parents or guardians are responsible for caring for you, you have a right to know both of your parents if it is safe; if adopted or in foster care, a child's needs must be first priority

5. **Education and working** . . . a right to an education with respectful discipline policies, an opportunity to develop personality and talents, a right to be protected from work that could be harmful

6. **Play and leisure** . . . a right to play and leisure such as sports, art, music, drama

7. **Well-being and health** . . . the right to live, to survive and grow up, a right to any special required health care, and to be healthy

8. **Being safe and protected** . . . a right to be protected from harm, not to be hurt by anyone, a right not to be abused or exploited, a right to be protected from war, and a right to defend yourself if accused of a crime

9. **Getting information and having a say** . . . a right to have opinions taken seriously, to find out about things and to share information, the right to meet and make friends, and the right to know your rights (Children's Rights Alliance, n.d.).

A careful examination of the irreducible needs and the rights of the child demonstrates overlaps in many areas. Thus, the foundation for children's rights can easily be seen as a connection to their absolute needs.

The Forum on Child and Family Statistics (2006) provides detailed information about national indicators of well-being of American children, offering a description of what is meant by the term *well-being*. The five broad areas of well-being, based on substantial research and detailed by this organization are the following:

■ Population and family characteristics—family structure, outside the home child care, environmental tobacco smoke

■ Economic security—poverty status, interactions of race and poverty, access to quality health care and health insurance

■ Health—vaccination, teen birth rates, infant and child mortality, childhood obesity, injuries

■ Behavior and social environment—participation in illegal or high risk activity, smoking, drinking alcohol, serious violent crime

■ Education—daily reading to preschoolers, center-based early childhood education and care, math and reading scores, high school completion (Forum on Child and Family Statistics, 2006).

The final segment of the professional mission in early childhood education, "with primary focus on the provision of educational and developmental services and resources," relates to the professional's position as a teacher of young children. Note that the mission refers to this as the *primary focus.* Although consideration must be given to the previously mentioned aspects of the mission of early childhood professionals, providing a high-quality, developmentally appropriate education is the most important element for teachers of young children. This mission is accomplished through knowledge, skills, and dispositions of teachers in the implementation of high-quality education for children from birth through eight years. An explanation of developmentally appropriate practice includes information about what early childhood professionals must know: "They must know about child development and the implications of this knowledge for how to teach, the content of the curriculum—what to teach and when—how to assess what children have learned, and how to adapt curriculum and instruction to children's individual strengths, needs, and interests. Further, they must know the particular children they teach and their families and be knowledgeable as well about the social and cultural context" (Guidelines for decisions, n.d.). NAEYC considers the criteria shown in Figure 2–5 to be integral for a definition of developmentally appropriate practice.

Chapter 4 provides a more complete explanation of the application of developmentally appropriate practices in early education programs.

- *creating a caring community of learners*
- *teaching to enhance development and learning*
- *constructing appropriate curriculum*
- *assessing children's development and learning*
- *establishing reciprocal relationships with families (guidelines for decisions, n.d.)*

Figure 2–5 NAEYC Criteria for Developmentally Appropriate Practice (DAP)

Disciplines Connected to Early Childhood Education

Although professional responsibilities for early childhood teachers are tremendous in scope, no teacher is an island. In order to best serve the young children and their families, early childhood professionals will be called on frequently to include professionals from connected disciplines. Some related professional roles are listed in Field Assignment 2–6.

Field Assignment 2–6 Seeking the Responsibilities of Related Professionals in Early Education Settings

In one or more field experience sites, find out the responsibilities of each of these professionals. Provide a brief description of the responsibilities for all related professionals.

Social worker

School counselor

Psychologist

Family service coordinator

Volunteer coordinator

Principal or director

Special educator

Early intervention specialist

Occupational therapist

Physical therapist

School nurse

(continues)

Field Assignment 2–6 (continued)

Physicians

Speech therapist

Audiologist

Reading specialist

Literacy coach

Math coach

Social services coordinator

Other _____

Other _____

An electronic version of each field assignment is available on the CD-ROM that accompanies this text.

COLLABORATION AND TEAMING

In the current high-tech, fast-paced world of education, collaboration and working with teams are standard practices. These approaches are in stark contrast to earlier paradigms of education in which a teacher often would be the only adult in the classroom for nearly 100% of the school year. Although the adage "two heads are better than one" is popular, many professionals are challenged by effective ways to collaborate in practice. Some even wonder why collaboration and teaming are necessary. One of the most important reasons has to do with the need for all professionals to become experts in a specific area, such as early childhood education. "Increasing levels of complexity require expertise in highly specialized fields" (21st century skills, n.d.).

Vast amounts of new knowledge in child development preclude professionals in related disciplines from knowing and applying all that early childhood educators know and do. The reverse is also true in that, because early childhood education is such a complex field, that knowing and applying related information is not typically possible for today's early educator.

Those candidates who are preparing to become early childhood professionals can begin to acquire and use dispositions that lead to effective collaboration even during their teacher preparation experiences. Some of the characteristics that are important to successful teamwork include the following:

- ability to take on different roles and tasks, sometimes leading and sometimes following, to realize the group objectives
- attention to open and honest communication
- considering past collaborations to make future ones more effective
- listening actively and offering constructive comment
- using disagreement and conflict in honest debate to reach the best conclusion (21st century skills, n.d.).

Field Assignment 2–7 Collaborating in Early Education Environments

1. Describe collaboration experiences that you have observed in early childhood environments. Be sure to include information about the characteristics that are important to effective teamwork.

   Collaboration experience #1:

   Collaboration experience #2:

   Collaboration experience #3:

   Collaboration experience #4:

---

2. Describe opportunities that you have had to collaborate with other adults in your early childhood field experiences. Be sure to include information related to characteristics that are important for successful teamwork. Also, identify challenges in each experience as well as ways that the challenges were or could have been overcome.

   Collaboration opportunity #1:

(continues)

Field Assignment 2–7 (continued)

Challenges:

Ways to overcome challenges:

Collaboration opportunity #2:

Challenges:

Ways to overcome challenges:

Collaboration opportunity #3:

Challenges:

Ways to overcome challenges:

Collaboration opportunity #4:

Challenges:

Ways to overcome challenges:

An electronic version of each field assignment is available on the CD-ROM that accompanies this text.

KNOWING AND USING ETHICAL GUIDELINES AND OTHER PROFESSIONAL STANDARDS RELATED TO EARLY CHILDHOOD PRACTICE

A Code of Ethical Conduct was created by NAEYC and was recently revised. This Code is intended to provide early childhood professionals with a compass for making ethical decisions and a guide for principled behavior. Definitions are provided for related terms. Among the most essential are the following:

- **"Professional ethics**—the moral commitments of a profession that involve moral reflection that extends and enhances the personal morality practitioners bring to their work, that concern actions of right and wrong in the workplace, and that help individuals resolve moral dilemmas they encounter in their work."

- **"Ethical responsibilities**—behaviors that one must or must not engage in. Ethical responsibilities are clear-cut and are spelled out in the Code of Ethical Conduct (for example, early childhood educators should never share confidential information about a child or family with a person who has no legitimate need for knowing.)"

- **"Ethical dilemma**—a moral conflict that involves determining appropriate conduct when an individual faces conflicting professional values and responsibilities" (NAEYC, April 2005).

Encompassing four sections, the Code provides information in the form of both Ideals and Principles. The sections provide guidelines and expectations for responsibilities to children, to families, to colleagues (including coworkers, employees, and employers), and to community and society.

Professional ideals are those that reflect *exemplary* or best practices. Examples of ideals from Section I of the Code are the following:

- To be familiar with the knowledge base of early childhood care and education . . .

- To recognize and reflect the unique qualities, abilities, and potential of each child . . .

- To appreciate the vulnerability of children and their dependence on adults . . .

Professional principles describe practices that are required, prohibited, or permitted. Examples of principles from Section I of the Code are the following:

- Above all, we shall harm no child . . .

- We shall care for and educate children in positive social and emotional environments . . .

- We shall not participate in practices that discriminate against children . . .

Individuals who are preparing to become early childhood professionals must be aware of the Code of Ethical Conduct as they begin to plan, implement, and evaluate their work with young children. The entire document can be found in Appendix B.

Field Assignment 2–8 Observing and Practicing Ethical Ideals

1. Review the Code of Ethical Conduct in Appendix B. Select at least two ideals from each of the four sections (responsibility to children, to families, to colleagues, and to community and society). Provide a brief description of a situation that you observed in an early childhood setting that either upheld or failed to uphold the ideal.

Responsibility to Children
Date: Time:
Ideal:
Summary of situation:

Date: Time:
Ideal:
Summary of situation:

Responsibility to Families
Date: Time:
Ideal:
Summary of situation:

Date: Time:
Ideal:
Summary of situation:

Responsibility to Colleagues
Date: Time:
Ideal:
Summary of situation:

Date: Time:
Ideal:
Summary of situation:

Responsibility to Community and Society
Date: Time:
Ideal:
Summary of situation:

Date: Time:
Ideal:
Summary of situation:

(continues)

Field Assignment 2–8 (continued)

2. Follow the same procedures as in #1, but relate the ethical ideals for each category to your own practice (rather than observations of others).

Responsibility to Children
Date: Time:
Ideal:
Summary of situation:

Date: Time:
Ideal:
Summary of situation:

Responsibility to Families
Date: Time:
Ideal:
Summary of situation:

Date: Time:
Ideal:
Summary of situation:

Responsibility to Colleagues
Date: Time:
Ideal:
Summary of situation:

Date: Time:
Ideal:
Summary of situation:

Responsibility to Community and Society
Date: Time:
Ideal:
Summary of situation:

Date: Time:
Ideal:
Summary of situation:

An electronic version of each field assignment is available on the CD-ROM that accompanies this text.

Although the Code of Ethical Conduct offers the most critical information for the profession, other standards exist to guide preparation of early childhood teachers and caregivers. Most notably, the National Council for the Accreditation of Teacher Education (NCATE) partners with several professional associations. NCATE is a highly respected national body that assesses and either awards or denies accreditation of teacher preparation programs based on documentation from the programs about ways in which they meet the required standards. Standards are based on current evidence from a research base in specific disciplines. For early childhood education, NAEYC is the professional association partner. Five broad standards listed in Figure 2–6 drive professional preparation at the associate degree level, the bachelor's degree level, and the advanced degree level, according to NAEYC and NCATE.

An additional set of principles for teacher preparation *for all disciplines*, and used in many states' teacher assessment systems, originated from the Interstate New Teacher Assessment and Support Consortium (INTASC). The ten INTASC principles and the related NAEYC standards are the following:

1. Subject matter
   NAEYC 4b, 4c, 4d

2. Student learning
   NAEYC 1, 4b, 4d

3. Diverse learners
   NAEYC 1, 2, 4b

4. Instructional strategies
   NAEYC 4b, 4d

5. Learning environment
   NAEYC 1, 3, 4b, 4d

---

1. *Promoting child development and learning*
2. *Building family and community relationships*
3. *Observing, documenting, and assessing to support young children and families*
4. *Teaching and learning*
   - *Connecting with children and families*
   - *Using developmentally effective approaches*
   - *Understanding content knowledge in early education*
   - *Building meaningful curriculum*
5. *Becoming a professional*

Figure 2–6 Standards for Early Childhood Education Professional Preparation

6. Communication
   NAEYC 4a, 4b

7. Planning instruction
   NAEYC 1, 2, 3, 4a, 4b, 4d

8. Assessment
   NAEYC 3

9. Reflection and professional development
   NAEYC 5

10. Collaboration, ethics, and relationships
    NAEYC 2, 4a, 5 (Hyson, 2003, p. 51).

These ten standards are derived from a current understanding of best practices for all teachers; they are widely viewed as minimal essentials in the preparation of highly effective teachers.

Another set of standards for practicing teachers has been created by the National Board for Professional Teaching Standards (NBPTS). While certification of teachers is a state function, the national set of standards is voluntary. Some states have adopted support systems or at least encouragement for practicing teachers to pursue national certification to demonstrate their proficiency. In order to apply to participate in this intensive portfolio assessment system, teachers must have successfully completed three years of experience. Early childhood teachers must be able to demonstrate content knowledge in these areas: (1) literacy and English language arts, (2) mathematics, (3) science, (4) social studies, (5) children's play, and (6) physical education, health, and safety.

Specific standards for the early childhood/generalist certification and the related NAEYC standards follow:

1. Understanding young children
   NAEYC 1

2. Equity, fairness, and diversity
   NAEYC 1, 2, 4b

3. Assessment
   NAEYC 3

4. Promoting child development and learning
   NAEYC 1

5. Knowledge of integrated curriculum
   NAEYC 4a, 4b, 4c, 4d

6. Multiple teaching strategies for meaningful learning
   NAEYC 1, 2, 4a, 4b, 4c, 4d

7. Family and community partnerships
   NAEYC 2, 3

8. Professional partnerships
   NAEYC 5

9. Reflective practice
   NAEYC 5

The mission of NBPTS includes having a system for recognizing accomplished teachers. In addition, the NBPTS standards provide a guide for continuing professional development in the teaching profession. The work of this professional association sends a clear message that continuing professional development, beyond initial certification and throughout a given teacher's career, is essential for a highly qualified work force.

Acting As Continuing, Collaborative Learners

How will you know that you are ready to be a teacher? It may be both comforting and disconcerting to understand that teachers must engage in ongoing professional development. This means that even as you continue to improve in your knowledge and skills, you will always have more to learn and do. This challenge is not a new one. In May 1990, the journal *Young Children* included a reprint of an article written by Jessie Stanton in 1920. In "The 'Ideal' Teacher and How She Grows," Ms. Stanton reflected with some humor on becoming a preschool teacher:

"A teacher 'should have a fair education. By this I mean she should have a doctor's degree in psychology and medicine. Socio-logy as a background is advisable. She should be an experienced carpenter, mason, mechanic, plumber, and thoroughly trained musician and poet. At least five years' practical experience in each of these branches is essential. Now, at eighty-three, she is ready'" (Stanton, 1990, p. 19).

Currently, both the NAEYC and the NBPTS standards demonstrate that it is expected that teachers will continue to participate in professional development throughout their careers. In addition to continuous learning, professional early educators must also expect to be collaborative learners. Collaboration with children, families, colleagues, administrators, communities, university faculty, and personnel in all of the related disciplines mentioned in this chapter leads to stronger, more knowledgeable teachers.

Field Assignment 2–9 Reflecting on Readiness to Teach

Keep a running account of how you feel ready to teach as well as how you feel that you need to continue to improve your knowledge and skills for teaching young children. Use the professional standards discussed in this chapter as a guide for your writing.

(continues)

Field Assignment 2–9 (continued)

How I feel ready to teach:	*How I need to improve:*
Date:	Date:
Description:	Description:
Date:	Date:
Description:	Description:
Date:	Date:
Description:	Description:
Date:	Date:
Description:	Description:
Date:	Date:
Description:	Description:
Date:	Date:
Description:	Description:
Date:	Date:
Description:	Description:
Date:	Date:
Description:	Description:

An electronic version of each field assignment is available on the CD-ROM that accompanies this text.

Thinking Reflectively and Critically

What does it mean to become a reflective teacher? Since the early 1980s, a great deal of professional literature has been directed toward defining reflection as well as categorizing various types of reflective thought and practice. However, the concept of reflective teaching does not belong only to contemporary teaching. Even in the 1930s, John Dewey (1933) considered reflective activity to be a particular form of the problem-solving process (Hatton & Smith, 1995). Three levels of reflection proposed by Van Manen (1977 as cited in Hatton & Smith, 1995) are the following:

- technical reflection
- practical or interpretive reflection
- critical reflection

Technical reflection is the most common type of reflection assigned in teacher preparation programs. Through technical reflection, students use a professional knowledge base to efficiently meet established goals. For example, in early childhood education, students who have a field assignment to teach a lesson to kindergartners might refer to resources for planning and implementing developmentally appropriate practices as they prepare to teach a lesson in literacy, math, or science. Student decisions about how and what to teach are often arrived at through the process of technical reflection, or using the current knowledge from the field to influence teaching.

Practical reflection is the second level of reflection in which teachers assess possibilities and outcomes of a variety of possible actions. It is likely that both knowledge and teaching experience influence a teacher's ability to effectively implement this type of reflection. For example, incorporating practical reflection during student teaching in a second grade classroom, Nicole found that introducing a system of conflict resolution yielded greater long-term effects than the previous system of reducing recess time for undesirable behaviors. This student teacher used her prior experience with outcomes for children who had reduced recess time as a consequence for their inappropriate behavior. Through systematic observation, Nicole noticed that almost every day, the same second graders were receiving the same consequences. This outcome indicates that the reduced recess time system was not effective in changing behavior over time. Nicole, then, considered alternatives from her professional knowledge base. She had read and analyzed a method of conflict resolution in an early childhood course that emphasized children's social and emotional development. Thus, practical reflection led Nicole to draw from both her field experiences and her professional knowledge base to derive a system that led to her second graders' increasing their ability to resolve conflicts and still maintain their optimal recess time.

Finally, critical reflection requires higher-order thinking that goes beyond teachers' previous experiences and immediate situations to consider the larger ethical, sociopolitical, and moral basis of practice in early childhood education. This type of reflection may require teachers to be familiar with the knowledge base, to have experience, and also to be well versed in the sociocultural contexts of education. Often, this type of reflection has led to the creation or modification of professional ethics as well as to changes in common practice. For example, current trends in special education to include all children in regular education classrooms as much as possible have been influenced not only by a professional knowledge base and best practices but also by concern for the rights of all children to receive an optimal education. In contemporary society, concerns about the epidemic proportions of childhood obesity is leading some teachers and administrators to critically reflect on existing practices related to nutrition, exercise, and wellness.

It is not uncommon for teacher preparation programs to implement reflective assignments for students in a more generic manner than indicated by these three categories. Zeichner (1992) describes generic reflection as "without much comment about what it is the reflection should be focused on, the criteria that should be used to evaluate the quality of the reflection, or the degree to which teachers' deliberations should incorporate a critique of the social and institutional contexts in which they work. The implication here is that teachers' actions are necessarily better just because they are more deliberate or intentional" (Zeichner, 1992, p. 167). Although this paradigm is a familiar one in teacher preparation programs, it leaves a great deal to be desired, particularly in terms of assessing both the teaching and reflection of pre-service teachers. Quite often, generic reflection leads students to teaching and reflecting positively on the ways in which they were taught as children instead of incorporating current understanding about how children learn best. Comments from students in this realm include the following:

"How can you grade my reflection assignment when I am just telling you what I think?"

"My favorite teacher was my third grade teacher, I want to teach exactly like he did."

"When I have my own preschool classroom, I'll make sure the children sit still and raise their hands. I prefer a structured setting, not a chaotic one like the campus school."

Although it is certainly true that some generic reflection may produce more analytical thought and effective practice, students might be better prepared to do so when an early childhood teacher education program provides direction, guidance, and support to develop highly qualified teachers. The risk of the generic approach is that it leaves to novice teachers only experience from their own schooling. In fact, when individuals who are preparing to become early childhood teachers learn to use technical, practical, and

---

Generic reflection does not provide comment about the focus, the criteria for evaluation, or degree to which deliberation should incorporate a critique of teaching context.

Technical reflection uses current knowledge in the field to reflect on planning and teaching.

Practical or interpretive reflection assesses possibilities and outcomes of a variety of possible actions.

Critical reflection requires higher-order thinking that goes beyond teachers' previous experiences and immediate situations to consider the larger ethical, sociopolitical, and moral basis of practice in early childhood education.

Figure 2–7 Types of Reflection

critical reflection in ways that ultimately impact their professionalism, this role for teacher preparation programs becomes imperative. Parsons and Brown (2002) summarize the primary goal of reflection as "systematic reflection on our teaching at any one time can provide the impetus and means for improving practice."

Field Assignment 2–10 Using Three Types of Reflection

1. Using the definition and explanation for *technical reflection*, summarize at least two field experiences in which you used this type of reflection to inform your practice or future practice.

   Technical reflection #1:

   Technical reflection #2:

   Technical reflection #3:

2. Using the definition and explanation for *practical reflection*, summarize at least two field experiences in which you used this type of reflection to inform your practice or future practice.

   Practical reflection #1:

   Practical reflection #2:

   Practical reflection #3:

3. Using the definition and explanation for *critical reflection*, summarize at least two field experiences in which you used this type of reflection to inform your practice or future practice.

   Critical reflection #1:

   Critical reflection #2:

   Critical reflection #3:

4. Describe one situation in which *generic reflection* was helpful to inform your practice and one situation when it was not helpful.

(continues)

Field Assignment 2–10 (continued)

Describe when generic reflection helped to inform practice:

Describe when generic reflection did not help to inform practice:

An electronic version of each field assignment is available on the CD-ROM that accompanies this text.

Advocating for Children, Families, and the Profession

Advocacy involves speaking and taking action for a cause. In the case of early educators, advocacy efforts must be threefold: for children, for families, and for the profession. In order to provide optimal care and educational environments for all young children, the needs of children and their families must be taken into consideration. Because young children are dependent on families for basic needs, nurturing, and socialization, advocacy efforts in early education frequently include not only the children but also their families. Further, advocating for the profession of early childhood education is necessary in order to ensure that all young children and families have access to high-quality, developmentally effective programs. Because early childhood encompasses many environments and many venues, it is not always clear to schools or communities that our discipline is based on what is best for children. Some interpret the emphasis on healthy social and emotional environments as teachers being "too nice" or lacking methods of discipline or management. When early childhood educators are proactive about best practices, knowledge of child development, and building partnerships with families, such advocacy supports children, families, and the profession.

It is sometimes difficult for developing and novice professionals to have confidence in their ability to speak for children, families, and the profession. As a starting place for content knowledge related to such advocacy for college students, Couchenour and Chrisman (2008) provide a list of Ten Big Ideas. See Figure 2–8 for a list of these concepts.

---

1. *Women's prenatal health is important to a child's optimal development.*
2. *Biological and environmental factors influence the process of development.*
3. *Families are children's first and most important teachers.*
4. *Experiences in children's daily lives have profound effects on their development.*

Figure 2–8 Ten Big Ideas About Child Development for College Student Advocates

5. *Individual differences in children must be understood.*

6. *Discrimination for or against any group of children must be avoided.*

7. *Infancy is a period of rapid growth and development.*

8. *Contrary to popular opinion, children ages 1–3 years are not "terrible twos," but rather "terrific toddlers."*

9. *Preschool children must have access to high-quality, developmentally effective education.*

10. *Primary education must be designed to meet the unique development of children of this age.*

Figure 2–8 Ten Big Ideas About Child Development for College Student Advocates *(continued)*

Field Assignment 2–11 Advocating for Children

1. Describe a time that you observed an early childhood professional advocate for children, families, or high-quality early childhood education.

2. Describe a time that you advocated for children, families, or high-quality early childhood education.

3. Select one of the Ten Big Ideas about child development from Figure 2–8. Plan a way to use this information as an advocacy tool in a field setting to which you are assigned. Write your plan, implementation, and reflective response to the advocacy here.

   Plan:

   Implementation:

   Reflection:

An electronic version of each field assignment is available on the CD-ROM that accompanies this text.

STAGES OF PROFESSIONAL DEVELOPMENT

For a student preparing to become an early childhood professional, the discussion of the various facets involved in professionalism may at first be overwhelming. It is important to understand that early childhood specialists typically go through a series of somewhat predictable phases of professional development in both their pre-service and in-service experiences. All early childhood professionals are continually evolving as lifelong learners.

Student teaching is typically the capstone experience in a teacher certification program. From the beginning of their programs, many students look forward to this culminating experience. As they proceed on this journey of developing a professional identity, they may experience "ambivalent feelings—joy, fear, love, guilt, frustration, and anger" (Caruso, 1977). Some notable phases that are common to student teachers are the following:

Phase 1: Anxiety/Euphoria. The first few days of student teaching may lead to greater anxiety or greater euphoria depending on the nature of the environment as a cold one or a supportive one.

Phase 2: Confusion/Clarity. It is common for student teachers to enter the second phase fairly early in their experience. Phase two may begin between the second and fourth weeks. Students might struggle with applying theory to practice, with timing, with school culture, with course requirements, with understanding the needs of individual children, and with the expectations of the cooperating teacher. Given some time and experience, student teachers often acclimate to their particular situations and see this as the essence of becoming a teacher. Although student teachers have a narrow perspective, based specifically on their own environments, it may be that this is a necessary perception in order to gain a more comprehensive view of the profession over time.

Phase 3: Inadequacy/Competence. During the third phase, student teachers rely on external means to increase their confidence and competence. Supportive suggestions and affirmation from the cooperating teacher, university supervisor, student teacher colleagues, family members, and sometimes the children help to decrease any sense of inadequacy. With experience, student teachers will internalize their sense of competence.

Phase 4: Criticism/New Awareness. This phase revolves around student teachers moving beyond themselves to greater attention to the well-being and positive outcomes with children. Further, issues surrounding professionalism are considered with more intentionality. "The ability to distance oneself from the intensity of one's emotions so as to be able to focus on children, to analyze critically the teaching performance of oneself and others, and to question the curriculum of the classroom and the philosophy of the school are signs of a maturing process" (Caruso, 1977, p. 61). It is in this phase that student teachers are moving from the narrow perspective given by their particular experience to a broader view of the profession.

Phase 5: Greater Inadequacy/More Confidence. This phase might be difficult for some student teachers to navigate because they have been continuously feeling increasing competence. At the same time, however, they have greater and greater expectations for themselves and they might not always live up to their goals. Sometimes competition with the cooperating teacher or other student teachers contributes to both feelings of confidence and inadequacy.

Phase 6: Loss/Relief. As student teaching comes to a close, it is not uncommon to feel both a sense of relief that the intensive experience is coming to an end and also a sense of loss because life as they have known it for several months will abruptly change. Relationships that have been built over this time come to a halting end. On the other hand, relief that one can now move on to the next stage of professionalism, and perhaps to earning a living, may be a source of delight (Caruso, 1977).

Phase 1: Anxiety/Euphoria

Phase 2: Confusion/Clarity

Phase 3: Inadequacy/Competence

Phase 4: Criticism/New Awareness

Phase 5: Greater Inadequacy/More Confidence

Phase 6: Loss/Relief

Figure 2–9 Caruso's Phases of Student Teaching

Field Assignment 2–12 Interviewing a Student Teacher

Identify a student teacher who you can follow through his or her extensive (10 weeks or more) experience. Keep a journal of the information. Interview the student teacher as follows:

After three to four days, ask "What were your strongest feelings during these early days of your student teaching assignment?"

After about one month of student teaching, ask "What do you recall over the past several weeks about

a)   applying theory to practice?

b)   timing of a lesson?

c)   observation of the particular school culture?

d)   management of all course requirements and expectations?

e)   understanding the needs of individual children?

f)   expectations of the cooperating teacher?"

After the halfway point of the student teaching assignment, ask "Did you receive affirming comments from

a)   cooperating teacher?

b)   university supervisor?

c)   family members?

d)   children?

e)   other school staff?

f)   other student teachers?"

(continues)

Field Assignment 2–12 (continued)

"If so, how did the affirmations impact your sense of competence as a student teacher?"
"If not, do you believe that such affirmations would have impacted your sense of competence as a student teacher?"
Near the end of student teaching

a) Explain critical reflection to the student teacher as described in this chapter. Ask whether the student teacher used critical reflection and how it improved his or her teaching.

b) Also ask whether the use of critical reflection influenced the student teacher's perception of himself or herself as a teacher.

c) As student teachers gain competence, they increase expectations of themselves. Ask about a time when the student teacher was feeling competent and then found additional goals to set for himself or herself. Were there ever any feelings of competition with other student teachers or staff? If so, ask for a description of the sense of competitiveness.

As student teaching ends, ask the student teacher about

a) a sense of relief

b) a sense of loss

What did you learn from the experience of interviewing a student teacher throughout his or her experience? Do you believe that this activity will influence your own student teaching experience?

An electronic version of each field assignment is available on the CD-ROM that accompanies this text.

Our understanding of professional development points to the likelihood that even after one is launched from teacher preparation programs to an early childhood education career, a sequence of adjustment or stages may be evident. Katz (1977) proposed four stages of professional development for teachers, noting that the length of any given stage will vary based on individual teacher characteristics and experiences.

Stage 1: Survival. Many experienced early childhood educators recall their first year on the job as basically surviving each day. Wondering whether one can make it through the school year may be diminished when provided with "support, understanding, encouragement, reassurance, comfort, and guidance" (Katz, 1977, p. 8).

Stage 2: Consolidation. Teachers consolidate the skills gained in the first year or so with their professional goals and directions for the future. In this stage, teachers have greater resources for assisting individual children's difficulties. Although support and encouragement are always helpful for professional development, specific information to address children's needs or various situations seems to be key for continuous learning of early childhood teachers.

Stage 3: Renewal. During the third or fourth year of professional experience, early childhood teachers reach toward new ideas, new resources, new information, new understanding. Meeting colleagues from different programs, attending workshops and conferences, and reading professional literature are at this stage stronger sources of support than they might have been at earlier stages.

Stage 4: Maturity. Teachers reach this stage at a variety of points in their professional lives. At this stage, reflection is required to understand where one has been, what has influenced one's teaching, and what one's mission is. Mature teachers are autonomous in that they will seek professional development from a range of possibilities, in terms of both format and content.

Stage 1: Survival

Stage 2: Consolidation

Stage 3: Renewal

Stage 4: Maturity

Figure 2–10 Katz's Four Stages of Professional Development for Early Childhood Teachers

Field Assignment 2–13 Interviewing Practicing Early Childhood Education Teachers

Interview five practicing early childhood teachers with different levels of experience about their memory of their first year of teaching.

A teacher with 1–2 years of experience: _____

What is the strongest memory from the first year of teaching?

Do you recall a special event or situation?

What was the most exciting part of the first year of teaching?

What was the most difficult?

How did your second and third years differ from the first year?

A teacher with 3–6 years of experience: _____

What is the strongest memory from the first year of teaching?

(continues)

Field Assignment 2–13 (continued)

Do you recall a special event or situation?

What was the most exciting part of the first year of teaching?

What was the most difficult?

How did your second and third years differ from the first year?

A teacher with 6–10 years of experience: _____
What is the strongest memory from the first year of teaching?

Do you recall a special event or situation?

What was the most exciting part of the first year of teaching?

What was the most difficult?

How did your second and third years differ from the first year?

A teacher with 10–20 years of experience: _____
What is the strongest memory from the first year of teaching?

Do you recall a special event or situation?

What was the most exciting part of the first year of teaching?

What was the most difficult?

How did your second and third years differ from the first year?

(continues)

Field Assignment 2–13 (continued)

A teacher with more than 20 years of experience: _____
What is the strongest memory from the first year of teaching?

Do you recall a special event or situation?

What was the most exciting part of the first year of teaching?

What was the most difficult?

How did your second and third years differ from the first year?

List any comments that you can relate to the Survival stage that most first year teachers experience:

List any comments that you can relate to the Consolidation stage that teachers in the second and third years typically experience:

2. Ask an early childhood teacher with about 3–5 years of experience whether the following sources of support are helpful. Also ask how, when, and under what circumstances they might be especially welcome.

   a) meeting colleagues from different (but similar) programs

   b) attending workshops or conferences

   c) reading professional literature

3. Interview three early childhood teachers with 10 or more years of teaching experience. Ask the following questions:

   a) How did each one of the teachers use reflection to understand his or her own professional development through the years?

   b) What has influenced changes in his or her teaching the most?

   c) What is his or her mission in teaching young children?

   d) How do the teachers view professional autonomy?

   e) What are some helpful sources of ongoing professional development?

(continues)

Field Assignment 2–13 (continued)

Write responses from each of the three teachers and create some conclusions about professional development for early childhood teachers.

An electronic version of each field assignment is available on the CD-ROM that accompanies this text.

Growth and development as a professional is an essential journey for you to take

Conclusion

The path to becoming an early childhood education professional is quite a journey! Having an understanding of external requirements related to professional standards and ethical conduct is essential for professional development in the field of early care and education. Such understanding has the potential to move developing professionals from acting on opinions, biases, or impulses to incorporating expectations, best practices, and continuous reflection in their work with young children, families, colleagues, and communities.

References

Brazelton, T. B., & Greenspan, S. I. (2000). *The irreducible needs of children: What every child must have to grow, learn and flourish.* Cambridge, MA: Perseus.

Caruso, J. J. (November 1977). Phases in student teaching. *Young Children,* 33(1).

Children's Rights Alliance. (n.d.) *Your rights.* Retrieved August 21, 2006, from http://www.childrensrights.ie/yourrights.php.

Couchenour, D., & Chrisman, K. (2008). *Families, Schools and Communities: Together for Young Children* (3rd Ed.). Clifton Park, NY: Thomson Delmar Learning.

Dewey, J. (1933). *How we think.* Chicago: Henry Regnery.

Forum on Child and Family Statistics. (2006). *America's children in brief: Key national indicators of well-being, 2006.* Retrieved August 21, 2006, from http://www.childstats.gov/americaschildren/index.asp.

Hatton, N., & Smith, D. (1995). *Reflection in teacher education: Towards definition and implementation.* The University of Sydney: School of Teaching and Curriculum Studies. Retrieved August 1, 2006, from http://alex.edfac.usyd.edu.au/LocalResource/originals/hattonart.rtf.

Hyson, M. (2003). *Preparing early childhood professionals: NAEYC's standards for programs.* Washington, DC: NAEYC.

Katz, L. (1977). *Talks with teachers.* Washington, DC: NAEYC.

National Association for the Education of Young Children. (April 2005). *Code of ethical conduct and statement of commitment: A position statement of the National Association for the Education of Young Children.* Retrieved August 15, 2006, from http://www.naeyc.org/about/positions/PSETH05.asp.

National Association for the Education of Young Children. (n.d.). *Guidelines for decisions about developmentally appropriate practice.* Retrieved August 21, 2006, from http://www.naeyc.org/about/positions/dap4.asp.

National Association for the Education of Young Children. (n.d.). *NAEYC Mission and Goals.* Retrieved August 21, 2006, from http://www.naeyc.org/about/mission.asp.

National Association for the Education of Young Children. (n.d.). *Using research on early childhood development and education.* Retrieved August 15, 2006, from http://www.naeyc.org/resources/research/.

North Central Regional Educational Laboratory. (n.d.). *21ˢᵗ century skills. Teaming and collaboration.* Retrieved August 21, 2006, from http://www .ncrel.org/engauge/skills/effcomm1.htm.

Parsons, R. D., & Brown, K. S. (2002). *Teacher as reflective practitioner and action researcher.* Belmont, CA: Wadsworth Thomson Learning.

Stanton, J. (May 1990). The "ideal" teacher—and how she grows. *Young Children,* 45(4).

Zeichner, K. M. (1992). Conceptions of reflective teaching in contemporary U.S. teacher education program reforms. In L. Valli (Ed.), *Reflective teacher education: cases and critiques.* Albany: State University of New York Press.

Chapter  3

Professional Behaviors in Field Settings

Objectives

After reading and reflecting on this chapter early childhood students will be able to:

- Begin to be reflective practitioners
- Better understand responsible decision-making
- Be prepared to work in a global & diverse society

Introduction

This chapter identifies and defines three categories of behavior in field settings: observational (you as an observer of young children), interactional (you as a participant with young children), and leadership (you as a model, guide, and teacher with young children). In each of these categories, professional behaviors vary due to the needs of the children and expectations of the task. These behaviors, as in all field settings, should be guided by both the NAEYC Code of Ethical Conduct and Statement of Commitment (April 2005) and NAEYC's Standards for Programs (Hyson, 2003). These documents are found in Appendix A and Appendix B. The goal of this chapter is to prepare professional practitioners as reflective, responsible decision makers for teaching young children in a global and diverse democratic society.

Learning about professional behaviors in field settings is important for children and families

OBSERVATIONAL BEHAVIORS

Completing observational tasks requires little interaction with children, but it does require careful attention to children's behavior, language, and interactions. It is critical in developing professional understanding, and it is important in all teaching careers.

Borich (2003, pp. 15–16) identified eight categories of observational areas (or lenses) for completing classroom assignments. See 3–1.

Abbreviated definitions that have been adapted for each lens are the following:

■ *Learning climate* refers to the physical and emotional environment

■ *Classroom management* refers to the ways that teachers organize space and anticipate and respond to student behavior

■ *Lesson clarity* refers to the teacher's ability both to speak clearly and to structure content at the student's current level of understanding

■ *Instructional variety* includes the use of attention-gaining devices, variation in eye contact and voice, and alternative modes through which learning occurs (seeing, listening, and doing)

■ *Task orientation* includes handling misbehavior with minimum disruption to the class, reducing time spent on clerical duties during instructional time, and maximizing time spent on content coverage

Eight areas, or lenses, to focus classroom observations:

1. *Consider the learning climate.*
2. *Focus on classroom management.*
3. *Look for lesson clarity.*
4. *Verify instructional variety.*
5. *Observe task orientation (time on task of both the teacher and the students).*
6. *Examine engagement (time and strategies in understanding the concept and content).*
7. *Measure student success.*
8. *Look for higher thought processes.*

Figure 3–1 Focusing Classroom Observations

- *Engagement* refers to the ways that teachers provide activities, problem sets, and projects that allow students to think about, act on, and practice what they learn
- *Student success* includes the pace of the classroom and its momentum that build toward major milestones (for example, projects, class meetings, and center activities)
- *Higher thought processes* includes collaboration and group activities, mental models, student projects, and student portfolios

Field Assignment 3–1 Observational Assignment

Using the lenses defined in Figure 3–1, observe in an early childhood classroom, and write a brief description in each category.

Lens	Brief Description
Learning climate	
Classroom management	
Lesson clarity	
Instructional variety	
Task orientation	
Engagement	

(continues)

Field Assignment 3–1 (continued)

Lens	Brief Description
Student success	
Higher thought processes	

An electronic version of each field assignment is available on the CD-ROM that accompanies this text.

Chrisman and Slattery (2005) asked pre-service teacher about their observational experiences and received the following comments about the benefits of observing in classrooms:

"Observing first-hand teaching techniques"

"Seeing principles in action"

"Seeing what methods 'look like'"

"Realistic view of how a classroom works"

"Helps to make concepts that I am learning clearer"

Consider your experiences in observing children, and compare them to the statements listed above. Are they similar? Consistent?

Using Self-Observation

Ayers (1989) has written about the benefits of self-observation. He notes that "[o]bservations can be formal and planned, or informal. They can be sustained or fleeting. Self-observation, journal-writing, and the like can contribute to the work." McNamee (2005) in writing about the work of Vivian Paley wrote, "The field of education needs this kind of personal depiction of where meaning in teaching comes from—from teachers looking within themselves as well as listening and speaking with their students . . ."

Consider your skill in self-observation. Can you identify some benefits to your own teaching?

INTERACTIONAL BEHAVIORS

Interactional tasks or assignments are those that require some preparation (tutoring one child or a small group of children) but do not require planning for the whole class or the whole day. These assignments are most often given to prepare students in particular content areas (teaching a reading lesson or math lesson) and often occur before student teaching or practicum semesters.

Field Settings require learning a full range of skills, attitudes, and dispositions for professional growth

Cooper (2003) identified three categories of skills that are required for learning how to teach. He stated that learning complex teaching skills requires (1) cognitive understanding of the skills needed to teach, (2) practice of those skills, and (3) knowledge of performance (feedback). Interactional assignments allow for each of these skills to develop in incremental and scaffolded situations.

There is also a growing body of research on student teachers that focuses on shared knowledge, struggles, and stories about becoming a teacher (Carroll, Conte, & Pam, 2000). This research is supportive of planning many opportunities during these interactional assignments for students to share concerns, questions, and suggestions with each other and with course instructors. Gross (2005), in a study of collaboration, identified the following characteristics of working with other student teachers: (1) solved practical, real-life problems, (2) worked in collaborative groups, (3) focused on projects that require problem-finding—what has succeeded, what needs to be refined, (4) experimented with resources (people and texts), (5) set personal goals, and (6) consulted with faculty and experts.

Field Assignment 3–2 Reflecting on Work with Peers and Colleagues

Consider the opportunities you have had to work with peers and colleagues. Were these helpful? How?

(continues)

Field Assignment 3-2 (continued)

Recall helpful experiences working with peers and colleagues:	Explain how they were helpful to you:

An electronic version of each field assignment is available on the CD-ROM that accompanies this text.

LEADERSHIP BEHAVIORS

Leadership tasks involve planning activities for the whole classroom throughout the day and responsibility for classroom management and daily routines. These tasks usually occur in practicum or student teacher placements. George (1978) constructed an instrument for measuring concerns of students as they performed various leadership duties in field placements (see Figure 3–2). Identifying concerns and reflecting on them can lead to increased effectiveness during extended teaching assignments in which you are placed. Review the following questionnaire and use it as a strategy for improving your teaching.

The ability to reflect on your own teaching is a critical skill to acquire during the leadership phase of becoming a professional teacher. Yoo (2001) has outlined the following skills & qualities for reflective teaching:

1. Be observers
2. Be self-critical
3. Conduct research
4. Collaborate
5. Allow room for mistakes
6. Be life-long learners

These skills take time and practice to accomplish, and the only way to gain them is to use them regularly. Field Assignment 3–3 provides opportunities to practice these skills and develop these qualities.

When I think about my teaching, how much am I concerned about each of the following?

Concerns Related to Myself

Doing well when a supervisor is present
Feeling more adequate as a teacher
Being accepted and respected by professional persons
Getting a favorable evaluation of my teaching
Maintaining the appropriate degree of class control

Concerns Related to Tasks

Lacking instructional materials
Feeling under pressure too much of the time
Having too many noninstructional duties
Working with too many students each day
Experiencing the routine and inflexibility of the teaching situation

Concerns Related to Impact on Others

Meeting the needs of different kinds of students
Diagnosing student learning problems
Guiding student toward intellectual and emotional growth
Understanding whether each student is getting what he or she needs

Figure 3-2 Relating Concerns about Role as Student Teacher

Field Assignment 3–3 Checklist of Professional Responsibilities to Be Completed Before Going into Field Experiences

1. Do you know the time of the observation, interaction, or leadership role?

   Yes: _____ The time is: _____

   No: _____

2. Do you know how to get there? Yes: _____ Directions: _____

   No: _____

3. Do you know the expected attire for this early childhood setting?

   Yes: _____ The attire is: _____

   No: _____

(continues)

Field Assignment 3–3 (continued)

4. Do you know the name(s) of the teacher, principal or director, and secretary?

Yes: _____   Teacher: _____

No: _____   Principal or Director: _____

                          Secretary: _____

5. Do you need to bring anything in order to be admitted (for example, letter from professor, criminal background checks, health cards)?

Yes: _____   Bring: _____

No: _____

6. Do you know what to do when you arrive at the school, sign-in procedures, security information (clearances), and so on?

Do you know what to do as you enter the classroom, where to sit, and so on?

Yes: _____ I know the procedures for entering.

No: _____

7. Read, sign, and date the following statement:

Statement of Commitment*

As an individual who works with young children, I commit myself to furthering the values of early childhood education as they are reflected in the ideals and principles of the NAEYC Code of Ethical Conduct. To the best of my ability I will

1. Never harm children.
2. Ensure that programs for young children are based on current knowledge and research of child development and early childhood education.
3. Respect and support families in their task of nurturing children.
4. Respect colleagues in early childhood care and education and support them in maintaining the NAEYC Code of Ethical Conduct.
5. Serve as an advocate for children, their families, and their teachers in community and society.
6. Stay informed of and maintain high standards of professional conduct.
7. Engage in an ongoing process of self-reflection, realizing that personal characteristics, biases, and beliefs have an impact on children and families.
8. Be open to new ideas and be willing to learn from the suggestions of others.
9. Continue to learn, grow, and contribute as a professional.
10. Honor the ideals and principles of the NAEYC Code of Ethical Conduct.

*This Statement of Commitment is not part of the code but is a personal acknowledgment of the individual's willingness to embrace the distinctive values and moral obligations of

(continues)

Field Assignment 3–3 (continued)

the field of early childhood care and education. It is recognition of the moral obligations that lead to an individual becoming part of the profession.

Name: _____

Date: _____

Source: NAEYC (2005). Code of Ethical Conduct and Statement of Commitment

An electronic version of each field assignment is available on the CD-ROM that accompanies this text.

Field Assignment 3–4 Sketching the Room Arrangement

Draw a sketch of each room in which you observe. Note the placement of equipment, desks, tables, chalkboards, computers, supplies, small group meeting spaces, and other items.

Include permanent features such as placement of doors, windows, and other environmental characteristics of the space.

Recommended resource: Hemmeter, Maxwell, Ault, & Schuster, 2001.

Field Assignment 3–5 Classroom Observation

What do you see in the classroom?

Daily schedule?
Helper charts?
Printed materials that teach (sounds of words, names of objects, and other literacy skills)? What types?

Printed materials that give direction (charts to show how things work)? What types?

Learning centers?
Individual spaces?

Small group meeting spaces?
What images are on the walls?

What book cover images do you see?
What are the visible cues for keeping materials organized?
What visible cues are present for managing behavior?

What do you hear?

What do you hear as instruction is presented?
What do you hear as children work in small groups?
Do transitional activities (songs, chants, games) that teach content occur throughout the day?
What types of child-to-child conversations do you hear?
Are there supportive words?
Are there words that scaffold understanding of concepts?
Are there open-ended as well as closed questions

(continues)

Field Assignment 3–5 (continued)

What do you feel?

What do you feel when you are in this environment? (Is the emotional climate warm, neutral, cold?)

An electronic version of each field assignment is available on the CD-ROM that accompanies this text.

Field Assignment 3–6 Comparing Teaching in Prekindergarten, Kindergarten, First, Second, and Third Grades

During each observation of the age groups, note differences in the following:

Room arrangement

Daily schedule

Teaching behaviors and styles

Curriculum

Lesson planning format

Classroom management

An electronic version of each field assignment is available on the CD-ROM that accompanies this text.

Field Assignment 3–7 Child Development As the Basis for Teaching in Early Childhood Classrooms

Review a child development textbook and consider each of the following questions:

1. What do I know about the development of language and literacy understanding for each of the following age groups?

    Prekindergartners

    Kindergartners

(*continues*)

Field Assignment 3–7 (continued)

First graders

Second graders

Third graders

2. What do I know about the development of numeracy and mathematical understanding for each of the following age groups?

Kindergartners

First graders

Second graders

Third graders

3. In what specific ways can I apply this developmental understanding to teach reading and math?

An electronic version of each field assignment is available on the CD-ROM that accompanies this text.

Field Assignment 3–8 Interviewing Professionals in the Field of Early Childhood Education

Interview teachers in prekindergarten, kindergarten, first, second, or third grade, asking the following types of questions:

1. What influenced your professional development in early childhood education?

2. What is your greatest concern about professional conduct in early childhood education?

3. What advice do you have for a beginning teacher?

(continues)

Field Assignment 3–8 (continued)

Interview principals or directors of early childhood programs, asking the following types of questions:

1. What influenced your professional development in early childhood education?

2. What is your greatest concern about professional conduct in early childhood education?

3. What advice do you have for a beginning teacher?

Cindy Forbes, an experienced third-grade teacher, wrote out each procedure in the daily schedule for a student teacher. She noted such items as her actions in preparing for each lesson, how she modified the room arrangement and prepared materials and equipment to teach the lesson, and the words she would stress in the lesson. As you begin to plan lessons, use the guide in this exercise to note the steps in each part of the lesson.

Lesson Steps

1. *Room arrangement:*

2. *Materials needed:*

3. *Equipment needed:*

4. *Words to use:*

    Key terms

    Definitions

5. *Children's abilities and interests:*

6. *Questions to ask (both open and closed):*

7. *Modifications to meet special needs:*

Figure 3–8 A Strategy from a Cooperating Teacher for a New Student Teacher

Field Assignment 3–9 Collaborating with Other Students, Faculty, and Cooperating Teachers

1. Describe ways to solve real-life problems in the classroom.

2. Work together in collaborative groups.

3. Work on projects that require problem-finding.

4. Experiment with matching resource to solving problems:

   a. list of texts

   b. list of people

5. Set personal goals.

An electronic version of each field assignment is available on the CD-ROM that accompanies this text.

Conclusion

Professional behavior in field settings varies with the roles and tasks that you will be performing as you work with children and other adults. Learning about, practicing, performing, and then reflecting on these roles and tasks will strengthen your abilities as an effective teacher in early childhood settings. As you know, hearing about professional behavior in a college classroom or reading about it in a book is different from performing it in the field. Working with children, families, and other adults always involves the unexpected, which is why it is good to practice professional behaviors with the support of faculty and field placement teachers before assuming your role as a classroom teacher.

References

Ayers, W. (1989). *The good preschool teacher: Six teachers reflect on their lives.* New York, NY: Teachers College Press.

Borich, G. D. (2003). *Observation skills for effective teaching* (4th ed.). Upper Saddle River, NJ: Prentice-Hall.

Carroll, S. Z., Conte, A. E., & Pam, A. C. (2000). Advice for student teachers. *Professional Educator, 23*(1), 1–7.

Chrisman, K., & Slattery, C. A. (2005). Analyzing classroom observation assignments. *National Association of Laboratory Schools Journal. 29*(2).

Cooper, J. M. (2003). *Classroom teaching skills* (7th ed.). pp.15–16. Boston, MA: Houghton Mifflin.

George, A. A. (1978). *Measuring self, task and impact concerns: A manual for use of the teacher concerns questionnaire.* The University of Texas at Austin: The University of Texas.

Gross, P. (Fall 2005). Learning collaboratively to construct curriculum. *National Association of Laboratory Schools Journal. 29*(2).

Hemmeter, M. L., Maxwell, K. L., Ault, M. J., & Schuster, J. W. (2001). *Assessment of practices in early elementary classrooms.* New York: Teachers College Press.

Hyson, M. (2003). *Preparing early childhood professionals: NAEYC's standards for programs.* Washington, DC: NAEYC.

McNamee, G. D. (2005). The one who gathers children: The work of Vivian Gussin Paley and current debates about how we educate young children. *Journal of Early Childhood Teacher Education. 25*(3).

National Association for the Education of Young Children (April 2005). *Code of ethical conduct and statement of commitment: A position statement of the National Association for the Education of Young Children.* Washington, DC: NAEYC.

Yoo, S. Y. (2001). Using portfolios to reflect on practice: Qualities of a reflective teacher. *Educational Leadership, 58*(8), 80.

Chapter 4

The Science of Teaching and Learning

Objectives

After reading and reflecting on this chapter, early childhood students will be able to:

- Describe key ideas and applications for related theories
- Explain how brain development research (neuroscience) influences an understanding of how children think and learn
- Discuss the rationale for inclusive practices in early education
- Demonstrate their understanding of the curric ulum and assessment cycle for teaching young children
- Apply principles of self-reflection and action research to classroom practice
- Practice classroom management skills based on an understanding of child development

Introduction

It is imperative that all early childhood teachers understand the scientific evidence supporting best practices when teaching young children and forming partnerships with families and communities. Although the ways in which effective teachers apply theoretical and research understanding often differs, professional behavior is always driven by the science of teaching and learning.

THEORETICAL FOUNDATIONS FOR EFFECTIVELY TEACHING YOUNG CHILDREN

All sciences have theories. The science of teaching is extensive because it draws from several scientific disciplines. Early childhood education draws not only from educational theory but also from psychology, sociology, family studies, and human development. This section of the chapter reviews key ideas and applications from theories that are believed to be central to early childhood educators' understanding for the scientific basis of teaching young children. (It is beyond the scope of this book to provide detailed descriptions of theories. Students are directed to child development and family involvement textbooks for further information or to review.)

Human Development Theories

Some of the developmental theories held in highest regard by early childhood professionals include Jean Piaget's cognitive developmental theory, Lev Vygotsky's contextualist theory, Urie Bronfenbrenner's bioecological theory, Erik Erikson's psychosocial theory, and Robert Selman's theory of social awareness and social competence. Although Albert Bandura's social learning theory does not emphasize development, it remains a useful theory for understanding children's behavior.

Piaget's Cognitive Developmental Theory: Key Ideas and Applications

Piaget's theory is known in education circles as constructivist. This denotation derives from the idea that humans construct their own knowledge as they interact with their environments. This theory is based in a biological understanding of humans as active learners; when people are in cognitive disequilibrium (or disequilibration), they seek knowledge as the path to equilibrium (or equilibration). Piaget noted that people adapt their thinking as they continue to interact with their environments. Adaptation occurs through assimilation and accommodation. According to Piaget, the purest form of assimilation is play that leads to integration of new information into a child's previous understanding. The purest form of accommodation is imitation, leading to changing the child's current understanding to accommodate new knowledge. One emphasis in education that has been derived from this approach is that children are becoming autonomous thinkers, or that they are constructing their own knowledge as they interact with their environments.

Piaget's observations led him to believe that children are internally motivated to acquire knowledge and that, from the beginning of life, infants think. In a unique classification of four developmental stages, Piaget

Piaget noted that people adapt their thinking as they continue to interact with their environments

described the manner in which thinking is qualitatively different from infancy through adulthood. This conception of thinking as not just more, bigger, or greater as children get older is at the essence of high-quality early education. If we are to be effective in teaching young children, we cannot teach them in the same manner as older children or adults. Piaget's four stages of cognitive development and approximate ages are senso-rimotor (birth–2 years), preoperational (2–7 years), concrete operational (7–11 years), and formal operational (adolescence through adulthood). Early childhood education encompasses children who are typically in the first three of these stages, birth through eight years.

Infants and young toddlers in the sensorimotor stage think through senses and motor activity. Senses include seeing, hearing, smelling, touching, and tasting as well as the proprioceptive (internal sense of body positioning) and vestibular (changing position) senses. Often, movement is indicative of thinking. Thus, in order to support cognitive development for very young children, teachers and families must provide continuous, safe opportunities to explore stimulating environments. Piaget believed that those in the sensorimotor stage had little ability to represent or use symbols in their thought processes. However, as children transition from this stage to preoperational, they typically use symbols in early forms of pretend play activities.

During toddlerhood, children move into the preoperational stage and function in some similar ways through first grade or even into second and third grade. While physical growth is tremendous during this period, it is essential that teachers understand how children think at this stage as well as the typical limitations in their thinking. The greatest new ability in this stage is the increasing ability to use symbols to represent the world. Children use symbols in the form of increasingly complex pretend play, oral language, and eventually, recognition of numbers and letters as well as the ability to write and read symbols. Piaget noted that children in this stage are limited in their ability to perform abstract cognitive activity. He used examples such as reversibility, conservation, classification, and seriation to demonstrate such constraints to preoperational thinking.

Children in primary grades are typically transitioning into the concrete stage of thought. This is a time when it is important to keep in mind that children develop in the same sequence but not at the same rate. While some children are moving from preoperational thinking at the middle or end of first grade, others might not do so until third grade. Putting this key idea into practice requires that early childhood teachers differentiate instruction in terms of both content and pedagogy. It is also necessary to keep in mind that children continue to think with concrete operational characteristics through about eleven years of age.

Evidence of concrete operational thinking in children can be observed in terms of their understanding of rules as standards for behavior. Piaget explained that children in this cognitive stage are capable and prefer games with rules when they are at play. For early childhood educators, this can be extrapolated to recognize that children can begin to apply rules to themselves and others. Figure 4–1 describes Piaget's stages of cognitive development.

Understanding both theory and research is important in understanding children's development

Sensorimotor (approximately birth–2 years): Children think through all of their senses and motor activity; little use of symbols to represent

Preoperational (approximately 2–7 years): Children increasingly make greater use of symbolic representation through pretend play, language, recognition of numbers and letters, ability to read and write; little use of abstract thought

Concrete Operational (approximately 7–11 years): Children can decenter, understand rules as standards for behavior; still lack ability to use abstraction and logic

Figure 4–1 Piaget's Stages of Cognitive Development for Children from Birth to Eight Years

Field Assignment 4–1 Observing Children's Cognitive Development

1. Observe three children who are between the ages of birth and one and one-half years. Describe scenarios related to sensorimotor thinking:

   Time: Date: Location: Age:
   Child #1:

   Time: Date: Location: Age:
   Child #2:

   Time: Date: Location: Age:
   Child #3:

2. Observe three children who are between the ages of two and six years. Describe scenarios related to preoperational thinking:

   Time: Date: Location: Age:
   Child #1:

   Time: Date: Location: Age:
   Child #2:

   Time: Date: Location: Age:
   Child #3:

3. Observe three children who are seven or eight years old. Describe scenarios related to concrete operational thinking:

   Time: Date: Location: Age:
   Child #1:

   Time: Date: Location: Age:
   Child #2:

(continues)

Field Assignment 4–1 (continued)

Time: Date: Location: Age:
Child #3:

An electronic version of each field assignment is available on the CD-ROM that accompanies this text.

Understanding the context of learning is important for your to appreciate as a beginning teacher

Vygotsky's Contextualist or Sociocultural Theory: Key Ideas and Applications

Vygotsky's theory is most often referred to as *contextualist*, but it is also called *sociocultural*. These terms have similar meaning in that Vygotsky's emphasis for thinking and learning was on the social environment or context. (In contrast, Piaget's focus was on the biological basis of cognition.) A major premise of contextualist theory is that social context influences thought. In contrast to Piaget's views about learners becoming autonomous, Vygotsky emphasized the role of social interaction in teaching and learning. In describing the Zone of Proximal Development (ZPD), he noted that this is the area between which learners are able to accomplish a task or skill for themselves and that for which they need assistance of another person. Teachers must be sensitive observers of individual children's abilities in order to pinpoint the ZPD in each area of learning for each child. Four stages of the ZPD explain Vygotsky's view about how development occurs:

Stage 1: A child's performance is assisted by others who have more ability with the task at hand.

Stage 2: The child assists his or her own performance, sometimes using private speech, as he or she moves to being able to do the task independently.

Stage 3: The child can perform the task so well that assistance from another person might actually interrupt the child's ability related to the specific task.

Stage 4: Throughout his or her lifetime, the child engages in recursive loops, going back to stage two and moving through to internalize the task or skill at a similar or higher level.

Some significant propositions from Vygotsky include the following:

- *People learn from each other.* This proposition implies that teachers are not the only ones who teach or cause learning to occur. Rather, all people in the learning community influence one another's knowledge at their individual ZPDs.

- *Knowledge comes from culture.* The way that children understand the world starts with their home experiences. All daily routines, including meal rituals, food choices, expected ways of interacting with one another, contact with the community or neighborhood, products used, roles of adults, and play activities, constitute a child's early knowledge. When children come to school with some familial and cultural experiences that have prepared them for that environment, the transition may be easier. Some of these experiences include adults reading to children, consistency in daily schedules, and opportunities for safe, supervised play with other children. When the home culture is vastly different from school expectations, children have a more difficult transition because their knowledge is not effective in the new environment. Partnerships between home and school help teachers to plan experiences so that children can use some of their cultural knowledge and adapt with support of both teachers and families.

- *Historical and social assumptions influence thought.* Many ideas are based in existing historical or social assumptions. Some children learn from their families, media, or communities that there is a difference between "men's work" and "women's work." Other children learn that all family members pitch in to get household work completed. Some children are seen as "the smart one," "the athletic one," "the good one," and a vast number of other identities that they may carry to school with them.

■ *Through play, children are able to know what they cannot know in reality.* "A child's greatest achievements are possible in play, achievements that tomorrow will become her basic level of real action" (Vygotsky, as cited in Leong & Bodrova, n.d.). Through imaginary or pretend play, children come to a greater understanding of the social world.

Implications for practice based on Vygotsky's contextualist theory include the following:

■ the importance of scaffolding for children's learning and cognitive development

■ the importance of individualizing classroom practices based on children's ZPDs in various areas

■ the necessity of forming family, school, and community partnerships to support children's academic achievement

■ the basis for collaborative projects and experiences in school

■ the need for young children to engage in pretend play

Teachers must be sensitive observers of children's individual abilities in order to pinpoint the Zone of Proximal Development (ZPD) in each area of learning

See Figure 4–2 for a summary of key points from Vygotsky's theory and Figure 4–3 for an illustration of the premises.

> ■ *The ZPD is the area between which learners can accomplish a skill by themselves and that for which they need assistance of another person.*
>
> ■ *People learn from each other.*
>
> ■ *Knowledge is based in culture.*
>
> ■ *Historical and social assumptions influence thought.*
>
> ■ *Through play, children know what they cannot know in reality.*

Figure 4–2 Key Points from Vygotsky's Sociocultural Theory

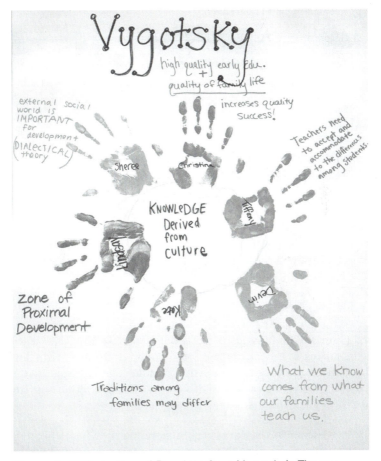

Figure 4–3 Illustration of Premises from Vygotsky's Theory

Field Assignment 4–2 Observing Examples of Children's ZPDs

1. Observe and describe examples of the ZPD in children of the following ages interacting with a more skillful peer or older child or adult:

   a) infant (birth to one year)

   b) toddler (one to two and one-half years)

   c) preschooler or kindergartner (two and one-half to five years)

   d) primary grade child (six to eight years)

2. Observe at least one child with a more skillful peer, older child, or adult and write an example for each of the following ideas:

   a) People learn from each other.

   b) Knowledge comes from culture.

   c) Historical and social assumptions influence thought.

   d) Through play, children are able to know what they cannot know in reality.

An electronic version of each field assignment is available on the CD-ROM that accompanies this text.

Bronfenbrenner's Bioecological Theory: Key Ideas and Applications

Urie Bronfenbrenner's bioecological theory places the individual at the center of various levels or systems that influence development. This theory provides important details about multiple influences on children's development as well as ways to help teachers understand that development is affected by systems in addition to homes and classrooms. Too often, solutions are sought by oversimplifying problems: "if only the parents would . . . ," "this child seems to lose focus for no reason at all . . . ," "Susie's mother is always late with the lunch money. . . . "

Viewing development as determined in part by various social contexts, Bronfenbrenner continuously worked to increase the role of biology or genetics in his theory. Essentially, the child is *influenced by* and *acts on* each of the systems, either directly or indirectly. The role of the child is active, not passive, according to this theory. The five levels of systems noted in this theory are the following:

▪ *Microsystem.* This is the social environment in which children are present, sometimes called the *near environment.* Young children typically have several microsystems in which they spend time on a daily or weekly basis, including home, school or child care, community association, faith-based experiences, and extended family visits. When we think of the influence of children's environments on their development and behavior, this is often the level that comes to mind.

- *Mesosystem.* This system is unique in that it is characterized by interactions between or among the microsystems. An understanding of child development thus includes influences from family, school, and community partnerships, as well as from any other interactions that occur with the child's microsystems. When such interactions and relationships are positive and supportive, children have better developmental outcomes than when the relationships are nonexistent or negative.

- *Exosystem.* This system is indirectly related to human development in that those who do not spend direct time in contexts from this system are still influenced by them. Parental workplaces often have a strong impact on children, even if they have never visited the site. The climate of the workplace as well as the existence of benefits for employees and their families are examples of such indirect influences. Other social contexts in which adult family members participate without children also lend influence, some positively and some negatively. When parents spend recreational time without children, it can replenish them in order to provide the consistent nurturing that children need. On the other hand, certain social interactions and contexts, such as those related to substance abuse, often have negative impacts on children's development, even if the children are safely cared for in another setting.

- *Macrosystem.* The system that accounts for the broader cultural context, macrosystem effects come from the political (social policy), economic, and sociohistorical positions in children's lives. In the pluralistic culture of the United States, not all children receive the same effects. Social policy often provides varying resources for different groups of people. Economic variables play a huge role in children's development because not all children have access to good schools, safe neighborhoods, or supportive families.

- *Chronosystem.* This system relates to the time period in which the child is born and develops as well as the events that serve as markers for that time period. It is sometimes viewed as a generation gap: children born in different decades are influenced by different histories. For example, the high level of technology use that is evident in the early part of the twenty-first century was unimaginable even three decades earlier.

This song was created by students in the ECH 460.02 course at Shippensburg University during the Fall 2006 semester. Use the tune of "The Farmer in the Dell."

The child is at the core,

The child is at the core,   *(continues)*

Figure 4-4 Bronfenbrenner's Bioecological Theory

With Bronfenbrenner's theory,

The child is at the core.

The family comes in,

The neighborhood comes in,

They make up the microsystem,

The school comes in, too.

The relationships come in,

The connections begin,

They make up the mesosystem,

Influencing the child.

The parent goes to work,

The kids watch TV,

That makes up the exosystem,

And has an indirect effect.

Politics come in,

History and change,

They make up the macrosystem,

Depends on where you live.

The time in which you live,

The history it give,

That makes up the chronosystem,

The era in which one lives.

Figure 4–4 Bronfenbrenner's Bioecological Theory *(continued)*

Taking all of the levels of these systems into consideration assists early childhood educators in seeing that children's development is complex. Multipledeterminants must be considered when school rules, policies, and expectations are decided. Avoiding oversimplified solutions to circumstances with complex contextual effects leads decision makers to more effective outcomes.

Specific applications that can be derived from this theory for early childhood education include the following:

- building strong family, school, community partnerships
- advocating for children and families both in their near environments and in macrosystem environments such as through social policy
- incorporating an understanding of the complex influences on each child's development into their educational lives

Field Assignment 4–3 Collecting Data about Effects of Bronfenbrenner's Systems

1. Observe three children (birth–eight years) for at least 15 minutes each in three different microsystems. Write a brief description of the observations.

   Date: Time: Location: Age:
   Description of microsystem #1:

   Observation of child:

   Date: Time: Location: Age:
   Description of microsystem #2:

   Observation of child:

   Date: Time: Location: Age:
   Description of microsystem #3:

   Observation of child:

2. Interview a parent of a young child about one of the following mesosystem scenarios:

   a) partnerships between home and school or child care
   Summary of parent comments:

   b) partnerships between families and communities
   Summary of parent comments:

   c) partnerships between families and extended family
   Summary of parent comments:

3. Interview the parent about an exosystem influence: workplace policies that support or inhibit the family's responsibilities for their children.

   Summary of parent comments:

4. Ask a parent or teacher about at least one of the following macrosystem influences on children's development:

   a) child care licensing or regulations
   Summary of comments:

   b) special education laws
   Summary of comments:

   c) the No Child Left Behind (NCLB) legislation
   Summary of comments:

(continues)

Field Assignment 4–3 (continued)

5. Ask a parent or teacher about the following chronosystem effects:

   a. What were the most important social influences on you as a child?

   How have those influences changed for children today?

   b. What do you believe were the most important social influences on the generation before you?

   Did you have any of the same influences, or had they changed completely? Describe.

An electronic version of each field assignment is available on the CD-ROM that accompanies this text.

Bandura's Social Learning Theory: Key Ideas and Applications

Albert Bandura focuses his social learning theory on how children incorporate modeling of others' behaviors into their own development and behavior. Just as Bronfenbrenner, over time, modified his theory to include a more active role for the individual, Bandura also has added new emphasis to the importance of a child's cognition in relation to who he or she chooses to model and when various models might be employed.

This theory emphasizes the reciprocal interactions among behavior, person (including cognition), and environment. That is, Bandura explains children's behavior as being influenced by watching what other people do and then imitating or modeling that behavior. Whether a child chooses to imitate a particular behavior is influenced by his or her own thinking as well as the environment in which the child is behaving. Behavior is modified not only through observation but also through the child's thinking and other environmental influences. Still, the old adage, "do as I say, not as I do" may be less effective than a strong adult role model. Demonstrating expected behaviors, along with explanations for those behaviors and a supportive environment, help children to exhibit those behaviors. Further, strong positive relationships seem to affect children's cognition in positive ways for modeling behavior. These relationships, however, may not always lead to positive behaviors for children. For example, a child who strongly identifies with a father who is a spouse abuser might view that behavior as desirable.

Applications for early childhood classrooms include the following:

- children need strong positive models as well as explanations and environmental supports for expected behavior
- some socially influenced behavior that is not appropriate for school may be difficult to change
- the environment must be examined to decrease negative effects and to increase positive effects for supporting children's expected behaviors

Field Assignment 4–4 Collecting Data about Children's Modeling Behaviors

1. Interview an early childhood teacher about the following:
   a) examples of children modeling behavior of others.
      List all persons mentioned by the teacher.

   b) how teachers can effectively change children's behaviors when their influential model is not appropriate for expected school behavior.
      List ways to change children's behaviors mentioned by the teacher.

   c) how teachers can increase the number of positive models for children both in and outside of school.
      List teacher ideas.

2. Provide a critical reflection of responses that you received from the teacher. Use the definition of critical reflection from Chapter 2.

An electronic version of each field assignment is available on the CD-ROM that accompanies this text.

Erikson's Psychosocial Theory: Key Ideas and Applications

Erik Erikson created a lifespan theory related to social and emotional development after a long professional association with Sigmund Freud. Expanding on Freud's notion of sexual motivation being related to emotional development, Erikson broadened the concept to social motivation as the key to social and emotional health. Taking a lifespan perspective, this theory comprises eight stages that describe emotional crises faced by individuals at different points in their lives. For the purpose of focus on the early childhood years, this text describes the first four stages, covering infancy through later childhood. (For information about all the stages, see Erikson, 1950, 1968.) Each stage is described in terms of contrasting outcomes, although it is likely that the best solution to each stage is not the absolute positive pole. For healthy development, the positive aspect of the stage will dominate, however. For example, infants must learn to have trust in their caregivers in order to move on to stage two, and toddlers must learn autonomy to move on to stage three.

Erikson labeled the first stage *Trust versus Mistrust*. This stage refers to the crisis to be resolved by infants during the first year of life. Very young children learn trust from their primary caregivers when their needs are met. Caregivers who are sensitive to the needs of the infant respond in a timely way and engage in mutual communication. A negative outcome on the side of mistrust makes it very difficult to proceed toward healthy emotional development.

The second stage is *Autonomy versus Shame and Doubt*. The approximate age range for addressing this crisis is one to three years of age. After learning to trust others to care for them, toddlers now need to learn to trust themselves. They do this through the pursuit of autonomy. Caregivers who support toddlers' drive to be autonomous will provide a balance of opportunities for children to explore their world, to do things for themselves, and to set limits for safety and security. The negative outcome related to this stage leads to toddlers having a sense of shame about desiring autonomy and doubt about their own abilities.

Initiative versus Guilt is Erikson's third stage of psychosocial development. Children from three to five years are involved in this crisis. Preschoolers who have achieved autonomy in the previous stage are now involved in the crisis of taking initiative. A sense of competence will prevail so that children can initiate both work and play activities. Knowledgeable caregivers understand that it is essential for preschoolers to initiate both their own play and helpful behaviors with others to meet the crisis of this stage. Guilt, the negative outcome related to the preschooler stage, often leads to stress and anxiety in children when they are unable to fulfill unreasonable adult demands.

The fourth stage of Erikson's theory is *Industry versus Inferiority*. This stage describes the crisis for children from six years until puberty. School-aged children who have met the initiative crisis move next to achieving a sense of industry. In our society, this crisis most often involves being successful at school—a complex set of capabilities. Caregivers, including parents and teachers, can best support children as they meet the crisis of industry by providing opportunities for success through teaching effectively, stating expectations clearly, and providing scaffolding and encouragement as necessary. A lack of school success, especially when it occurs repeatedly, may lead children to feeling incompetent and inferior.

Trust versus Mistrust (approximately birth–1 year)

Autonomy versus Shame and Doubt (approximately 1–3 years)

Initiative versus Guilt (approximately 3–6 years)

Industry versus Inferiority (approximately 7–11 years)

Figure 4–5 Erikson's Stages of Psychosocial Development (Birth–Eight Years)

Field Assignment 4–5 Collecting Data about Erikson's Psychosocial Stages of Development

1. Observe three children from birth to twelve months of age in the presence of a teacher, caregiver, or parent. Describe a situation that may relate to trust or mistrust. In all cases, note child behaviors and adult behaviors that seem to support or inhibit the child's behaviors.

   Date: Time: Location: Age of child:
   Description:

(continues)

Field Assignment 4–5 (continued)

Relate to trust or mistrust:

Date: Time: Location: Age of child:
Description:

Relate to trust or mistrust:

Date: Time: Location: Age of child:
Description:

Relate to trust or mistrust:

2. Observe three children who are from one to three years old in the presence of a teacher, caregiver, or parent. Describe a situation that may relate to autonomy or shame and doubt. In all cases, note child behaviors and adult behaviors that seem to support or inhibit the child's behaviors.

Date: Time: Location: Age of child:
Description:

Relate to autonomy or shame and doubt:

Date: Time: Location: Age of child:
Description:

Relate to autonomy or shame and doubt:

Date: Time: Location: Age of child:
Description:

Relate to autonomy or shame and doubt:

3. Observe three children who are from three to five years old in the presence of a teacher, caregiver, or parent. Describe a situation that may relate to initiative or guilt. In all cases, note child behaviors and adult behaviors that seem to support or inhibit the child's behaviors.

Date: Time: Location: Age of child:
Description:

Relate to initiative or guilt:

Date: Time: Location: Age of child:
Description:

Relate to initiative or guilt:

Date: Time: Location: Age of child:
Description:

Relate to initiative or guilt:

(continues)

Field Assignment 4–5 (continued)

4. Observe three children who are from six to eight years old in the presence of a teacher, caregiver, or parent. Describe a situation that may relate to industry or inferiority. In all cases, note child behaviors and adult behaviors that seem to support or inhibit the child's behaviors.

Date: Time: Location: Age of child:
Description:

Relate to industry or inferiority:

Date: Time: Location: Age of child:
Description:

Relate to industry or inferiority:

Date: Time: Location: Age of child:
Description:

Relate to industry or inferiority:

An electronic version of each field assignment is available on the CD-ROM that accompanies this text.

Selman's Theory of Social Awareness and Competence: Key Ideas and Applications

In addition to understanding how children think, according to the cognitive theorists, and how they develop emotionally, it is also necessary for early childhood teachers to understand how children's understanding influences their sociomoral actions. Robert Selman (1980) developed a series of five stages related to children's ability to take the perspective of another person.

The first stage (Stage 0) includes children from about three to six years and is referred to as *Egocentric Viewpoint.* In this stage, children do differentiate themselves from others in a physical sense, but they typically cannot separate thoughts and feelings of others from their own. Even when children are able to identify another's feelings, they cannot internalize an understanding of the reasons for those feelings when they differ from their own.

Selman's second stage (Stage 1), *Social-Informational Role Taking,* is typically observed in children from six to eight years of age. At this point, children often can understand that each person has his or her own reasoning, some similar to and some different from their own. Children focus on each of the views separately and cannot apply the complex thought that is necessary to coordinate the views.

The third stage related to perspective-taking ability (Stage 2) is *Self-Reflective Role Taking,* and it is evident in children from about 8 to 10 years of age. It is not until this stage that children can cognitively put themselves in the place of another. Although this is a major new capability that is essential for developing authentic concern for others, children are still limited in their ability to see the perspectives in a way that demonstrates mutuality. That is, children's own points of view are still eminent in their minds.

It is not until most children are older than the early childhood years, about 10 or 12 years of age, that they have the ability to engage in *Mutual Role Taking* (Stage 3). After 12 years of age and through adolescence, individuals come to understand not only that various individual perspectives are relevant but also that it is necessary to have knowledge of social conventions (*Social and Conventional System Role Taking*, Stage 4).

Successful early childhood teachers apply this theory in daily routines and procedures for effective behavioral management as well as in partner or group pedagogical frameworks.

Egocentric Viewpoint (3–6 years). *Children differentiate themselves from others in a physical sense, but they typically cannot separate thoughts and feelings from themselves and others.*

Social-Informational Role Taking (6–8 years). *Children often can understand that each person has his or her own reasoning, some similar to and some different from their own reasoning. Children at this stage focus on each of the views separately and cannot apply the complex thought that is necessary to coordinate their views with those of others.*

Self-Reflective Role Taking (8–10 years). *Children can cognitively put themselves in the place of another; however, they are still limited in their ability to see the perspectives in a way that demonstrates mutuality. Each child's own point of view is still eminent in his or her mind.*

Figure 4–6 Selman's Stages of Social Awareness and Competence

---

Field Assignment 4–6 Collecting Data about Children's Perspective-Taking Behavior

1. Observe two children from three to six years of age for behaviors that may be related to Selman's egocentric stage of perspective taking (see Figure 4-6). Note the child's behavior as well as the behavior of anyone else with whom the child is interacting at the time of observation.

Date: Time: Location: Age of child:
Description:

Date: Time: Location: Age of child:
Description:

(continues)

Field Assignment 4–6 (continued)

2. Observe two children from six to eight years of age for behaviors that may be related to Selman's social-informational stage of perspective taking. Note the child's behavior as well as the behavior of anyone else with whom the child is interacting at the time of observation.

Date: Time: Location: Age of child:
Description:

Date: Time: Location: Age of child:
Description:

3. Observe two children from 8 to 10 years of age for behaviors that may be related to Selman's self-reflective stage of perspective taking. Note the child's behavior as well as the behavior of anyone else with whom the child is interacting at the time of observation.

Date: Time: Location: Age of child:
Description:

Date: Time: Location: Age of child:
Description:

An electronic version of each field assignment is available on the CD-ROM that accompanies this text.

Family Systems Theories: Key Ideas and Applications

In addition to understanding major child development theory and applications, early childhood professionals must also have knowledge about family systems theory and application. Two major frameworks of family systems are included here: *family life cycle* and the *circumplex* or *family mapping* model.

The family life cycle approach emphasizes the challenges and strengths of families over time. Major life periods are marked, such as courtship and marriage, transition to parenthood, rearing young children and school age children, parenting adolescents, the empty nest family, and grandparenting. Emphasis is on the family system and the ways in which all roles change as families experience various stages in their life cycle. For example, new parents are adjusting to their dramatic new roles as mothers or fathers at the same time that grandparents are adjusting to some similar changes. New parents observing their own parents move into the role of grandparents often requires adjusting relationships and interactions (Carter & McGoldrick, 1999). See Figure 4–7 for illustration of this theory.

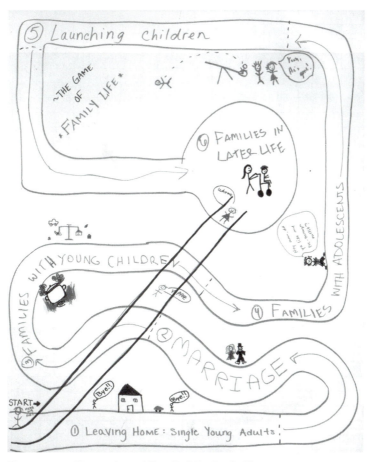

Figure 4–7 Illustration of Family Life Cycle Theory

Field Assignment 4–7   Collecting Data about the Transition to Parenthood

Interview two new parents about this transition to parenthood stage of the family life cycle. Ask the following questions and record the responses:

Date: Time: Location: Parent:

a) How did you adapt to your role as a parent? What was your biggest challenge?

b) How have the grandparents or other extended family members reacted to their new roles?

c) How have your extended family relationships changed with the addition of the new baby?

(continues)

Field Assignment 4–7 (continued)

d) How has your relationship with the child's other parent changed?

e) How have you accommodated your life to meet the needs of the child?

Date: Time: Location: Parent:

a) How did you adapt to your role as a parent? What was your biggest challenge?

b) How have the grandparents or other extended family members reacted to their new roles?

c) How have your extended family relationships changed with the addition of the new baby?

d) How has your relationship with the child's other parent changed?

e) How have you accommodated your life to meet the needs of the child?

Compare and contrast responses of the parents.
Similarities

Differences

An electronic version of each field assignment is available on the CD-ROM that accompanies this text.

Another framework that has been used extensively to study family systems is the *circumplex* model that was developed by Olson and his associates (Olson, 2000). This model emphasizes the importance of communication as a tool for healthy family interaction. Also, a balance of cohesion or togetherness is examined as well as a balance of flexibility or adaptability. In building this theory, Olson has demonstrated that the amounts of cohesion or flexibility a family exhibits may be related to the family life cycle. For example, families with young children are often more cohesive and less flexible than families with teens. The greater closeness when children are younger is necessitated by the everyday nurturing needed by children. Also, less flexibility is often a hallmark of families with young children as parents keep busy schedules for work, child care, school, community activities, and other family priorities on track. A close look at families with adolescents is likely to show significant differences in relation to both cohesion and flexibility. However, communication is a staple for healthy family functioning. Figure 4-8 provides an illustration of this theory.

Figure 4–8 Illustration of Olson's Circumplex Model

Field Assignment 4–8 Collecting Data about Family Communication, Cohesion and Flexibility

Interview two families with at least two children. Be sure that at least one of the children is in the early childhood age range (birth–8 years). Ask the following questions and record your responses.

Family #1
Date: Time: Location: Family members:

a) How important is effective communication with family members? What are challenges to effective communication? What helps communication?

b) How much time does your family spend together in a typical day or week? Is the amount of time that you spend together satisfactory? What do you do to ensure that you get to have enough togetherness? Are there any negative effects from too little or too much togetherness for your family?

c) How has your family been flexible or adaptable at times? Is there a specific recent occurrence when flexibility was necessary? What makes it hard to be flexible? What are some things that help support flexibility?

Family #2
Date: Time: Location: Family members:

a) How important is effective communication with family members? What are challenges to effective communication? What helps communication?

(continues)

Field Assignment 4–8 (continued)

b) How much time does your family spend together in a typical day or week? Is the amount of time that you spend together satisfactory? What do you do to ensure that you get to have enough togetherness? Are there any negative effects from too little or too much togetherness for your family?

c) How has your family been flexible or adaptable at times? Is there a specific recent occurrence when flexibility was necessary? What makes it hard to be flexible? What are some things that help support flexibility?

Compare and contrast responses from the two families:
Similarities:

 Differences:

An electronic version of each field assignment is available on the CD-ROM that accompanies this text.

When early childhood teachers understand the challenges and strengths of families, efforts to form partnerships to support children's school achievement have a greater possibility for success. Sensitivity to demands that families face and to variations in their challenges leads to stronger relationships among educators and family members.

Current Research Related to Teaching Young Children

Relevant, current research literature must be examined by early childhood teachers in order to be effective practitioners. This section of the chapter reviews current research related to brain development, the curriculum-assessment cycle for teaching, the basis for developmentally appropriate practice, inclusive educational practices, classroom management practices based on a knowledge of child development, and reflective practice and action research.

Brain Development

Recent progress in understanding how the brain develops has contributed to a scientific understanding of teaching young children. Information has been gained about the rapid changes that the brain undergoes from prenatal development through school entry. The plasticity of the brain is both a positive and a negative force because it leads to both adaptation and vulnerability. It is known that the brain is so adaptable that meaningful experiences across expansive periods of time can have a positive influence on neurological development. It is also known that children with sensory or other physical and motor disabilities will need greater attention and intervention for their brains to adapt in the most efficient, effective ways. Finally, the brain is vulnerable to dangers of abusive or neglectful care, toxic or violent environments, and other extremes of nonnormative environments (National Research Council and Institute of Medicine, 2000).

The influence of early experiences on brain development points to the ongoing interactions of nature and nurture. In addition to various nutrients and biological attributes, healthy brain development is known to require sensory stimulation, activity, and social interaction. Those factors that are detrimental or toxic to the brain include infectious diseases, neurotoxins such as alcohol, insufficient nutrition, prematurity, and stress. Without appropriate methods of early intervention (nurture), the negative impact of these biological (nature) effects can be expected to be greater (National Research Council and Institute of Medicine, 2000).

Curriculum and Assessment Cycle

In addition to understanding child development and neuroscience, the science of teaching in early childhood education draws from our understanding of best practices in terms of curriculum and assessment. For all effective teaching, a cycle of curriculum and assessment informs teachers about what and how content should be taught as well as when to individualize for various learners. Consideration of children's development is the basis for all developmentally appropriate curriculum and assessment practices.

Developmentally Appropriate Practice (DAP) Developmentally appropriate or effective practice is based on two dimensions: (1) typical development of children at various ages from birth through age eight, and (2) individual differences in children that include abilities, personalities, learning styles, cultural contexts, language, family structure, and similar factors. Based on "five interrelated dimensions of early childhood professional practice" (Bredekamp & Copple, 1997, p. 16) the guidelines for DAP consist of the following components:

- *Creating a caring community of learners.* Environments that provide high-quality early education are supportive and caring of all members: children, families, and staff. Positive relationships are essential as the foundation for excellence in early childhood education.

- *Teaching to enhance development and learning.* In addition to creating an intellectually interesting and challenging environment, early childhood teachers demonstrate explicit respect for all children and families. Through continuous observation, they gain deep knowledge of each child's development, strengths, needs, stress levels, and competencies.

- *Constructing appropriate curriculum.* Early childhood curriculum is multifaceted. Not only will early childhood teachers consider child development but they will also plan content from all disciplines (subject areas) in a manner that indicates intellectual integrity. Considerations are given to home culture and language, differences in abilities, and technology use that is integrated with other aspects of the curriculum.

■ *Assessing children's development and learning.* "Accurate assessment of young children is difficult because their development and learning are rapid, uneven, episodic, and embedded within specific cultural and linguistic contexts" (Bredekamp & Copple, 1997, p. 21). Assessment is used as a mechanism to inform teachers about children's development and learning so that teachers can plan effectively for all children. Methods of assessment must be appropriate to the developmental level of the children.

■ *Establishing reciprocal relationships with families.* Young children are inextricably tied to their families. Early childhood teachers must forge relationships that support reciprocity and partnership with family members. Active programs of family involvement are necessary for high-quality early education.

See Appendix C for the NAEYC Position Statement, *Developmentally Appropriate Practice in Early Childhood Programs Serving Children from Birth through Age 8.*

Field Assignment 4–9 Observing and Incorporating the Five Dimensions of DAP

1. Observe in a variety of early childhood environments and write examples related to each of the five dimensions of developmentally appropriate practice (DAP). Use Appendix C to check for details about each of the dimensions.

   Creating a caring community of learners
   Date: Time: Location:

   Example 1:

   Date: Time: Location:

   Example 2:

   Date: Time: Location:

   Example 3:

   Teaching to enhance development and learning
   Date: Time: Location:

   Example 1:

   Date: Time: Location:

(continues)

Field Assignment 4–9 (continued)

Example 2:

Date: Time: Location:

Example 3:

Constructing appropriate curriculum
Date: Time: Location:

Example 1:

Date: Time: Location:

Example 2:

Date: Time: Location:

Example 3:

Assessing children's development and learning
Date: Time: Location:

Example 1:

Date: Time: Location:

Example 2:

Date: Time: Location:

Example 3:

Establishing reciprocal relationships with families
Date: Time: Location:

Example 1:

Date: Time: Location:

Example 2:

Date: Time: Location:

Example 3:

(continues)

Field Assignment 4–9 (continued)

2. When you have an assignment to participate in an early childhood setting, describe how you considered each of the five dimensions. Also, note any challenges that you faced in considering each dimension.

Creating a caring community of learners
Date: Time: Location:

Example 1:

Date: Time: Location:

Example 2:

Date: Time: Location:

Example 3:

Teaching to enhance development and learning
Date: Time: Location:

Example 1:

Date: Time: Location:

Example 2:

Date: Time: Location:

Example 3:

Constructing appropriate curriculum
Date: Time: Location:

Example 1:

Date: Time: Location:

Example 2:

Date: Time: Location:

Example 3:

(continues)

Field Assignment 4–9 (continued)

Assessing children's development and learning
Date: Time: Location:

Example 1:

Date: Time: Location:

Example 2:

Date: Time: Location:

Example 3:

Establishing reciprocal relationships with families
Date: Time: Location:

Example 1:

Date: Time: Location:

Example 2:

Date: Time: Location:

Example 3:

An electronic version of each field assignment is available on the CD-ROM that accompanies this text.

Inclusive Early Childhood Environments

The current educational movement to include all children in early education environments is based on "research that contributes to our knowledge of recommended practice" (DEC Position Statement, 2000, p. 1). All high-quality early education environments make an effort to practice *inclusion*, the practice of placing children with identified disabilities into regular education settings. "Inclusive programs provide the opportunity to preserve individualized approaches to developing goals and objectives for children with disabilities, and for assessing outcomes, within the context of developmentally appropriate practices" (Klein & Gilkerson, 2000). Figure 4–9 provides the entire text of the Division for Early Childhood's Position Statement on Inclusion.

Division for Early Childhood, June 2000

Inclusion, *as a value, supports the right of all children, regardless of abilities, to participate actively in natural settings within their communities. Natural settings are those in which the child would spend time had he or she not had a disability. These settings include, but are not limited to home, preschool, nursery schools, Head Start programs, kindergartens, neighborhood school classrooms, child care, places of worship, recreational (such as community playgrounds and community events) and other settings that all children and families enjoy.*

DEC supports and advocates that young children and their families have full and successful access to health, social, educational, and other support services that promote full participation in family and community life. DEC values the cultural, economic, and educational diversity of families and supports a family-guided process for identifying a program of service.

As young children participate in group settings (such as preschool, play groups, child care, kindergarten) their active participation should be guided by developmentally and individually appropriate curriculum. Access to and participation in the age appropriate general curriculum becomes central to the identification and provision of specialized support services.

To implement inclusive practices **DEC** *supports: (a) the continued development, implementation, evaluation, and dissemination of full* **inclusion** *supports, services, and systems that are of high quality for all children; (b) the development of preservice and inservice training programs that prepare families, service providers, and administrators to develop and work within inclusive settings; (c) collaboration among key stakeholders to implement flexible fiscal and administrative procedures in support of* **inclusion;** *(d) research that contributes to our knowledge of recommended practice; and (e) the restructuring and unification of social, educational, health, and intervention supports and services to make them more responsive to the needs of all children and families. Ultimately, the implementation of inclusive practice must lead to optimal developmental benefits for each individual child and family.*

Figure 4–9 Position Statement on Inclusion.

Field Assignment 4–10 Observing and Practicing Inclusion in Early Education

1. Observe in two inclusive early childhood settings. Describe ways in which the early childhood teaching staff include all children with "access to and participation in the age appropriate general curriculum" and provide specialized support services to meet the individual needs of children.

   Date: Time: Location:

   Description of how teachers included all children:

   Description of specialized services to meet individual needs:

(continues)

Field Assignment 4–10 (continued)

Date: Time: Location:

Description of how teachers included all children:

Description of specialized services to meet individual needs:

2. In your own practice, describe at least two different times that you included all children in the "general curriculum" and provided specialized services to meet the needs of all children.

Date: Time: Location:

Description of how you included all children:

Description of how you used specialized services to meet individual needs:

Date: Time: Location:

Description of how you included all children:

Description of how you used specialized services to meet individual needs:

An electronic version of each field assignment is available on the CD-ROM that accompanies this text.

Classroom Management and Guiding Children's Behavior

The very term *classroom management* brings about differing ideas to teachers. In early childhood education, it is critical to base methods of management and guidance of children's behavior on what is known about the development of young children. In *The Power of Guidance*, Dr. Dan Gartrell (Gartrell, 2004) provides a compelling framework for the basis of classroom management in early education. With a strong basis in understanding the nature and development of young children, Gartrell reframes common misconceptions about children's behavior by identifying "mistaken behavior" (rather than misbehavior) and classifying causes of behavior. Although mistaken behavior is sometimes intentional, not accidental, children often do not have the knowledge, experience, or self-control that is necessary to change such behaviors on their own.

Based on theoretical and research evidence about how young children think and learn, Gartrell's conception of guiding children's behavior, versus the commonly practiced rewards and punishments approach, is held in high regard by knowledgeable early childhood educators. Effective guidance of children's behavior is always based on the teacher or caregiver having built a positive relationship with each child. In addition, early childhood professionals must understand reasons for children's mistaken behaviors in order to effectively guide children. Three categories of mistaken behaviors are explained:

Experimental. Children engage in mistaken behavior because they do not know what to do or not do; children engage in mistaken behavior to see what will happen. This is generally the easiest type of mistaken behavior for early childhood professionals to guide children to change.

Socially influenced. Children observe others—parents, media heroes, peers, teachers—engaging in these behaviors and mistakenly assume that they are appropriate for them to model. This type of mistaken behavior is more strongly ingrained in children's behavioral repertoires and may be more difficult to engage children to change.

Strong needs. Children engage in mistaken behavior because they have a great deal of pain, they have learned that the world is not a safe place. Children's pain may be either biologically based, socially based, or both. Typically, in order to support children in changing these strong needs mistaken behaviors, teachers must involve various combinations of others such as families, counselors, psychologists, special educators, or administrators (Gartrell, 2004).

The tools that teachers will incorporate with the guidance approach are those that encourage children, rather than those that offer rewards or threaten punishments. When children feel encouraged, they are more likely to believe in their own ability to engage in positive behaviors. Some of the ways that teachers can offer encouragement include the following:

- individual and group communication that builds positive relationships with children: the use of encouragement rather than punishment and reinforcement

- contact or guidance talks: one-on-one teacher–student conversations used to teach and support children's positive, prosocial behaviors and attitudes

- conflict resolution strategies: children learn how to cool down and identify problems with others, to brainstorm solutions, to choose a solution for implementation. Teachers follow up by monitoring and providing encouragement

- partnerships with families: teachers communicate continuously with families about children's behavior and ways to encourage and support positive behaviors that lead to school success

- class meetings: guidelines are established so that children speak and listen respectfully in efforts to solve whole group issues or concerns

▓ self-removal: children learn self-control through the process of moving themselves to a quiet place specifically identified in the classroom for short-term self-removal

In addition, strategies for crisis management, especially for children with strong needs mistaken behavior are included (Gartrell, 2004). When emotions are out of control and communication is breaking down, crisis management strategies are put into effect in order to be able to effectively communicate and to solve the problem. Gartrell (2004) emphasizes these approaches for crisis management:

▓ Be direct. Describe objectively what you see, express displeasure without insulting anyone, and correct by direction. Use a combination of these approaches as necessary.

▓ Command a choice. Teachers give children two choices, but not an ultimatum. One choice is what the child chooses in order to continue involvement; the other choice allows the child to stay out of the activity but to choose another with a follow-up discussion.

▓ Calm everyone involved.

▓ Use physical restraint, if necessary. Specialized training should be required for teachers so that they use this approach wisely and correctly.

Types of Mistaken Behavior:
   Experimental
   Socially influenced
   Strong needs

Methods Teachers Use to Offer Encouragement As They Guide Children's Behavior:
   Contact or guidance talks
   Conflict resolution strategies
   Partnerships with families
   Class meetings
   Self-removal

Crisis Management Methods
   Be direct.
   Command a choice.
   Calm everyone involved.
   With appropriate training, use physical restraint.

Figure 4–10 Highlights of Gartrell's Guidance Approach.

Field Assignment 4–11 Collecting Data about Children's Mistaken Behaviors and Teachers' Use of Guidance Procedures

1. Using Figure 4–10, observe at least three examples of children's mistaken behavior in each of the following categories:

a) experimental
Date: Time: Location:
Description:

Date: Time: Location:
Description:

Date: Time: Location:
Description:

b) socially influenced
Date: Time: Location:
Description:

Date: Time: Location:
Description:

Date: Time: Location:
Description:

c) strong needs
Date: Time: Location:
Description:

Date: Time: Location:
Description:

Date: Time: Location:
Description:

2. Provide details about a time that you observed a teacher or caregiver use the following strategies in an early childhood setting.

Encouragement
Date: Time: Location:
Description:

Outcome:

(continues)

Field Assignment 4–11 (continued)

Contact or guidance talk
Date: Time: Location:
Description:

Outcome:

Conflict resolution strategy
Date: Time: Location:
Description:

Outcome:

Partnership with families
Date: Time: Location:
Description:

Outcome:

Class meetings
Date: Time: Location:
Description:

Outcome:

Self-removal
Date: Time: Location:
Description:

Outcome:

Crisis management
Date: Time: Location:
Description:

Outcome:

---

3. Describe a time when you implemented the following strategies.

Encouragement
Date: Time: Location:
Description:

Outcome:

Contact or guidance talk
Date: Time: Location:
Description:

Outcome:

(continues)

Field Assignment 4–11 (continued)

Conflict resolution strategy
Date: Time: Location:
Description:

Outcome:

Partnership with families
Date: Time: Location:
Description:

Outcome:

Class meetings
Date: Time: Location:
Description:

Outcome:

Self-removal
Date: Time: Location:
Description:

Outcome:

Crisis management
Date: Time: Location:
Description:

Outcome:

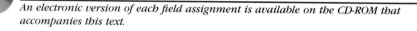

An electronic version of each field assignment is available on the CD-ROM that accompanies this text.

Self-Reflection and Inquiry

Teachers are always learning and refining their ability to support children's learning. A great deal of information is available about the importance of implementing an inquiry approach to teaching and learning. Current best practice in many fields of teaching emphasizes a learner- and learning-centered approach in contrast to a more traditional teacher-centered approach. In practice, this means that teachers must be prepared to observe and collect evidence about each child's learning in order to reflect upon what and how to teach. In contrast, the teacher-centered approach is simpler in that decisions about what and how to teach are driven by sequencing of curriculum or program philosophy, often emanating from sources outside the classroom.

Field Assignment 4–12 Interviewing Teachers about Teaching Expectations

Interview at least three teachers of young children (birth to 8 years), using the following questions:

1. How do you know what to teach and when to teach it?
2. Who makes decisions about the following?
   a. choice of curricula
   b. sequencing of each curriculum
   c. program philosophy
3. What guidelines are used to make such decisions?
4. Are teachers expected to observe and collect evidence about each child's learning? If so, how are teachers doing this? If not, would this be effective in meeting standards for every child?

Summarize the responses from each of the three teachers:

Summary from teacher #1:

Summary from teacher #2:

Summary from teacher #3:

An electronic version of each field assignment is available on the CD-ROM that accompanies this text.

Reflective practice requires knowledgeable teachers who understand children and are capable of designing learning experiences to meet each of their needs. Reflective teachers engage in continuous processing about their teaching throughout their professional lives. Grossman and Williston (2001) define reflection as "the act of creating a mental space in which to contemplate a question or idea, such as, 'What do I know about teaching young children?' This moment allows a mental transformation to a time and a situation that leads to a deeper perspective" (p. 236). With this definition in mind, those who are preparing to become early childhood professionals must have instructional and content knowledge about children and pedagogy in order to reflect in professionally meaningful and accountable ways. One sequence that has been used to teach pre-service teachers about reflection includes the following:

- *reflecting on self:* pre-service teachers discover their own personal identities
- *reflecting on child development and pedagogy:* pre-service teachers use content knowledge to develop professional skills and dispositions for working with children, families, and colleagues
- *reflecting on professionalism:* pre-service teachers practice reflection in order to construct ethical teaching behaviors, skills, and attitudes (Grossman & Williston, 2001).

Field Assignment 4–13 Reflecting on Yourself as a Teacher, on Child Development and Pedagogy, and on Professionalism

1. Reflect on your personal identity
   a) Who are you as a teacher?

   b) As you gain knowledge and skills, how has your perspective about teaching young children changed?

   c) How do your personal values connect with or conflict with the Code of Ethical Conduct?

   d) What personal values do you hold that might be challenged by the Code of Ethical Conduct?

2. Reflect on child development and pedagogy
   a) How has your understanding of children changed since you began your teacher preparation program?

   b) How do you understand the relationship of children's development to your teaching strategies?

3. Reflect on professionalism
   a) How do you use reflection to construct professional behavior?

   b) How do you use reflection to construct professional knowledge?

   c) How do you use reflection to construct professional attitudes?

An electronic version of each field assignment is available on the CD-ROM that accompanies this text.

Effective teaching of young children is based in our scientific understanding of child development, family systems, and appropriate pedagogy

Conclusion

Effective teaching of young children is based in our scientific understanding of child development, family systems, and appropriate pedagogy. Professionalism requires that early educators know and practice implications from current evidence in the field. Possessing the disposition of a lifelong learner aids teachers in the important work of staying current in their profession.

References

Bredekamp, S., & Copple, C. (Eds.). (1997). *Developmentally appropriate practice in early childhood programs, revised edition*. Washington, DC: NAEYC.

Carter, E. A., & McGoldrick, M. (1999). *The expanded family life cycle: Individual, family and social perspectives*. Boston: Allyn and Bacon.

Division for Early Childhood, Council on Exceptional Children. (June 2000). *Position statement on inclusion*. Retrieved on April 30, 2007, from http://www.dec-sped.org/pdf/positionpapers/PositionStatement_Inclusion.pdf.

Erikson, E. H. (1950). *Childhood and society*. New York: W. W. Norton.

Erikson, E. H. (1968). *Identity: Youth and crisis*. New York: W. W. Norton.

Gartrell, D. J. (2004). *The power of guidance: Teaching social-emotional skills in early childhood classrooms*. Clifton Park, NY: Thomson Delmar Learning.

Grossman, S., & Williston, J. (Summer 2001). Strategies for teaching early childhood students to connect reflective thinking to practice. *Childhood Education, 77*(4), 236–240.

Klein, N. K., & Gilkerson, L. (2000). Personnel preparation for early childhood intervention programs. In J. P. Shonkoff & S. J. Meisels (Eds.), *Handbook of early childhood intervention* (2nd ed.). New York: Cambridge University Press.

Leong, D. J., & Bodrova, E. (n.d.). Lev Vygotsky: Playing to learn. *Early Childhood Today.* Retrieved September 12, 2006, from http://content .scholastic.com/browse/article.jsp?id=3549.

National Research Council and Institute of Medicine. (2000). *From neurons to neighborhoods: The science of early childhood development.* Committee on Integrating the Science of Early Childhood Development. J. P. Shonkoff and D. A. Phillips (Eds.), Board on Children, Youth, and Families, Commission on Behavior and Social Sciences and Education. Washington, DC: National Academy Press.

Olson, D. H. L. (2000). *Circumplex model of marital and family systems.* Warrington, England: Association of Family Therapy and Systemic Practice.

Selman, R. L. (1980). *The growth of interpersonal understanding: Development and clinical analysis.* New York: Academic Press.

Chapter 5

The Art of Teaching

Objectives

After reading and reflecting on this chapter, early childhood students will be able to

- Explain how teachers' personal characteristics influence their teaching
- Discuss the meaning and application of teacher beliefs
- Demonstrate an understanding of the relationships of personal characteristics and how they affect professional dispositions
- Describe differences between personal values and professional values and ethics
- Apply aspects of their own personal style in ways that support them to teach through the scientific knowledge base

Introduction

It is clear that even though a broad array of scientific evidence exists about effective teaching of young children, the actual practice of individual teachers often looks quite different. Good teachers, using this same knowledge base, convey themselves in a variety of ways in early childhood classrooms. Teachers implement best practices in ways that make the classroom their own. Personal preferences and belief systems are at the core of the art of teaching.

Relationships form the basis for teaching and learning in early education. When teachers develop positive relationships, children are more likely to be successful in school (Pianta & Stuhlman, 2004). "Children who develop warm, positive relationships with their kindergarten teachers are more excited about learning, more positive about coming to school, more confident, and achieve more in the classroom" (Young children, 2004, p. 4).

"Someone's got to be crazy about that kid. That's number one. First, last, and always."–Urie Bronfenbrenner

Effective teaching requires an understanding of existing information about best practice in early education. It also requires that teachers have a healthy sense of themselves and their own identities. This is the emotional basis necessary to form positive relationships with children, families, colleagues, community members, and administrators. The umbrella of healthy emotional status and principled values for teachers encompasses many different styles and beliefs.

 PERSONAL IDENTITY

Grossman and Williston (2001) note that one way to scaffold an understanding of personal identity is through reflection. The following reflective exercises in Figure 5–1 are described by these authors.

---

1. Preprofessional self-assessment. *Write at least eight sentences that include your personal qualities, dispositions and behaviors for each of these time periods:*
  - *The way I am now*
  - *The way I was as a child*
  - *The way I will be in my fifth year of teaching.*

2. Questions to ask yourself throughout your teacher preparation program:
  - *What do I think I know?*
  - *What do I want to learn?*
  - *How can I find out about _____?*
  - *How will I demonstrate what I have learned?*
  - *What problems may arise with the situation I am planning for the classroom?*
  - *How will I be proactive or resolve problem situations with children? With families? With colleagues?*

3. Draw yourself in an early childhood classroom. *Do this at the beginning of your field experiences, sometime before student teaching, and as a student teacher.*

Figure 5–1 Understanding Personal Identity through Reflection

Field Assignment 5–1 Preprofessional Self-Assessment

Complete the reflective exercises described in Figure 5–1.

1. For the preprofessional assessment, provide eight sentences for each of the three prompts.

    a) the way I am now

    b) the way I was as a child

    c) the way I will be after five years of teaching

2. Questions to ask yourself throughout your teacher preparation program. Respond to these questions at least four times:

    a) What do I already know?

    Date:

    Date:

    Date:

    Date:

    b) What do I want or need to know?

    Date:

    Date:

    Date:

    Date:

    c) What have I learned?

    Date:

    Date:

    Date:

    Date:

    d) How can I find out what I want or need to know?

    Date:

    Date:

(continues)

Field Assignment 5–1 (continued)

Date:

Date:

e) How will I demonstrate what I have learned?

Date:

Date:

Date:

Date:

3. Draw yourself in an early childhood setting four times throughout your teacher preparation program.

Date:

Date:

Date:

Date:

An electronic version of each field assignment is available on the CD-ROM that accompanies this text.

TEMPERAMENT

One way of discerning temperament, or behavioral style preferences, of teachers is through the Myers-Briggs Type Indicator (MBTI) (Sears & Kennedy, 1997). The MBTI defines four dimensions of temperament dichotomously, with the underlying notion that individuals have preferences for behaving more in one way or the other on each of the four preferences:

- Extraversion (E)–Introversion (I): how one interacts with the world, mostly through others or through introspection

- Intuition (N)–Sensing (S): how one takes in information, through a global sense of intuition or through concrete mechanisms of the senses

- Thinking (T)–Feeling (F): how one makes decisions, through logic or subjective personal values

■ Perception (P)–Judgment (J): how one works, using process to guide the outcome or planning and organizing first

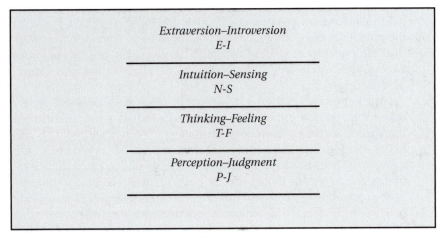

Extraversion–Introversion
E-I

Intuition–Sensing
N-S

Thinking–Feeling
T-F

Perception–Judgment
P-J

Figure 5–2 Four Dimensions and Abbreviations of the Myers-Briggs Type Indicator (MBTI)

A variety of studies have found that most teachers select the following preferences, abbreviated ESFJ:

■ extraversion

■ sensing

■ feeling

■ judgment

However, no systematic information is available that relates temperament to teaching effectiveness. Rather, temperament is best used to understand oneself and ways to work with others of similar or different styles. For more detail about temperament or to complete a preliminary form of the questionnaire without cost, go to http://www.keirsey.com. (There is a charge for completing the comprehensive form.)

Generally, extraverted teachers get energy from their interactions with others, and introverted teachers become sapped of energy after lengthy or intense interactions with others. Teachers of both styles, though, can develop good communication patterns and healthy relationships with children, families, and colleagues. Sensing teachers gather their information in a linear fashion through observation, whereas intuitive teachers use a more global approach based on introspection. Both sensing and intuitive teachers can effectively assess needs of children and support their learning; they are likely to go about it in different ways. Teachers with a feeling preference typically make decisions based on their values, whereas teachers with a thinking preference are more likely to use an external basis of reasoning from past experience. Few individuals are so extreme in their ability to be rational or merciful that it is a detriment to teaching and learning. Finally, judging teachers are often product-oriented with strict deadlines, and perceiving teachers are likely to place the emphasis on the process, sometimes with more fluid deadlines. When teachers with either of these preferences understand child development and communicate their expectations to children, both types can be effective teachers (http://www .keirsey.com).

An important reason to be aware of one's own personal style preferences is to be aware that these preferences impact what teachers plan and implement in their classrooms or centers. When attempting to meet the needs of all learners, an extraverted teacher must be certain to include some activities and assessments that are sensitive to students with an introversion preference as well as those who are more extraverted. Similar understanding of the remaining three sets of preferences can help teachers to provide more balance in the types of learning experiences that they offer.

Field Assignment 5–2 Four Dimensions of Temperament

Consider information about each of the four dimensions of temperament and hypothesize about your personal preferences:

Extraversion–Introversion
Explain your hypothesis about your personal preference:

Sensing–Intuition
Explain your hypothesis about your personal preference:

Feeling–Thinking
Explain your hypothesis about your personal preference:

Judging–Perceiving
Explain your hypothesis about your personal preference:

---

2. Go to http://www.keirsey.com and read more about temperament. Check to see whether you decide to keep your previous hypotheses or if you want to make a change.
   Explain which of your previous hypotheses you are maintaining:
   E–I:

(continues)

Field Assignment 5–2 (continued)

S–N:

T–F:

J–P:

Explain which of your previous hypotheses you wish to change:
E–I:

S–N:

T–F:

J–P:

3. How do you believe that each aspect of your temperament will influence your role as an early childhood teaching professional?
E–I:

S–N:

T–F:

J–P:

4. How can understanding the dimensions of temperament help to create a balance of instructional strategies in the classroom?

5. Reflect on a time that you spent with children. Consider all aspects of your temperament, and describe how these preferences might have influenced your interactions and expectations.

Reflecting on your disposition about children's development and learning is essential for your professional growth

EARLY CHILDHOOD TEACHER DISPOSITIONS

Lilian Katz, a venerable leader in early childhood education, defines dispositions for teaching as tendencies "to exhibit frequently, consciously, and voluntarily a pattern of behavior that is directed to a broad goal" (Katz, 1993). Further, Katz notes that it is important to attend to dispositions for all levels of learners, including young children in early education programs and candidates in early childhood teacher preparation programs. One essential application regarding dispositions is that teachers visibly demonstrate their own dispositions as they are teaching young children. Thus, children are not typically taught about dispositions for learning through methods of direct instruction, but rather in the climate of the classroom created by the teacher.

In addition to content knowledge and pedagogical skills, teacher effectiveness is influenced by various attitudes about children, teaching, and the profession. Information about dispositions currently is drawn from a variety of sources (Schulte, Edick, Edwards, & Mackiel, n.d.). For several decades, Good and Brophy (1987, 1997, as cited in Schulte et al., n.d.) have countered that there are ten teaching behaviors that are particularly important. These ten behaviors are the following:

- imparting clear lessons
- using a variety of instructional strategies

- maintaining orientation to tasks
- engaging children in their learning
- keeping a high rate of success for each student
- encouraging student ideas and contributions
- structuring the day
- questioning throughout the day
- probing for clear answers
- maintaining positive affect.

Field Assignment 5–3 Observing and Incorporating Ten Behaviors for Effective Teaching

1. Observe at least two early childhood teachers and provide examples about how they incorporate the ten teaching behaviors espoused by Good and Brophy (Schulte et al., n.d.).

   Date: Time: Location:
   Description of early childhood setting:

   imparting clear lessons

   using a variety of instructional strategies

   maintaining orientation to tasks

   engaging children in their learning

   keeping a high rate of success for each student

   encouraging student ideas and contributions

   structuring the day

   questioning throughout the day

(continues)

Field Assignment 5–3 (continued)

probing for clear answers

maintaining positive affect

Date: Time: Location:
Description of early childhood setting:

imparting clear lessons

using a variety of instructional strategies

maintaining orientation to tasks

engaging children in their learning

keeping a high rate of success for each student

encouraging student ideas and contributions

structuring the day

questioning throughout the day

probing for clear answers

maintaining positive affect

---

2. In your own teaching, describe how you incorporate these ten teaching behaviors.

imparting clear lessons

using a variety of instructional strategies

(continues)

Field Assignment 5–3 (continued)

maintaining orientation to tasks

engaging children in their learning

keeping a high rate of success for each student

encouraging student ideas and contributions

structuring the day

questioning throughout the day

probing for clear answers

maintaining positive affect

An electronic version of each field assignment is available on the CD-ROM that accompanies this text.

Listening with understanding and empathy is one of the Sixteen Habits of Mind in action

More recently, Costa and Kalick (2000, as cited in Schulte et al., n.d.) have developed 16 habits of the mind that they have found to be relevant to teaching and learning. These habits of the mind are connected to various aspects of personal preferences and understanding of others. See Figure 5–3 for a list of relevant habits of the mind.

1. *Persisting*
2. *Managing impulsivity*
3. *Listening with understanding and empathy*
4. *Thinking flexibly*
5. *Metacognition (knowing about knowing; thinking about thinking)*
6. *Striving for accuracy*
7. *Questioning and posing problems*
8. *Applying past knowledge to new situations*
9. *Thinking and communicating with clarity and precision*
10. *Gathering data through all senses*
11. *Creating, imagining, innovating*
12. *Responding with understanding and awe*
13. *Taking responsible risks*
14. *Finding humor*
15. *Thinking interdependently*
16. *Remaining open to continuous learning*

Figure 5–3 Sixteen Habits of the Mind (Costa & Kalick, 2000)

Field Assignment 5–4 Observing and Incorporating Habits of the Mind for Effective Teaching

1. Observe several early childhood teachers to find examples for all 16 habits of the mind listed in Figure 5-3. Write your observations here.

   Persisting
   Date: Time: Location:
   Description:

   Managing impulsivity
   Date: Time: Location:
   Description:

(continues)

Field Assignment 5–4 (continued)

Listening with understanding and empathy
Date: Time: Location:
Description:

Thinking flexibly
Date: Time: Location:
Description:

Metacognition
Date: Time: Location:
Description:

Striving for accuracy
Date: Time: Location:
Description:

Questioning and posing problems
Date: Time: Location:
Description:

Applying past knowledge to new situations
Date: Time: Location:
Description:

Thinking and communicating with clarity and precision
Date: Time: Location:
Description:

Gathering data through all senses
Date: Time: Location:
Description:

(continues)

Field Assignment 5–4 (continued)

Creating, imagining, innovating
Date: Time: Location:
Description:

Responding with understanding and awe
Date: Time: Location:
Description:

Taking responsible risks
Date: Time: Location:
Description:

Finding humor
Date: Time: Location:
Description:

Thinking interdependently
Date: Time: Location:
Description:

Remaining open to continuous learning
Date: Time: Location:
Description:

2. Reflect on your own habits of the mind and provide specific examples about how you have incorporated each one into your teaching and learning. Also, how will you consider these habits of the mind in your future teaching?

Persisting:

Managing impulsivity:

Listening with understanding and empathy:

Thinking flexibly:

Metacognition:

(continues)

Field Assignment 5–4 (continued)

Striving for accuracy:

Questioning and posing problems:

Applying past knowledge to new situations:

Thinking and communicating with clarity and precision:

Gathering data through all senses:

Creating, imagining, innovating:

Responding with understanding and awe:

Taking responsible risks:

Finding humor:

Thinking interdependently:

Remaining open to continuous learning:

Schulte, et al. (n.d.), drawing from current understanding of best practices in education, have developed the Teacher Dispositions Index. The index is composed of two subscales: the student-centered subscale and the professionalism, curriculum-centered subscale. Some points from the 25-item student-centered subscale include:

- I believe it is important to learn about students and their community.
- I view teaching as an important profession.
- I believe it is important to include all students in learning.
- I demonstrate qualities of humor, empathy, and warmth with others.
- I understand that students learn in many different ways.
- I believe that the classroom environment a teacher creates greatly affects students' learning and development.
- I respect the cultures of all students.

The 20-item professionalism, curriculum-centered subscale includes the following:

- I provide appropriate feedback to encourage students in their development.
- I value both long-term and short-term planning.
- I stimulate students' interests.
- I select material that is interesting for students.
- I communicate effectively with students, parents, and colleagues.

Considering the items from the Teacher Dispositions Index may help teachers and teacher candidates to gain increased understanding about what is meant by dispositions. Although they are somewhat difficult to objectively measure, dispositions are not elusive. Continuing research and strong emphasis in the teacher preparation literature in this area is likely to lead to better forms of measurement in the near future.

One effort to objectively measure dispositions for teacher candidates has been undertaken by Martin, Smith, and Ezell (2005) from the University of Arkansas at Fort Smith. These teacher educators created an eight-point scale based in part on the Interstate New Teacher Assessment and Support Consortium (INTASC) standards and criteria from the National Board for Professional Teaching Standards (NBPTS), in addition to professional behaviors and communication skills valued by this teacher preparation program. Items from this assessment are presented in Figure 5–4.

Dispositions

1. *Understands and values the discipline(s) he or she teaches.*
2. *Is willing to utilize multiple teaching methodologies because of a belief that all children can learn and that there are multiple ways children do learn.*
3. *Is committed to planning effective units of curriculum that are aligned with assessment strategies and utilize appropriate technology.*
4. *Is committed to providing a classroom environment in which the diverse needs, interests, and talents of students are appreciated and utilized to create a learning climate fostering attainment of high standards.*
5. *Is committed to a democratic school environment in which positive attitudes, respect for all students and adults, and two-way communication are the norm.*
6. *Values continuous educational improvement that includes research, reflection, assessment, and learning as an ongoing process.*
7. *Is committed to integrity, ethical behavior, and professionalism as the foundation for all that takes place in the school and classroom.*
8. *Believes that close cooperation and collaboration with parents and the community are critical to maximum student learning for all students.*

Figure 5–4 Dispositions Assessment Items (Martin, Smith & Ezell, 2005)

Professional Behaviors

1. Promptness

2. Appropriate dress and grooming

3. Positive attitude

4. Caring and respectful of others

Communication Skills

1. Demonstrates professional content in all writing assignments

2. Demonstrates accurate mechanics in all writing assignments

3. Demonstrates professional oral communication skills, including correct verb usage

Figure 5–4 Dispositions Assessment Items (Martin, Smith & Ezell, 2005) *(continued)*

Field Assignment 5–5 Self-Assessment of Dispositions

Dispositions

1. Understands and values the discipline(s) he or she teaches.
   Rarely   Sometimes   Often
   Evidence:

2. Is willing to utilize multiple teaching methodologies because of a belief that all children can learn and that there are multiple ways children do learn.
   Rarely   Sometimes   Often
   Evidence:

3. Is committed to planning effective units of curriculum that are aligned with assessment strategies and utilize appropriate technology.
   Rarely   Sometimes   Often
   Evidence:

4. Is committed to providing a classroom environment in which the diverse needs, interests, and talents of students are appreciated and utilized to create a learning climate fostering attainment of high standards.
   Rarely   Sometimes   Often
   Evidence:

(continues)

Field Assignment 5–5 (continued)

5. Is committed to a democratic school environment in which positive attitudes, respect for all students and adults, and two-way communication are the norm.
   Rarely   Sometimes   Often
   Evidence:

6. Values continuous educational improvement that includes research, reflection, assessment, and learning as an ongoing process.
   Rarely   Sometimes   Often
   Evidence:

7. Is committed to integrity, ethical behavior, and professionalism as the foundation for all that takes place in the school and classroom.
   Rarely   Sometimes   Often
   Evidence:

8. Believes that close cooperation and collaboration with parents and the community are critical to maximum student learning for all students.
   Rarely   Sometimes   Often
   Evidence:

Professional Behaviors

1. Promptness
   Rarely   Sometimes   Often
   Evidence:

2. Appropriate dress and grooming
   Rarely   Sometimes   Often
   Evidence:

3. Positive attitude
   Rarely   Sometimes   Often
   Evidence:

(continues)

4. Caring and respectful of others
   Rarely   Sometimes   Often
   Evidence:

Communication Skills

1. Demonstrates professional content in all writing assignments
   Rarely   Sometimes   Often
   Evidence:

2. Demonstrates accurate mechanics in all writing assignments
   Rarely   Sometimes   Often
   Evidence:

3. Demonstrates professional oral communication skills, including correct verb usage
   Rarely   Sometimes   Often
   Evidence:

An electronic version of each field assignment is available on the CD-ROM that accompanies this text.

EARLY CHILDHOOD TEACHER BELIEFS

In her review of the research literature about beliefs of teachers, Vartuli (2005) refers to them as the "heart of teaching." In the review, Vartuli separates beliefs into two categories: beliefs about one's ability to teach, and beliefs about the nature of teaching and learning.

Those teachers who have confidence in their ability to teach are known to have a good degree of self-efficacy. Teachers who have such confidence are more likely to take time and effort and not to give up in their efforts to teach all children. On the other hand, teachers with lower self-efficacy do not believe that they can help all children to learn or achieve.

"Beliefs are the heart of teaching" (Vartuli, 2005, p. 82).

The characteristics of teachers with high and low self-efficacy are specifically related to beliefs about effective teaching and how children learn. Teachers who experience high levels of competence in teaching children are more likely to have a higher sense of self-efficacy, and thus be willing to take appropriate risks, persist with all children, and bounce back after their

Teachers with High Self-Efficacy
- *believe they can help children learn new concepts*
- *value and appreciate individual differences in children*
- *have confidence in themselves*
- *build warm relationships with children*
- *mirror positive reflections back to children*
- *are found to have positive correlations with children's academic progress and social-emotional development*
- *are found to have positive correlations with children's self-esteem, self-direction, and positive attitudes toward school*
- *see children with lower abilities as being worthy of attention and effort that it takes to help them learn*
- *have more positive attitudes toward children who are low achievers*
- *are associated with high scores on measures of developmentally appropriate practice*
- *set higher standards of performance for themselves*
- *accept responsibility when they do not meet their high expectations*
- *meet failure with renewed effort and persistence*
- *select a variety of teaching strategies based on the need to increase all children's learning*
- *know the subject matter and effective pedagogy*
- *promote autonomy in children*
- *implement democratic decision-making and conflict resolution*
- *demonstrate higher levels of family involvement, including conferencing, volunteering, and home tutoring*

Teachers with Low Self-Efficacy
- *do not believe that more time or effort on their part help children to learn*
- *focus teaching efforts on students who easily succeed in school*
- *view children who struggle in school as disruptive*
- *often cover the curriculum, with attention to reducing noise and confusion in the classroom*
- *spend more time on containment and less time on academics*
- *criticize children for failures*
- *believe that there is little they can do for children who do not have support at home or in their communities*
- *believe that families of children who do not do well in school are uncaring and unconcerned about the importance of education*

Figure 5–5 Characteristics of Teachers with High and Low Self-Efficacy
Source: Vartuli (2005).

own failures. It seems imperative, then, that teachers be provided with and supported in their confidence and ability.

Can inappropriate beliefs be changed? According to Woolfolk, Hoy, and Murphy (2001, as cited in Vartuli, 2005), four steps are necessary for changing such beliefs: awareness, analysis, discussion, and reconsideration. Awareness of beliefs that affect teaching efficacy must first be made explicit. Student journals and reflection assignments can lead to an awareness of their beliefs about children and teaching. These assignments can be analyzed by students themselves, peers, cooperating teachers, and teacher educators for beliefs that help to increase efficacy as well as those that reduce efficacy. Discussions must occur at various levels of teacher preparation, both pre-service and in-service. Teacher candidates must then reconsider their belief systems in light of scientific understanding about child development and the teaching–learning dialectic.

"... beliefs about good teachers seem to form as early as second grade and stay consistent, even throughout teacher preparation" (Murphy, Delli, & Edwards, 2004, as cited in Vartuli, 2005, p. 80).

Field Assignment 5-6 Reflecting on Your Self-Efficacy

1. Summarize a time when you worked with children and felt a high level of success.

2. View the list of characteristics of teachers with high self-efficacy in Figure 5-4. Select items from the list that you believe to be descriptive of you in this situation.

3. Summarize a time when you worked with children and felt more a sense of failure than success.

4. View the list of characteristics of teachers with low self-efficacy in Figure 5-4. Select items from the list that you believe to be descriptive of you in this situation.

5. What support systems will be helpful to you to increase your sense of self-efficacy in your journey to become a professional early childhood educator?

(continues)

Field Assignment 5–6 (continued)

6. Think back to teachers who taught you in earlier years. Describe one example of a teacher who might have had a positive sense of self-efficacy and one who may have had a negative sense of self-efficacy.

7. Add comments about your understanding of the relationship between your self-efficacy and your ability to support children's learning.

An electronic version of each field assignment is available on the CD-ROM that accompanies this text.

All individuals bring much of themselves to the children and systems in which they teach

Conclusion

All individuals bring much of themselves to the children and systems in which they teach. Classrooms look different, sound different, and feel different, based on personal variations in teachers. Variations in temperament, dispositions. and beliefs will produce diverse environments. Yet for effective teaching to exist in all of these settings, a common foundation based on current evidence guides teachers toward best practices. Early childhood practitioners must understand and reconsider when their beliefs are incongruent with current evidence in early education.

References

Grossman, S., & Williston, J. (Summer 2001). Strategies for teaching early childhood students to connect reflective thinking to practice. *Childhood Education, 77*(4), 236–240.

Katz, L. (1993). *Dispositions as educational goals.* Retrieved May 8, 2007, from http://ceep.crc.uiuc.edu/eecearchive/digests/1993/katzdi93.html.

Kiersey, D. (n.d.). *The four dimensions of Myers.* Retrieved May 9, 2007, from http://www.keirsey.com/pumII/dimensions.html.

Martin, T., Smith, R., & Ezell, G. (September 2005). *Utilizing comprehensive assessments as the basis for promoting positive dispositions.* Paper presented at the British Educational Research Association Annual Conference, University of Glamorgan, South Wales, UK. Retrieved January 27, 2007, from http://www.leeds.ac.uk/educol/documents/143621.htm.

National Scientific Council on the Developing Child. (2004). *Young children develop in an environment of relationships.* Working Paper No. 1. Cambridge, MA: Author. Retrieved May 9, 2007, from http://www.developingchild.net/pubs/wp/Young_Children_Environment_Relationships.pdf.

Pianta, R. C., & Stuhlman, M. W. (2004). Teacher-child relationships and children's success in the first years of school. *School Psychology Review, 33*(3), 444–458.

Schulte, L., Edick, N., Edwards, S., & Mackiel, D. (n.d.). *The development and validation of the teacher dispositions index.* Retrieved January 27, 2007, from http://www.usca.edu/essays/vol122004/Schulte.pdf.

Sears, S. J., & Kennedy, J. J. (1997). Myers-Briggs personality profiles of prospective educators. *The Journal of Educational Research, 90*(4), 195–202.

Vartuli, S. (September 2005). Beliefs: The heart of teaching. *Young Children, 60*(5), 76–86.

Chapter 6

Teaching Content in Early Childhood Education

Objectives

After reading and reflecting on this chapter early childhood students will be able to:

■ Review content of appropriate lessons and activities in each of the content area and make decisions regarding their age appropriateness

■ Understand and use state or national standards and professional association recommendations to plan curriculum and instruction

■ Evaluate practices that have been observed

Introduction

This chapter focuses on teaching content in early childhood classrooms. The content areas included in this chapter are (1) literacy, (2) the arts, (3) science, (4) mathematics, (5) physical education and health, and (6) social studies.

 LITERACY

Literacy is a broad term that includes a variety of skills, attitudes, practices, and development. As discussed in this chapter, it is not limited to reading instruction, but it is certainly related to reading ability.

In many early childhood classrooms, teachers practice age-appropriate methods that support literacy by using (1) conversations with young children, (2) rich and varied language in group times through the inclusion of songs,

Planning for a variety of literacy experiences is important

stories, and transitions, and (3) language experiences in centers, including environmental print and books. Children are also given opportunities to write with the teacher in a structured session in methods such as the Kid Writing (Felgus & Cardonick, 1999) approach, but also throughout the room in many places. Opportunities to recall and retell stories are also frequently provided, as are interactions with other children and adults.

Take the early literacy self-assessment to check your support and integration of literacy experiences in classrooms:

Field Assignment 6–1a Early Literacy Self-Assessment for Teaching in the Preschool Years

1. The classroom provided positive, nurturing relationships that encouraged responsive conversations with children.

   _____ Always _____ Sometimes _____ Need To Work On

2. The classroom provided a print-rich environment.

   _____ Always _____ Sometimes _____ Need To Work On

3. The classroom provided a variety of writing tools for children to use with letters, words, and sounds.

   _____ Always _____ Sometimes _____ Need To Work On

(continues)

Field Assignment 6–1a (continued)

4. The classroom schedule included the reading of high-quality books each day to individual children, small groups, or both.

   _____ Always _____ Sometimes _____ Need To Work On

5. Some books reflected children's identity, home language, and cultures.

   _____ Always _____ Sometimes _____ Need To Work On

6. I provided opportunities for children to focus on sounds and parts of language as well as the meaning.

   _____ Always _____ Sometimes _____ Need To Work On

7. The daily schedule included teaching strategies and experiences that developed phonological and phonemic awareness, such as
   ■ singing songs
   ■ using fingerplays
   ■ reading or listening to poems
   ■ using stories (that include rhyme and alliteration)

   _____ Always _____ Sometimes _____ Need To Work On

8. Opportunities for children to engage in play that integrated literacy tools were included in the daily plan, such as
   ■ writing grocery lists in dramatic play
   ■ making signs in block building
   ■ using icons and words in exploring computer games

   _____ Always _____ Sometimes _____ Need To Work On

9. Firsthand experiences that expand children's vocabulary were planned, such as:
   ■ taking trips in the community
   ■ exposure to a variety of tools, objects, and materials.

   _____ Always _____ Sometimes _____ Need To Work On

Field Assignment 6–1b Early Literacy Self-Assessment for Teaching in Kindergarten and Primary Grades

In addition to many of the same activities in the preschool list, I have also observed:

1. Planned daily experiences of being read to

   _____ Always_____ Sometimes _____ Need To Work On

2. Planned daily experiences of independent reading of meaningful stories and informational texts

   _____ Always _____ Sometimes _____ Need To Work On

(continues)

Field Assignment 6-1b (continued)

3. Time for systematic code instruction and meaningful reading, balanced throughout the daily schedule to support writing of
   - ▣ stories
   - ▣ lists
   - ▣ messages to others
   - ▣ poems
   - ▣ reports
   - ▣ responses to literature
   - ▣ graphs and charts

   _____ Always _____ Sometimes _____ Need To Work On

4. Writing experiences that allowed for flexibility in using nonconventional forms of writing (invented or phonic spelling) and, over time, moving to conventional forms.

   _____ Always _____ Sometimes _____ Need To Work On

5. Work in small groups that adapted instructional strategies for more individualized approaches (if the expected progress in reading was not evident *or* if the child's literacy skills were advanced).

   _____ Always _____ Sometimes _____ Need To Work On

6. Intellectually engaging and challenging curriculum each day

   _____ Always _____ Sometimes _____ Need To Work On

Adapted from Learning to Read and Write: Developmentally Appropriate Practice for Young Children (1998). A joint position statement of the International Reading Association and the National Association for the Education of Young Children. Washington, DC: NAEYC. http://www.naeyc.org/about/positions/pdf/PSREAD98.pdf.

An electronic version of each field assignment is available on the CD-ROM that accompanies this text.

ENGLISH LANGUAGE LEARNERS

In many communities throughout the country, the number of English language learners (ELLs) has increased over the last decade. Planning for and responding to the needs of young ELL children is a reality for many early childhood programs. Bredekamp & Copple (1997), in *Developmentally Appropriate Practice,* state that "teachers bring each child's home culture and language into the shared culture of the school so that children feel accepted and gain a sense of belonging." This statement is an important guiding principle for all children, but it is especially important for English language learners.

Literacy activities can be planned throughout the day

Take the ELL self-assessment to check your involvement in planning appropriate experiences.

Field Assignment 6–2 Self Assessment for Support of English Language Learners

1. I support the use of first language and am not misled by students' ease of use with predictable language.

   _____Always _____ Sometimes _____ Need To Work On

2. I do not over-correct errors.

   _____ Always _____ Sometimes _____ Need To Work On

3. I do not encourage families to speak only English.

   _____ Always _____ Sometimes _____ Need To Work On

4. I do not assume that students' understand because they appear to be listening.

   _____ Always _____ Sometimes _____ Need To Work On

5. I do not force students to speak.

   _____ Always _____ Sometimes _____ Need To Work On

Adapted from Lee (2006). Using children's texts to communicate with parents of English-Language Learners. *Young Children.*

Lee (2006) also states that "parents' interactions with children in their home language must be appreciated and valued by the teacher in the classroom in ways that enable children to actively participate in classroom activities and thereby have greater access to the curriculum...." When teachers value cultural and linguistic diversity, they can

- Make sense of young children's texts, enabling them to make informed decisions about literacy instruction and assessment
- Gain better understanding of the children's culture and their time at home

Resources for Literacy Activities

Beaty, J. J. (2005). *50 Early Childhood Literacy Strategies.* Upper Saddle River, NJ: Pearson/Merrill Prentice-Hall.

Feldman, J. (2005). *Puppets & storytime: More than 100 delightful, skill-building ideas and activities for early learners (Pre K–K).* New York: Scholastic.

Hanson, J. (2004). *Tell me a story: Developmentally appropriate retelling strategies.* Newark, DE: International Reading Association.

Heroman, C., & Hones, C. (2004). *Literacy: The creative curriculum approach.* Washington, DC: Teaching Strategies.

Machado, J. M. (2007). *Early childhood experiences in language arts* (8th ed.). Clifton Park, NY: Thomson Delmar Learning.

Nelsen, M., & Nelsen-Parish, J. (2002). *Peak with books: An early childhood resource for balanced literacy* (3rd ed.). Clifton Park, NY: Thomson Delmar Learning.

Owocki, G. (2001). *Make way for literacy: Teaching the way young children learn.* Portsmouth, NH: Heinemann and Washington, DC: NAEYC.

Sawyer, W. E. (2003). *Growing up with literature* (4th ed.). Clifton Park, NY: Thomson Delmar Learning.

Schickedanz, J. A., & Casbergue, R. M. (2004). *Writing in preschool: Learning to orchestrate meaning and marks.* Newark, DE: International Reading Association.

Strickland, D., & Morrow, L. (2000). *Beginning reading and writing.* New York: Teachers College.

Vukelich, C., & Christie, J. (2004). *Building a foundation for preschool literacy: Effective instruction for children's reading and writing development.* Newark DE: International Reading Association.

Resources for Instruction of English Language Learners

Dragan, P. B. (2005). *Teaching English language learners in the primary classroom.* Portsmouth, NH: Heinemann.

Hill, J. D., & Flynn, K. M. (2006). *Classroom instruction that works with English language learners.* Alexandria, VA: Association for Supervision and Curriculum Development.

■ Understand what is important to the parents in terms of cultural values and literacy development

■ Keep connected to the parents through authentic activity on a daily (or weekly) basis, not just twice a year during parent–teacher conferences

For parents, such practices strengthen the connections between home and school and allow them to:

■ Stay connected to the work their children are doing at school

■ Support and strengthen literacy skills in the home language

■ Communicate with the teacher on an ongoing basis through both oral and written language

■ Have a certain level of influence in their children's schooling by using the "funds of knowledge" that they and their communities hold (Moll, Amanti, Neff, and Gonzalez, 1992).

 ## THE ARTS IN EARLY CHILDHOOD

The arts for young children include singing, dancing, moving, painting, and playing instruments in group times and centers. It includes multimedia experiences such as painting and working with clay and play dough in the art center, and choices are available each day.

Field assignment 6–3 is a self assessment for the arts that has been adapted from the work of Mary Renck Jalongo (1995).

Music and the Arts give children opportunities for expression and creativity

Field Assignment 6–3 Self-Assessment of Classroom Practice in the Arts

1. I have observed high-quality art forms in classrooms, such as:
   - prints of work by famous artists
   - recordings of quality music
   - award-winning picture books
   - displays of work by children or original drawings

   _____ Always _____ Sometimes _____ Still Need To Observe

2. I have seen activities that support and celebrate children's artistic expression:

   _____ Always _____ Sometimes _____ Still Need To Observe

3. I have seen a variety of painting opportunities throughout the week.

   _____ Always _____ Sometimes _____ Still Need To Observe

4. I have seen the availability of clay or play dough choices every day.

   _____ Always _____ Sometimes _____ Still Need To Observe

5. I have observed a variety of crayons, markers, and colored pencils available each day.

   _____ Always _____ Sometimes _____ Still Need To Observe

6. I have observed a variety of papers, foils, bags, and other media for drawing and painting available each day.

   _____ Always _____ Sometimes _____ Still Need To Observe

7. In my classroom observations, simple musical instruments are available for group times and in centers.

   _____ Always _____ Sometimes _____ Still Need To Observe

8. A variety of dramatic play props are available (not just in housekeeping).

   _____ Always _____ Sometimes _____ Still Need To Observe

9. A variety of CDs and tapes, representing a wide range of musical styles and cultures, is available for group times, music centers, and listening centers

   _____ Always _____ Sometimes _____ Still Need To Observe

10. Have I seen
    - singing songs in group times with children?
    - planning for creative movement (in group time circle)?
    - planning for dramatic plays?

    _____ Always _____ Sometimes _____ Still Need To Observe

Adapted from Jalongo, M. R. (Fall 1995). Awaken to the artistry within young children. *Dimensions of Early Childhood*, p. 14.

Resources for Supporting the Arts in Early Childhood Classrooms

Hussain, D. (1996). *Art for young children.* Nashville, TN: Incentive Publications.

Koster, J. B. (2005). *Growing artists: Teaching art to young children* (3rd ed.). Clifton Park, NY: Thomson Delmar Learning.

Mayesky, M. (2006). *Creative activities for young children* (8th ed.). Clifton Park, NY: Thomson Delmar Learning.

Schirrmacher, R. (2006). *Art & creative development for young children* (5th ed.). Clifton Park, NY: Thomson Delmar Learning.

Planning for art experiences is important each day

SCIENCE

Science is one of those subjects that may be left out of the curriculum much of the time or may be relegated to special experiences a few times a year. This is unfortunate because young children benefit from rich exploration of materials, objects, and processes in appropriately designed activities.

Field Assignment 6–4 provides opportunities for you to check your understanding of science and determine your familiarity with age–appropriate science activities. The use of discovery or science centers can give children time each day for such opportunities. In addition, discussions, stories, and songs during group times can expand children's ideas, vocabulary, and reasoning.

In Field Assignment 6–4, check your experiences with science activities with young children.

Look for Science materials that are available each day in classrooms

Field Assignment 6–4 Science Checklist

The five items below are based on the National Science Education Standards for K-4 (1996).

1. I plan science activities that encourage children to ask questions about objects, organisms, and events in the environment.

   _____ Always _____ Sometimes _____ Need To Work On

(continues)

Field Assignment 6–4 (continued)

Sample questions to ask when planning science activities to help children understand science. Crockett (2004) suggests that we ask the following questions:
- What do you think?
- What makes you think that?
- What made you decide to do it this way?
- Can you think of any other ways to do that?

Adapted from Crockett (2004). What do kids know—and misunderstand—about science? *Educational Leadership.*

2. Materials are available for simple investigations.

   _____ Always _____ Sometimes _____ Still Need To Work Observe

3. Simple equipment and tools to gather data and extend the investigation are included for skill development in other content areas (math, writing, and so on).

   _____ Always _____ Sometimes _____ Still Need To Work Observe

4. Children use data to construct reasonable explanations (charts, graphs, and so on).

   _____ Always _____ Sometimes _____ Still Need To Work Observe

5. Children's abilities to communicate (written and oral) investigations and explanations are encouraged.

   _____ Always _____ Sometimes _____ Still Need To Work Observe

National Research Council (1996). *National Science Education Standards.* Washington, DC: National Academic Press.

Caroline V. Owens (1999) included in her article "Conversational Science 101A: Talking It Up!" a thorough description of how language can be facilitated through science activities. Her description is excerpted in the following section.

Teaching Science through Language

- *Children need to know that science is a way of looking at the world,* not a string of facts or a series of grades on worksheets. Show children that you are a curious learner also. Let your children see you struggle to solve problems; model questioning, brainstorming, and experimenting.

- *Children need to have experiences to talk about.* Make sure you create an environment that is rich with open-ended possibilities such as water play, art, outdoor play, and block building. Encourage children to bring in objects from home or from walking field trips for study in the classroom.

▪ *Children need tools for making observations and comparisons.* Create an observer's corner containing tools such as containers with clear lids, magnifying glasses, measuring tapes, reference books such as bird guides and nonfiction picture books, and drawing and writing materials.

▪ *Children need to know that their ideas are valued.* Listen rather than tell, model open questioning, and encourage children to share ideas with other children.

▪ *Children need new ways to express their thoughts.* Encourage talking, drawing, and writing. Allow time in the schedule for sharing ideas as well as for sharing pictorial and written examples of your children's thinking.

▪ *Children need to be able to trust others with incomplete ideas.* Model respect for the ideas of others and point out that many of the greatest scientific advances were first dismissed with laughter. Validate the courage of speakers by discussing and writing down every child's thoughts, not only those that seem consistent with adult ideas.

▪ *Children need large blocks of time free to devote to wondering about their world* without adult constraints about subject matter, curricular areas of study, or the mastery of factual content.

Excerpted from Owens (1999). Conversational Science 101A: Talking It Up! *Young Children,* September 1999. (54)5, p. 7.

Some Science Resources That May Be Helpful in Your Work with Children

Colker, L. J. (2005). *The cooking book: Fostering young children's learning and delight.* Washington, DC: NAEYC.

Goldish, M. (1996). *101 Science poems & songs for young learners.* Broadway, NY: Scholastic. Inc.

Lind, K. K. (2005). *Exploring science in early childhood education* (4th ed.). Clifton Park, NY: Thomson Delmar Learning.

Matricardi, J. & McLarty, J. (2005). *Science activities a to z.* Clifton Park, NY: Thomson Delmar Learning.

Pottenger, F. M., Young, D. B., Brennan, C. A., & Pottenger, L. M. (2000). *DASH: Developmental approaches in science, health and technology. Instructional Guide.* University of Hawaii, HI: Curriculum Research and Development Group. (ERIC Document Reproduction Service No. ED482953)

Prairie, A. P. (2005). *Inquiry into math, science, and technology: For teaching young children.* Clifton Park, NY: Thomson Delmar Learning.

SOCIAL STUDIES

Social studies in early childhood is sometimes inappropriately construed to mean memorizing the continents, making Thanksgiving ornaments, or having a guest from another country come for a one-time visit to the class. Social studies, like science, is often relegated to the end of the day or the end of the week (if then) type of activity.

Planning for social studies activities for young children, as for other content areas, needs to consider children's developmental levels—especially their cognitive, social, and language abilities. In early childhood classrooms, we must listen to children's ideas about the world and help them grow in their understanding.

Taking the social studies assessment (Field Assignment 6-5) can help you decide and reflect on your understanding of teaching social studies with young children. Brewer (2007) listed these social studies themes that are consistent with the thematic approach recommended by the National Council for the Social Studies (NCSS).

Field Assignment 6–5 Social Studies Checklist

When I am in classrooms, I typically see the following types of social studies activities and projects with young children.

1. Activities are often planned to walk around the school.

   _____Yes _____ How? _____ No Comments: _____
   _____

2. Activities are planned to document & record services that families use.

   _____Yes _____ How? _____ No Comments: _____
   _____

3. Activities are planned to record, map, and sketch recreational facilities for children in the community.

   _____ Yes _____ How? _____ No Comments: _____
   _____

4. Activities that include graphing the types of vehicles that drive by the school during an observation are planned.

   _____Yes_____How? _____ No Comments: _____
   _____

5. Investigations to identify and then solve as a class a problem in the school neighborhood are planned.

   _____ Yes _____ How? _____ No Comments: _____
   _____

(continues)

Field Assignment 6–5 (continued)

6. Families are involved in planning holiday studies.

_____ Yes _____ How? _____ No Comments: _____

_____

Brewer (2007, p. 472). *Introduction to Early Childhood Education: Preschool through Primary Grades.* Part Two: The Curriculum Chapter.

An electronic version of each field assignment is available on the CD-ROM that accompanies this text.

Additional Resources for Social Studies

The following are some resources for planning social studies with young children:

Derman-Sparks, L. & the A.B.C Task Force. (1989). *Anti-bias curriculum: Tools for empowering young children.* Washington, DC: NAEYC.

Seefeldt, C. & Galper, A. (2006). *Active experiences for active children.* Upper Saddle River, NJ: Pearson/Merrill-Prentice Hall.

Teaching Tolerance Project (1997). *Starting small: Teaching children tolerance in preschool and early grades.* Montgomery, AL: Southern Poverty Law Center. Retrieved May 9, 2007, from http://www.teachingtolerance.org/teach/resources/starting_small.jsp.

Wallace, M. (2006). *Social Studies: All day every day in the early childhood classroom.* Clifton Park, NY: Thomson Delmar Learning.

PHYSICAL EDUCATION AND YOUNG CHILDREN

In many districts in the United States, recess is being reduced or eliminated. In some districts, physical education instruction is being removed from early childhood and elementary curricula. At the same time in our country, we have had an increase in the numbers of children being identified with Type II diabetes and obesity.

Physical activity in early childhood programs can be included in a variety of ways: (1) set up age-appropriate outdoor space on playgrounds, (2) plan inside movement centers each week, (3) use transition activities that involve movement throughout the day, (4) use movement songs in group time activities several times in the day.

Using Field Assignment 6–6, review your plan for physical activity by comparing it with the list of goals developed by the Council for Physical Education for Children (COPEC) of the National Association for Sport and Physical Education (NASPE).

Corbin and Pangrazi (2004), in a document developed for COPEC, provide physical activity guidelines for teachers, administrators, parents, and others who see the value of promoting such activity among children. *Physical activity* is broadly defined to include not only exercise and sports but also dance and movement activities. The authors provide four guidelines. Read their recommendations and then complete the field assignment.

Field Assignment 6–6 Physical Education

Each day children should:

1. Accumulate at least 60 minutes of age-appropriate physical activity.
   List ways you have seen this recommendation being met.

   _____

   _____

   _____

2. Participate in several bouts of physical activity lasting 15 minutes or more.
   List ways you have seen this recommendation being met.

   _____

   _____

   _____

3. Participate in a variety of age-appropriate physical activities designed to achieve optimal health, wellness, fitness, and performance benefits.
   List ways you have seen this recommendation being met.

   _____

   _____

   _____

4. Not have extended periods (two hours or more) of inactivity.
   List ways you have seen this recommendation being met:

   _____

   _____

   _____

Corbin & Pangrazi (2004). *Physical activity for children: A statement of guidelines for children ages 5–12,* 2nd ed., as cited in Brewer (2007). *Introduction to Early Childhood Education: Preschool through Primary Grades.* Part Two: The Curriculum Chapter.

Resources for Physical Activities for Your Planning with Young Children

Clements, R. L. & Schneider, S. L. (2006). *Movement-based learning: Academic concepts and physical activity for ages three through eight.* Reston, VA: National Association for Sport and Physical education.

Feldman, J. (2000). *Transition tips and tricks for teachers.* Beltsville, MD: Gryphon House.

Pica, R. (2007). *Moving and learning across the curriculum* (3rd ed.). Clifton Park, NY: Thomson Delmar Learning.

Planning a variety of mathematical experiences is important for children's understanding of concepts

MATHEMATICS AND YOUNG CHILDREN

Helping children to think mathematically is a goal in some early childhood programs. This goal has implications for planning activities and selecting materials that create environments for children to act on, sort into groups, identify patterns, notice differences, and use symbols. Mathematical experiences for young children are planned group times, small groups, learning centers, transitional activities, games, and songs.

This type of planning is different from simply modeling an arithmetic equation on the chalkboard and then assigning pages of problems for children to work on. Review the sample of *Principles and Standards* developed by The National Council of Teachers of Mathematics (Appendix D), list skills in each category, and then reflect on your experiences with these types of mathematical activities that you have observed in classrooms for young children.

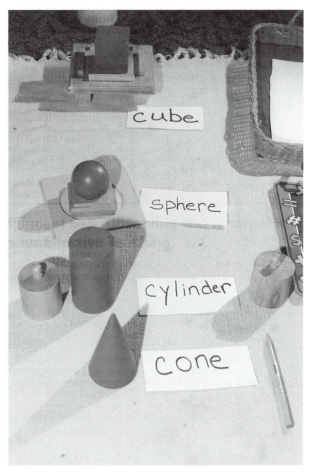

Teaching math with a variety of materials helps all children learn

---

Field Assignment 6–7 Analysis of Mathematical Expectations

Category	Skills for each	Your experiences with mathematical activities in each category
Numbers and operations		
Algebra		

Field Assignment 6–7 (continued)

Category	Skills for each	Your experiences with mathematical activities in each category
Measurement		
Data analysis and probability		

Adapted from National Council of Teachers of Mathematics (2000). Standards for Grades Pre-K–2, *Principles and Standards for School Mathematics.* Reston, VA: NCTM.

An electronic version of each field assignment is available on the CD-ROM that accompanies this text.

Sources for Games and More

The following are helpful Web sites and resources for planning mathematics experiences for young children.

Math Perspectives—http://www.mathperspectives.com. The Math Perspectives teacher development center provides prekindergarten to sixth grade mathematics educators with tools, strategies, and assessments that will ensure that all children are successful in the study of mathematics and are able to use mathematics to solve problems and to think and reason mathematically.

NAEYC—This Web address leads to *Early Childhood Mathematics: Promoting Good Beginnings,* a joint position statement of the NAEYC and the National Council of Teachers of Mathematics (NCTM).

National Council of Teachers of Mathematics—http://www.nctm.org. Here you will find the math standards, *Principles and Standards for School Mathematics* (http://standards.nctm.org) and many activities, Web-based software environments, and videos. Also see the Teacher's Corner and Family Corner sections at www.figurethis.org.

U.S. Department of Education—Read *Early Childhood: Where Learning Begins—Mathematics.* There are also mathematical activities for parents and their two- to five-year-old children. Also explore http://www.figurethis.org and http://www.lhs.berkeley.edu/equals.

Charlesworth, R. (2005). *Experiences in math for young children_*(5th ed.). Clifton Park, NY: Thomson Delmar Learning.

Matricardi, J. & McLarty, J. (2005). *Math activities a to z.* Clifton Park, NY: Thomson Delmar Learning.

From Sarama & Clements (2006). Mathematics in kindergarten. *Young Children,* 61(5).

Conclusion

Content in early childhood programs can be included as separate subjects or integrated in the same activities. Observing and understanding how children learn in each area can lead to better planning and instruction. By planning activities that are varied, the educational needs of many children are met each day.

Note: An excellent resource for adapting materials and classrooms for all children is *The Inclusive Early Childhood Classroom* (Gould & Sullivan, 1999).

References

Allen, R. (2006). *The essentials of science, grades K–6: Effective curriculum, instruction and assessment (Priorities in practice).* Association for Supervision and Curriculum Development (ASCD).

Bredekamp, S., & Copple, C. (Eds.). (1997). *Developmentally appropriate practice in early childhood programs (revised edition).* Washington, DC: NAEYC.

Brewer, J. A. (2007). *Introduction to early childhood education: Preschool through primary grades* (6th ed.). Boston, MA: Allyn and Bacon.

Corbin, C. & Pangrazi, R. (2004). *Physical activity for children: A statement of guidelines for children ages 5–12* (2nd ed.). Reston, VA: National Association for Sport and Physical Education (NASPE).

Crockett, C. (2004). What do kids know—and misunderstand—about science? *Educational Leadership.* 21(5), 34–37.

Felgus, E. G. & Cardonick, I. (1999). *Kid writing: A systematic approach to phonics, journals, and writing workshop.* Bothell, WA: Wright Group/McGraw-Hill.

Gould, P. & Sullivan, J. (1999). *The inclusive early childhood classroom: Easy ways to adapt learning centers for all children.* Beltsville, MD: Gryphon House.

Jalongo, M. R. (1995). Self-assessment of classroom practice in the arts. *Dimensions of Early Childhood.* 23(4), 8–14. Little Rock, AR: Southern Early Childhood Association.

Lee, S. (2006). Using children's texts to communicate with parents of English-language learners. *Young Children,* 61(5), 18–25.

Moll, L. C., Amanti, C., Neff, D., & Gonzalez, N. (1992). Funds of knowledge for teaching: Using a qualitative approach to connect homes and classrooms. *Theory into Practice.* 31(2), 132–141.

National Association for the Education of Young Children. (1998). *Learning to read and write: Developmentally appropriate practice for young children.A joint position statement of the* International Reading Association *and the* National Association for the Education of Young Children. Washington, DC: NAEYC. Retrieved May 9, 2007, from http://www.naeyc.org/about/positions/pdf/psread98.pdf.

National Council of Teachers of Mathematics. (n.d.). Standards for Grades Pre-K–2, *Principles and Standards for School Mathematics.* Retrieved May 9, 2007, from http://standards.nctm.org.

National Research Council (1996). National Science Education Standards. Washington, DC: National Academic Press.

Owens, C.V. (1999). Conversational science 101A: Talking it up. *Young Children,* 54(5), 4–9.

Sarama, J., & Clements, D. H. (2006). Mathematics in kindergarten. *Young Children* 61(5).

Chapter 7

Partnerships with Families

After reading and reflecting on this chapter, early childhood students will be able to:

- Define family involvement in early childhood classrooms
- Discuss ways to involve families with young children
- Identify strategies for literacy and home language

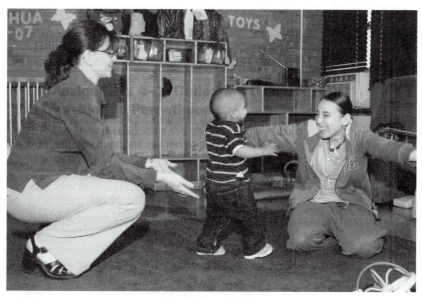

Understanding family involvement takes practice

Introduction

This chapter looks at family involvement in early childhood programs. Sections of the chapter examine the following topics: (1) understanding family involvement, (2) ideas for working with families, (3) valuing and connecting with home language and culture, (4) transforming communities into family-centered places, and (5) strategies for family literacy.

UNDERSTANDING FAMILY INVOLVEMENT

Families are children's first teachers. Couchenour and Chrisman (2008) emphasize the need for early childhood educators to understand families from a scientific perspective. That is, teachers must understand current stresses on and practices of contemporary families. (See Couchenour and Chrisman, 2008 for extensive information about theory and research related to families.) It is this depth of understanding that will lead to the formation of authentic partnerships among teachers, schools, and families.

As you read this chapter, reflect on coursework, previous readings, and your own experiences with families of young children. Think about the following statements, and decide on your level of agreement with each one.

1. Family involvement determines a significant amount of a child's success in school.
   Agree _____ Somewhat agree _____ Disagree _____

2. Family involvement attitudes can be related to specific content (literacy and reading, numeracy and math, discovery and science, and so on).
   I know how to relate content to families _____
   A great deal: _____ Somewhat: _____ Not much: _____

3. Family involvement means more than parents; it also includes grandparents, other adults living in the home, siblings and other family members.
   Agree _____ Somewhat agree _____ Disagree _____

4. Family involvement means more than attendance at parent conferences and open houses; it also means interaction of the family at home, and in the community with the child.
   I know how to promote a wide variety of types of family involvement with children:
   Somewhat: _____ Yes: _____ No: _____

5. Family involvement is especially important when children have special needs (learning disabilities, English Language Learners, physical disabilities and other types of exceptionalities).

Agree _____ Somewhat agree _____ Disagree _____

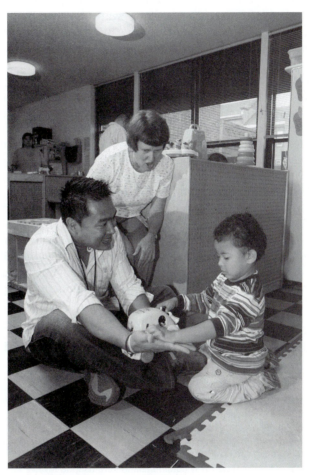

It is important to involve all family members

Joyce Epstein, a professor of sociology and a researcher at Johns Hopkins University, has written extensively about the ways families can be involved in schools and schools with families (Epstein, Coates, Salinas, Sanders, and Simon 1997). The following are the six types of involvement that Epstein's family involvement framework encompasses.

Epstein's Six Types of Involvement

Read and consider each type of family involvement delineated by Epstein and her colleagues.

Parenting of: Assist families with parenting and childrearing skills, their understanding child and adolescent development, and setting home conditions that support children as students at each age and grade level.

Communicating: Communicate with families about school programs and student progress through effective school-to-home and home-to-school communications. Two-way communications are necessary for effectively incorporating this type of family involvement.

Volunteering: Develop efforts for recruiting, training, and scheduling for involving families as volunteers and audiences at the school or in other locations to support students and school programs.

Learning at home: Involve families with their children in learning activities at home, including homework and other curriculum-related activities. Include activities that encourage families to learn new information as they work together.

Decision making: Include families as participants in school decisions, governances, and advocacy through PTA or PTO, school councils, committees, action teams, and other parent organizations.

Collaborating with the community: Coordinate community resources and services for students, families, and the school with businesses, agencies, and other groups that provide services to the community. Families may serve others in the community or be served by community groups.

Field Assignment 7–1 Interviewing Teachers about Epstein's Six Types of Family Involvement

Interview at least 3 teachers from a variety of early childhood settings (community programs, child care, preschool, Head Start, kindergarten, primary grades) about their experiences with different types of family involvement.
Use these questions:

1. How do you (or your school) support families in understanding children's development and in their parenting skills?
2. What methods of two-way communication are used to involve families in school programs and their children's progress?
3. How are volunteers recruited, trained, and scheduled at school or other locations to support children's learning and school programs?
4. How are family members supported to be involved in their children's learning at home?
5. In what ways are family members included in school decision making?
6. How do you (or your school) coordinate community resources and services for families to access or to contribute?

(continues)

Field Assignment 7–1 (continued)

Summarize responses of teacher #1:

Summarize responses of teacher #2:

Summarize responses of teacher #3:

What ideas did you learn about regarding family involvement that you may be able to implement in the future?

What ideas do you have for increasing family involvement in addition what you learned from the teachers that you interviewed?

Ideas for Working with Families

Christian (2006) identified six categories related to the operation of family systems. These categories and ideas are useful as you interact with families and plan activities or events. Additionally, teachers may observe behaviors of children that are indicative of their understanding about the role that they have in their families. Review each category for working with families as shown in Figure 7–1.

Hierarchy

Hierarchy *helps answer the question "Who's the boss?" and is related to decision making, control, and power in the family.*
   Classroom applications for teachers:
1. *Engage in keen and careful observation of child-to-child interactions.*
2. *Note information that you have about a family's hierarchy that may be in the process of changing.*
3. *Watch out for hierarchies emerging in the classroom, on the playground, in the cafeteria, and in other school venues.*

Climate

Climate *includes both the emotional and physical environment in which a child grows.*
   Classroom applications for teachers:
1. *Provide opportunities for families to discuss their beliefs about children with teachers.*
2. *Create a classroom climate of safety, positive feedback, and guidelines.*

(continues)

Figure 7–1 Ideas for Working with Families

Equilibrium

Equilibrium *is the balance within a family that is essential for children's sense of security and trust. Rituals and customs often support this need for balance.*

Classroom applications for teachers:

1. *Consider inviting a trained family professional to facilitate discussion.*

2. *Provide as much consistency of rituals and schedules as possible.*

3. *Encourage families to plan ways to increase stability and security.*

Boundaries

Boundaries *are related to limits, togetherness, and separateness—what or who is "in" or "out" of the family.*

Classroom applications for teachers:

1. *Recognize different parenting styles and family boundaries.*

2. *Avoid stereotypes (such as speaking only to the mother about child performance at school or not speaking to custodial grandparents about school performance).*

3. *Recognize that, for some families, everything is a family affair.*

4. *Balance children's attitudes and curriculum to incorporate both individual and group identities.*

5. *Respect families' need for control.*

Roles

Roles *learned within families can be carried over to work, school, and social settings.*

Classroom applications for teachers:

1. *Give children ample opportunity for role play in both structured and unstructured situations.*

2. *Observe children carefully.*

3. *Help families recognize their children's many and varied strengths.*

Rules

Rules *are sets of standards, laws, or traditions that tell us how to live in relation to one another.*

Classroom applications for teachers:

1. *Make distinctions between home rules and school rules.*

2. *Be aware that children have learned and act on unspoken rules.*

3. *Ask for families' input and assistance when conflict arises over rules.*

Figure 7–1 Ideas for Working with Families *(continued)*

Adapted from Christian (2006). Understanding families: Applying family systems theory to early childhood practice. *Young Children.* 61(1).

Field Assignment 7–2 Reflecting on Categories Related to Family Systems Understanding

Based on your experiences and thoughts, provide a reflection related to each of the six categories explained by Christian (2006).

1. Hierarchy
   Your reflection:

2. Climate
   Your reflection:

3. Equilibrium
   Your reflection:

4. Boundaries
   Your reflection:

5. Roles
   Your reflection:

6. Rules
   Your reflection:

An electronic version of each field assignment is available on the CD-ROM that accompanies this text.

Three common ways of incorporating family involvement into educational settings are through parent or family conferences, meetings, and newsletters. Although it is essential that teachers look beyond these three frequent approaches to be sure that all families are included and that a variety of opportunities exist for forming strong partnerships, these practices remain valuable.

Parent or Family Conferences

Many schools require that teachers participate in parent conferences once or twice per school year. In addition to these contracted obligations, many effective teachers invite parents to request conferences and request conferences with parents as the needs arise. The primary goal for conferences is providing a mechanism for two-way communication so that family and school partners can best serve children's learning. Specific goals for such conferences will be based on the needs and strengths of individual children and may include concerns about the child's academic progress, behavioral situations, health issues, or family transitions. When it is deemed appropriate, parent–teacher conferences can be transformed into family conferences with children or other family members attending. Because of the variety of concerns and age ranges of children, one conference format does not meet the need for every situation. It is important that teachers give thought to the format that they believe might be optimal.

Many teachers report that they have been expected to conduct conferences without any specific professional preparation for doing so. This is unfortunate because conferencing with families requires many complex skills and interpersonal communication abilities.

Field Assignment 7–3 Interviewing Teachers about Conducting Parent or Family Conferences

Interview at least three teachers. Ask the following questions and record all responses.

1. How did you learn about procedures and expectations for parent or family conferences?
   Teacher 1:
   Teacher 2:
   Teacher 3:

2. What do you see as the most beneficial aspect of conducting parent or family conferences?
   Teacher 1:
   Teacher 2:
   Teacher 3:

3. What do you find to be the most challenging aspect of conducting parent or family conferences?
   Teacher 1:
   Teacher 2:
   Teacher 3:

4. How do you prepare for conferences?
   Teacher 1:
   Teacher 2:
   Teacher 3:

5. Have you ever conducted conferences with variations of family members present, including children? If so, what are your thoughts about such conferences?
   Teacher 1:
   Teacher 2:
   Teacher 3:

(continues)

Field Assignment 7–3 (continued)

Add two questions of your own:
Your question #1:
Teacher 1:
Teacher 2:
Teacher 3:
Your question #2:
Teacher 1
Teacher 2
Teacher 3:

What do you believe to be the most important idea that you learned about conducting parent or family conferences from these interviews? How will that affect your practice as an early childhood teacher?

An electronic version of each field assignment is available on the CD-ROM that accompanies this text.

Parent or Family Meetings

Many early childhood programs hold meetings for families on a regular basis, some monthly or less frequently. Goals for such meetings typically include information of interest to families of children in the program. Such meetings can use a variety of formats and focus on many types of topics. Some of the more common topics for such meetings include the following:

- information about a field trip
- schoolwide endeavors
- expert guest speakers
- fund-raising
- new curriculum
- supporting children's learning at home

As families become increasingly pressed for time, many early childhood programs report difficulty in holding successful meetings. Although changes for contemporary families are real and should not be discounted, it is also possible that the nature of such meetings need to be examined and modified to meet the evolving needs of families. To do this, the first step in planning for any family meeting must include a needs assessment (Couchenour & Chrisman, 2008). Needs assessments are often sent home with children early in the school term and request that families include information about best times to schedule meetings, topics of interest, and preferences such as child care, meals provided, or children's work on display. Use of information from needs assessments is especially helpful to busy teachers to help in planning successful meetings.

Field Assignment 7–4 Attending and Analyzing a Family Meeting

■ Obtain permission from an early childhood teacher to attend a meeting for families. Be sure to dress and behave in a professional manner.

■ Note the location and time of the meeting:

■ Describe who was in attendance at the meeting (teachers, family members, children) and the numbers of each:

■ Note the purpose of the meeting:

■ Describe the organization of the meeting. Was there a written agenda? Was child care available? Sketch the physical environment with as many details as possible.

■ In ten-minute segments, describe the key happenings during the meeting.

First 10 minutes:

Second 10 minutes:

Third ten minutes:

Fourth 10 minutes:

Fifth 10 minutes:

Sixth ten minutes:

(Add increments as necessary.)

■ How did the meeting conclude?

■ Was any mention made of a follow-up meeting or event?

Reflect on the following:

(continues)

Field Assignment 7–4 (continued)

■ What was the best part of this meeting?

■ What evidence did you see of authentic partnerships between families and teachers?

What have you learned that you plan to use in the future?

What would you change when you are in charge?

An electronic version of each field assignment is available on the CD-ROM that accompanies this text.

Sending Newsletters Home

Teachers often find that, when time is short, one-way methods of communication are better than no communication. Newsletters often are sent home to provide information to families. The importance of building partnerships with families cannot be overlooked, so even though newsletters are an efficient means of communication, it is vital to also implement additional methods that provide for two-way communication. That being said, an effective newsletter has several components. Components include both content and form.

Some suggestions for topics to include in newsletter columns:

■ activities for learning at home (children alone, with siblings, with parents)

■ descriptions of activities and routines at school (special events, outdoor play, and others)

■ announcements about community activities of interest to families with young children

■ bios or recent professional development activities of school staff

■ announcements about school calendar or schedule changes

■ articles to support positive parenting, guiding children's behavior, and health or safety issues

■ reminders for school expectations such as tuition due dates, updated policies

■ announcements of parent or family association activities

■ children's corner to include new learning, drawings, ideas (Couchenour & Chrisman, 2008).

Design tips for getting family members' attention for newsletters should be heeded to increase efficiency of this communication strategy. Some tips include the following:

- Graphic organizers such as bulleted lists, page borders, column dividers, and short paragraphs captures attention.

- Readers use a Z-shaped path when looking at a page. The upper left quadrant of the page is viewed first, and the upper left is viewed second. Place the most important information in these two areas. The bottom left is a good place for a photo or other graphic to maintain interest. The lower right is the best place to communicate to the readers any actions you are requesting from them.

- The most readable fonts are Times New Roman and Courier; use Helvetica or Tahoma for titles, headlines, and captions; use bold font and underlining sparingly (5-7 consecutive words) since both forms slow the rate of reading.

- Color is powerful and is used to establish balance on a page (Krech, 1995).

Field Assignment 7–5 Critiquing Newsletters

Contact four or five early childhood teachers and request copies of their most recent newsletters. Using information about content and form provided in this section, critique the newsletters as follows:
List all topics included in the newsletter:

Place a check beside topics listed below that were included:

Activities for home

Explanations of activities and routines at school

Announcements of community activities for families

Information about school staff

School changes or announcements

Articles to support parenting

Reminders

Parent or family association announcements

Children's corner

Consider the format:

What information is included in the top two quadrants?

Is there an item of interest or graphic in the lower left?

Are requested actions placed in the lower right?

What fonts are used? How much bold or underlining is included?

Is color used? If so, describe.

(continues)

Field Assignment 7–5 (continued)

Is color used? If so, describe.

What is the most effective aspect of each newsletter for communicating with families?

What would you change about each newsletter to increase the effectiveness of communication?

An electronic version of each field assignment is available on the CD-ROM that accompanies this text.

Valuing Home Language and Culture

Moll, Amanti, Nett, & Gonzalez (1992) refer to the social and linguistic capital that children bring to school from their family lives, "funds of knowledge." This idea originated through observations of Mexican-American households that, through collaboration with family members, friends, and neighbors, developed an economic system referred to as funds of knowledge. Each cluster of households then exchanges information and resources about all sorts of services, including plumbing, vehicle and appliance repair, medical information, and first aid. Applying this model to schools and classrooms, social and linguistic capital can be thought of as families' resources that early childhood teachers can tap into in order to best help children learn.

Examples of such funds of knowledge are listed below. These were generated from an Institute that was structured to guide parents and teachers in understanding how simple daily routines in families are beneficial for children's performance in school and reported by Riojas-Cortez, Huls, and Clark (2003).

The themes selected for the Institute's five sessions reflect the socialization patterns of children within families.

1. In the Morning / En la Mañana
2. Let's Go to the Market / Vamos al Mercado
3. Afternoon Snack / La Merienda
4. Watching TV? Instead, Let's Tell a Story /¿Viendo La Televisión? Mejor Vamos a Contar un Cuento
5. The Weekend / El Fin De Semana

Excerpted from Riojas-Cortez, Huls, and Clark (2003). Valuing and Connecting Home Cultural Knowledge with an Early Childhood Program. *Young Children* 58(6).

Using a funds of knowledge approach in classrooms provides teachers with insight into children's language and thinking about the world and how things work. This connection to home will also give teachers a way to further support children's development and competency at school. Rueda and DeNeve (n.d.) explain that a funds of knowledge approach is an effective way to accommodate cultural diversity at school, as it helps to "build bridges between the home cultures of students and the cultures of their schools" (p. 2).

Community Involvement for Family Support

Swick (2008) notes that early childhood professionals can provide the necessary leadership to stimulate community transformation toward becoming family-centered locales in which to live and develop. Several important starting points are suggested below that provide the foundation for such transformations:

- Teachers, administrators, and staff provide a model of family-centered functioning in the school and in relations with families and community members.
- Members of the community are engaged in the total school programs in ways that empower them to take ownership of creating the very best schools for children and families.
- The community is educated on key educational, social, and family needs that exist, and on strategies for addressing these needs.
- Early childhood educators advocate for policy change that will strengthen families in the community.
- Early childhood teachers participate in actions that help reshape the community as a positive force in the lives of families

Excerpted from Swick Foreword in Couchenour & Chrisman (2008). *Families, Schools, and Communities: Together for Young Children*, 3rd ed.

Field Assignment 7–6 Examining Roles of Early Childhood Educators with Communities

Describe your observations of the following:

1. teachers providing models of family-centered functioning at school or in the community
   Description of example:

(continues)

Field Assignment 7–6 (continued)

2. teachers encouraging community members to be engaged in school programs in ways that empower them to take ownership for helping to create the very best schools for their children and families
Description of example:

3. teachers educating community members on key educational, social, and family needs that exist, including strategies for addressing the needs
Description of example:

4. teachers advocating for policy changes to strengthen families in the community
Description of example:

5. teachers participating in actions that help reshape the community to increase positive forces in the lives of families
Description of example:

Family Literacy

From the beginning of children's lives, families have a profound effect on their literacy development. Early childhood teachers have an essential role in supporting and encouraging families to provide literacy-rich environments for their children. Some of the ways that families do this include the following:

- engaging in authentic conversations with their children
- having regular reading times during the day or evening
- making books and writing materials available on a regular basis
- attending to everyday opportunities to point out traffic signs, words on cereal boxes. closed captioning on television
- taking regular trips to libraries and bookstores
- singing songs and reading poems (Couchenour & Chrisman, 2008).

When early childhood teachers and families work in partnerships to support children's literacy learning, children benefit in a multitude of ways. Because we know this, it is imperative that teachers make every effort to work with parents to establish strong partnerships for children's learning. "[T]eachers must actively reach out to families, building on their strengths while guiding them toward the kinds of home language and literacy activities that will help their children achieve the educational success that families desire for their children" (Dickinson & Tabors, 2002).

Field Assignment 7–7 Helping Families Facilitate Language and Literacy Development—A Checklist

Field assignment 7–7 is a self-assessment of your knowledge of family literacy strategies, adapted from Vukelich, Christie, and Enz (2002). Consider your knowledge in each category by completing each item.

I know how to design a needs assessment survey to determine family literacy needs.

Yes _____ Describe:

Somewhat _____ Describe:

No _____ Find a source to help and list it here:

I know how to organize family workshops on literacy.

Yes _____ Describe:

Somewhat _____ Describe:

No _____ Find a source to help and list it here:

I know how to conduct conferences for specific language and literacy problems.

Yes _____ Describe:

Somewhat _____ Describe:

No _____ Find a source to help and list it here:

I know how to send home informal weekly notes.

Yes _____ Describe:

Somewhat _____ Describe:

No _____ Find a source to help and list it here:

I know how to write newsletters to support literacy.

Yes _____ Describe:

Somewhat _____ Describe:

No _____ Find a source to help and list it here:

I know how to create a classroom lending library.

Yes _____ Describe:

Somewhat _____ Describe:

No _____ Find a source to help and list it here:

I know how to create a writing or book buy program.

Yes _____ Describe:

Somewhat _____ Describe:

(continues)

Field Assignment 7–7 (continued)

No _____ Find a source to help and list it here:

Adapted from Vukelich, Christie, and Enz (2002). *Helping Young Children Learn Language and Literacy.*

An electronic version of each field assignment is available on the CD-ROM that accompanies this text.

Conclusion

Teachers in early childhood programs can support children's learning by communicating, supporting, and understanding families and family systems. Although this takes some effort and time, its benefits to children are worth it. This chapter has attempted to show you ways to increase the application of family involvement in classroom practices.

Resources

Couchenour, D., & Chrisman, K. (2008). *Families, schools and communities: Together for young children,* 3/e. Clifton Park, NY: Thomson Delmar Learning.

Powell, D. R., & Gerde, H. K. (2006). Considering kindergarten families. In D. F. Gullo (Ed.), *Teaching and learning in the kindergarten year.* Washington, DC: NAEYC.

National Association for the Education of Young Children. *Relationships: A guide to the NAEYC early childhood program standard and related accreditation criteria.* (2005). Washington, DC. NAEYC.

Southern Early Childhood Association. Literacy and young children. (1993). *Dimensions of early childhood.* Little Rock, AR: Southern Early Childhood Association.

U.S. Department of Education. (2002). *Helping your child become a reader.* Washington, DC: Office of Intergovernmental and Interagency Affairs.

U.S. National Institute on Early Childhood Development and Education. (1997). *Read with me: A guide for student volunteers starting early childhood literacy programs.* Washington, DC: Department of Education.

Winston, L. (1997). *Keepsakes: Using family stories in elementary classrooms.* Portsmouth, NH: Heineman.

References

Christian, L. G. (2006). Understanding families: Applying family systems theory to early childhood practice. *Young Children,* 61(1). Washington, DC: NAEYC.

Couchenour, D., & Chrisman, K. (2008). *Families, schools and communities: Together for young children,* 3rd ed. Clifton Park, NY: Thomson Delmar Learning.

Dickinson, D. K., & Tabors, P. O. (2002). Fostering language and literacy in classrooms and homes. *Young Children,* 57 (2), 10-18. Washington, DC: NAEYC.

Epstein, J. L., Coates, L., Salinas, K. C., Sanders, M. G. & Simon, B. S. (1997). *School, family and community partnerships: Your handbook for action.* Thousand Oaks, CA: Corwin Press.

Krech, B. (1995). Improve parent communication with a newsletter. *Instructor* (September).

Moll, L.C., Amanti, C., Nett, D., & Gonzalez, N. (1992). Funds of knowledge for teaching: Using a qualitative approach to connect homes and classrooms. *Theory into Practice,* 31(2), 132–141

Riojas-Cortez, M., Hals, B. B., Clark, E. R. (2003). Valuing and connecting home cultural knowledge. *Young Children,* 58(6). Washington, DC: NAEYC.

Rueda, R., & DeNeve, C. (n.d.) How paraeducators build cultural bridges in diverse classrooms. Reprinted from the *Community Circle of Caring Journal,* 3(2), 53-55. Retrieved June 1, 2007, from http://www.usc.edu/dept/education/CMMR/paraed/Rueda_DeNeve_article.html.

Swick, K. (2008). Foreword. In Couchenour, D., & Chrisman, K. *Families, schools, and communities together for young children* (3rd ed.). Clifton Park, NY: Thomson Delmar Learning.

Vukelich, C., Christie, J., & Enz, B. (2002). *Helping young children learn language and literacy.* Boston, MA: Allyn & Bacon.

Chapter 8

Understanding the Goals and Roles of Supervision in Field Placements and Student Teaching

Objectives

After reading and reflecting on this chapter, early childhood students will be able to:

- Implement the goals of supervision
- Identify the roles of supervisors
- Understand the pre-service teacher's role and the goals during supervision

Introduction

Supervision of pre-service teachers in early childhood settings is important because young children count on adults for their safety and well-being. Margie Carter (2003) discusses the difference between supervising and coaching or mentoring. She draws the distinction between the two, stating that "supervising and training has a focus of upholding standards and managing resources, while coaching and mentoring keeps the focus on the staff person as a learner, working from his or her strengths, learning styles, and desired goals." Aspects of both of these perspectives are included in this chapter.

It is likely that as a pre-service student you will be supervised in a variety of settings before a full-time placement in a practicum or student teaching setting is made. It is also likely that supervision will be more intensive during these experiences. Supervision is defined in this chapter in terms of both goals and roles. Goals communicate meanings for both the supervisor and for you, the student, in field settings. The goals set the parameters that then identify and define the roles during supervision.

Caruso and Fawcett (2007) discuss the value that supervisees place on effective supervision. Characteristics that have been found to be important in helpful supervisors include the following:

- honesty and trustworthiness
- willingness to spend time, listening to thoughts and concerns
- knowledgeable in the field of early education
- understanding about how to help families being served
- skillful at direct, constructive feedback
- willingness to ask for feedback, from supervisee's
- supportive of supervisees' abilities
- capable of encouraging creativity
- behaving professionally as a good role model.

Effective supervisors help supervisees to become less dependent and more confident in their teaching of young children and working with families.

This chapter outlines the following components of supervision that are important for you to consider as a pre-service student:

1. Understanding written expectations
   a. contained in course syllabi (written requirements, schedules, due dates, forms)
   b. contained in student teaching handbooks (policies, schedules, and forms to be completed before, during, and after field experiences)
   c. contained in the NAEYC Code of Ethical Conduct and Statement of Commitment (see Appendix C)

2. Understanding expectations shared during classes or meetings:
   a. from the university instructor or supervisor
      – reflection strategies
      – decision-making strategies
      – self-assessment strategies
   b. from the classroom teacher
      – daily organization tasks
      – suggestions for meeting special needs
      – classroom management methods
      – lesson or unit planning formats
      – assessment
   c. from the site supervisors (directors or principal)
      – professional expectations (behavior, dress, and so on)

Styles of supervision vary in different early childhood settings

- training
- legal issues
- confidentiality issues
- health and safety procedures

Use Field Assignment 8–1 as a self-assessment tool to better understand the goals of supervision in a field setting.

Field Assignment 8–1 Self-Assessment Tool Based on your Experiences

Check the items that are used on your campus.
1. Understanding written expectations
    ____a. contained in course syllabi (written requirements, schedules, due dates, forms, etc.)

(continues)

Field Assignment 8–1 (continued)

_____b. contained in student teaching handbooks (policies, schedules, forms to be completed before, during and after field experiences)

_____c. contained in the NAEYC Code of Ethical Conduct and Statement of Commitment (see Appendix C)

2. Understanding expectations shared during classes or meetings:
   a. from the university instructor/supervisor
   _____ ■ reflection strategies
   _____ ■ decision-making strategies
   _____ ■ self-assessment strategies
   b. from the classroom teacher
   _____ ■ daily organization tasks
   _____ ■ meeting special needs
   _____ ■ classroom management methods
   _____ ■ lesson or unit planning
   _____ ■ assessment*
   c. from the site supervisors (directors or principal)
   _____ ■ professional expectations (behavior, dress, etc.)
   _____ ■ training
   _____ ■ legal issues
   _____ ■ confidentiality issues
   _____ ■ health and safety procedures

---

*Assessment

Meisels and Atkins-Burnett (2005) provided the following guidelines about developmental screening instruments. Because assessment of children's abilities is an important way to plan, it is important to understand its meaning.

A developmental screening instrument should
   1. be a brief procedure that identifies children at risk for learning problems or disabilities
   2. focus on developmental tasks, rather than academic readiness tasks
   3. sample a wide range of developmental areas
   4. provide classification data concerning the reliability and validity of the instrument

---

An electronic version of each field assignment is available on the CD-ROM that accompanies this text.

ROLES OF STUDENTS IN THE FIELD SETTING

Consider the following competencies that will be observed during field placements or student teaching in early childhood settings:

- demonstrates understanding of research, theories, and philosophies supporting developmentally appropriate practice in early childhood education and teaching
- demonstrates knowledge of developmentally appropriate guidance and guidance strategies
- demonstrates knowledge of the use of observation to understand and support children's development
- demonstrates skills in creating environments that support, guide, and encourage young children.
- demonstrates ability to use both open-ended and closed questioning techniques with children
- demonstrates skills in making adaptations for children with special needs
- demonstrates skills in making adaptations for children with unique language or cultural needs
- demonstrates ability to analyze data collected and to plan from this data

Adapted from Barbour et al. (n.d.). *Developing Quality Field Experiences: Landmines and Lessons from Early Childhood Teacher Educators.*

Field Assignment 8–2 Self-Assessment Tool

To prepare for observations by a supervisor, use this field assignment as a self-assessment tool.

_____ I demonstrate an understanding of research, theories, and philosophies supporting developmentally appropriate practice in early childhood education and teaching by

_____

_____ I demonstrate knowledge of developmentally appropriate guidance and guidance strategies by

_____

_____ I demonstrate knowledge of the use of observation to understand and support children's development by

_____

_____ I demonstrate skills in creating environments that support, guide, and encourage young children by

_____

(continues)

Field Assignment 8–2 (continued)

_____ I demonstrate ability to use both open-ended and closed questioning techniques with children by

_____ I demonstrate skills in making adaptations for children with special needs by

_____ I demonstrate skills in making adaptations for children with unique language or cultural needs by

_____ I demonstrate ability to analyze data collected and to plan from this data by

---

 ## GOALS OF SUPERVISION

Understanding and reflecting on the goals of supervisors may help you appreciate the expectations of a supervisor. Here are some goals that supervisors may have:

- ▓ to prepare students to teach in positions in early childhood settings
- ▓ to meet the needs of students (pre-service teachers) in the context of their developmental stage (Katz, 1999): survival, consolidation, renewal, maturity
- ▓ to help students understand the roles, tasks. and responsibilities of working with children, families. and other adults in field settings
- ▓ to deepen ethical understanding of professional conduct.

 ## ROLES IN SUPERVISION

Understanding and reflecting on the roles during supervision is also important. Here are examples of roles that your supervisor may perform:

- ▓ The supervisor emphasizes constructivist methods (problem-solving, reflection, collecting evidence, etc.) so that student teachers learn to be self-directed in their learning.
- ▓ Supervisors act as cognitive coaches to promote the student teacher's learning.
- ▓ Supervisors provide student teachers with frequent opportunities for collaboration, inquiry and reflection about their own teaching, as well as students' learning.
- ▓ Supervisors teach student teachers how to reflect on their own teaching.

■ The supervisor understands that evaluation is a necessary component of student teaching, but an important criterion should be the student teacher's ability to reflect upon and assess his or her own teaching and learning.

Adapted from Quick & Dasovich (1994). *The role of the supervisor: Meeting the needs of early childhood pre-service teachers.*Paper presented at the annual meeting of the Mid-South Education Research Association, Nashville, TN.

Field Assignment 8–3 Expanding your Understanding of the Roles of Supervisors

Read each assignment and its corresponding definition.

1. Provide at least three examples of self-direction that you have demonstrated.

    Definition of *self-direction:* the ability to synthesize knowledge and experiences and apply them to the current situation to plan actions

2. Provide at least three examples of cognitive coaching that you have received from a supervisor.

    Definition of *cognitive coaching:* the process of supervision that involves helping students develop conceptual frameworks to enhance teaching (such as developmentally appropriate practice, antibias approaches, or methods of inquiry)

3. Describe opportunities for collaboration, inquiry, and reflection you have had for in your field placement.

    Definition of *collaboration:* opportunities to talk with other students in similar situations and stages of professional development

4. Explain how you have developed in your abilities to use methods of inquiry in your own teaching.

    Definition of *inquiry:* the process of teaching that promotes problem-defining, evidence collection, and action research to plan curriculum and meet children's needs

5. Describe ways that you have developed self-assessment and reflection tools to use in your own teaching.

    Definition of *reflection:* an active process of contemplating a question or idea; examples include reflection as events occur, reflection after events occur, and reflection to plan for the future

---

Observing and Conferencing: Two Major Roles in Supervision

Two major roles for supervisors are to observe teaching and to conference with students. The following are brief samples of formats for observing and conferencing that may be similar to those used in your field supervision.

A Sample Form for Observations

Student name: _____

Date: _____ Time: _____

Setting/room/ age group: _____

_____

Observation Notes:	Specific Suggestions:
	Comments:
	Next Scheduled Observation:

Sample Guidelines for Conferencing

- Conferences are scheduled during a quiet time of the day (when the student teacher does not have classroom responsibilities).
- The conference is scheduled with the cooperating teacher (when possible).
- The supervisor and the student identify strengths and successes together.
- The following methods are suggested for use during conferencing:
  - Focus on problem-finding and problem-solving strategies.
  - Use child-centered observational methods or authentic checklists to assess developmental needs of children.
  - Use evidence gathering (inquiry methods) to plan.
  - Identify resources (people, texts*, materials).
  - Consider videotaping to analyze interactions.
  - Write action plans to document next steps.

*Note: See the Resources section of this chapter for early childhood citations.

Possible Barriers to Effective Supervision

Understanding and reflecting on barriers to effective supervision is also important. Here are some barriers to consider.

- Students in the early childhood setting decide that working with young children is not a good match for them
- Students in the early childhood setting decide that teaching is not a good match for their professional goals
- Students are not yet ready for placement with children in field settings
- There are sufficient personal factors that prevent students from acting professionally in a school setting

Words from Two Practicing Cooperating Teachers and a Field Supervisor

"As a mentor and cooperating teacher for undergraduate students I believe my biggest role is as a model. When undergraduates enter my classroom they are coming in with many "text book" ideas on how to manage a classroom full of students and how to teach those students at the same time. Showing an undergrad student how these ideas work in the classroom and how they may need to be modified is what I do. Modeling allows the student to see how these practices play out in real life and how students respond to them. I have found that often a small change in a plan or idea is all it takes to have that plan work for a child. Because teachers come in contact with so many students with so many different needs seeing all the adaptations and modifications they can will help the teacher and the students in the long run."

"My second role as a mentor or cooperating teacher is as a giver. My hope is that as the undergraduates enter my classroom they see something they like or something they have not thought of before and then take that idea with them for their own classroom. I have often been told not to reinvent the wheel; most of the ideas that I use in my classroom I have gotten from other teachers and they have all been great ideas. Now sharing and giving those ideas to a future teacher is part of my job."

"Finally my role as mentor or cooperating teacher is to be a set of eyes. Being in front of your first group of children can be very intimidating especially when you are thinking of what to do, how to do it, and when to do it. I can watch a new teacher and see things both good and bad that he or she may not have noticed. Together as a team we can then work through that list to make future lessons even better. I enjoy being a mentor and being a part of the learning for new teachers."
—Angie Britcher, Cooperating Teacher in a Kindergarten Classroom

"Walking into a classroom filled with conversations, laughter, singing and learning all at the same time is a wonderful experience for a person to see and be a part of. There are not many classrooms that you can experience a world of a 5 or 6 year olds on their developmental level in these new times of teaching to the test. It is a benefit for pre-student teachers to be actively involved in an Early Childhood Classroom to see that you can teach the standards while taking into consideration and implementing developmentally appropriate activities for the students. Pre-service teachers hear about developmentally appropriate practices all through their classes and reading, but to see it in action is a very different perspective. Being able to talk and interact with children is another benefit. It allows them to really interact and see if this is where their heart is, because if you are going to be a great teacher to children, especially young children who look up to you and hold every word you say as gold, you have to be willing to give 110% each and every day. Personally, I enjoy sharing ideas and hearing what the pre-service teachers are learning about and the requirements. All good teachers share and borrow ideas."

—Stacy Hart, Kindergarten Teacher and Practicum Cooperating Teacher

"I ask that each student teacher reflect daily on their classroom management styles, lesson planning, effectiveness, and feelings. This reflective process allows students to examine their thoughts and their teaching on a daily basis. I also expect that they email me regularly with updates and information. Student teaching is a time to practice . . . with all of the support and encouragement needed from the supervisor. It is also a time for taking risks, making mistakes, feeling success, and growing daily to become a competent and caring professional in the field of teaching children."

—Jennifer Chestnut, University Supervisor

Field Assignment 8–4 Listening, Cooperating, and Developing Your Own Professional Voice

Listening to the University Supervisor

The following exercise has been developed to provide you with greater understanding of the supervision process.

Check your listening ability by asking yourself these questions:

1. As your supervisor is speaking, are you considering the advice or directions?

2. How do you actively try to understand the concerns or expectations stated by the supervisor?

List the guiding words that your supervisor stressed	List the actions you plan to take (based on these words)
1.	1.

(continues)

Field Assignment 8–2 (continued)

2.   2.

3.   3.

Cooperating with Others
Check your ability to cooperate by asking yourself these questions:
1. When your supervisor asks you to participate in an activity, do you agree?
2. Do you cooperate fully in activities assigned by the supervisor to the best of your ability?

Listening to the Cooperating Teacher

List the guiding words   List the actions you
that your cooperating   plan to take (based on these words)
teacher has stressed

1.   1.

2.   2.

3.   3.

Listening to Your Own Voice:
After listening to others, write out your own ideas and thoughts. Share these with trusted peers. Finding a balance between your own voice and the voices of others takes some practice. Here is a chart that may help:

List the words that guide you: List the actions you will take:

1.   1.

2.   2.

3.   3.

Considering all of the voices, how do you get to decision-making throughout your teaching day?

An electronic version of each field assignment is available on the CD-ROM that accompanies this text.

Learning to work with supervisors in constructive ways is important for professional growth

Conclusion

You may have considered some of the roles and expectations in field settings, but you may not have considered the roles and goals of supervision. This chapter has attempted to present some of those to you to help you relate to your supervisor. Supervision is an important part of your professional growth in field placements.

Resources

Copple, C. & Bredekamp, S. (2006). *Basics of developmentally appropriate practice: An introduction for teachers of children 3 to 6.* Washington, DC: NAEYC.

Derman-Sparks, L., & the A.B.C. Task Force. (1989). *Antibias curriculum: Tools for empowering young children.* Washington, DC: NAEYC.

Gartrell, D. (2001). *The power of guidance: Teaching social-emotional skills in early childhood classrooms.* Washington, DC: NAEYC.

Harvard Project Zero. (2003). *Making teaching visible: Documenting individual and group learning as professional development.* Cambridge, MA: Harvard University Graduate School of Education.

Helm, J. H., & Beneke, S., (Eds.). (2003). *The Power of projects: Meeting contemporary challenges in early childhood classrooms.* New York: Teachers College Press.

McAfee, O., Leong, D. J., & Bodrova, E. (2004). *Basics of assessment: A primer for early childhood educators.* Washington, DC: NAEYC.

Rog, L.J. (2001). *Early literacy instruction in kindergarten.* Newark, DE: International Reading Association.

References

Barbour, N., Catlette, C., McMullen, M., Cassidy, D. J. Huss-Gage, E., & Schulte, R. *Developing quality field experiences: Landmines and lessons from early childhood teacher educators.* Handout from the 13th Annual NAEYC Institute for Early Childhood Professional Development. Retrieved February 1, 2006, from http://www.fpg.unc.edu/~scpp/pdfs/Dev_Qual_Field_Exps.pdf

Carter, M. (2003). Supervising or coaching—what's the difference? Ideas for staff training. *Child Care Information Exchange,* (151) pp. 20–22. Redmond, WA: Child Care Information Exchange. Retrieved February 1, 2006 from http://www.childcareexchange.com.

Caruso, J. J. & Fawcett, M. T. (2007). *Supervision in early childhood education: A developmental perspective,* 3rd. ed. New York: Teachers College Press.

Katz, L. G. (1998). Developmental stages of preschool teachers. *The Elementary School Journal.* In Paciorek, K. M., & Munro, J. H. (1998). *Sources: Notable Selections in Early Childhood Education.* Guildford, CT: McGraw-Hill/Dushkin.

Meisels, S. J. & Atkins-Burnett, S. (2005). *Developmental screening in early childhood: A guide* (5th. ed.). Washington, DC: NAEYC.

Quick, B. N., & Dasovich, J. A. (1994, November 9–11). *The role of the supervisor: Meeting the needs of early childhood pre-service teachers.* Paper presented at the annual meeting of the Mid-South Education Research Association: Nashville, TN.

Chapter 9

Beyond Student Teaching and the Practicum Experience

Objectives

After reading and reflecting on this chapter, early childhood students will be able to:

■ Anticipate some of the conditions of first year teaching

■ Be prepared for teaching and professional development opportunities in the first year

Introduction

This chapter reviews selected research and best practices for beginning professionals in early childhood programs. The chapter is intended to be helpful to you as you transition from pre-service experiences to first-year teaching experiences. Each piece of research and best practice is followed by a reflection or activity to personalize its significance for your teaching career.

TRANSITIONING TO THE FIRST YEAR OF TEACHING

As you consider your first year of teaching, read the list of concerns in Figure 9–1 that have been identified by first-year teachers (Giovacco-Johnson, 2005). To deal constructively with any concerns you may have, it may be helpful to use the field assignment worksheet based on these findings.

> ■ *understanding themselves as teachers*
> ■ *supporting children's learning and development*
> ■ *partnerships with families*
> ■ *collaborating with professionals*
> ■ *influence of program variables (mentors, team members, and so on)*
> ■ *influence of external system variables (district guidelines, state standards)*
>
> *From the findings of Giovacco-Johnson (2005). I just don't feel like a teacher: Struggling to figure out the first year as an early childhood special educator.* Journal of Early Childhood Teacher Education, 26(2).

Figure 9-1 Concerns from First-Year Teachers

Field Assignment 9–1 Worksheet for Identifying Concerns

1. How do you think about yourself as a teacher? Explain.

   _____

   _____

2. How do you support children's learning and development?

   _____

   _____

3. How do you partner with families?

   _____

   _____

4. How do you collaborate with other professionals?

   _____

   _____

5. What are the influences of program variables (mentors, team meetings, and so on) ?

   _____

   _____

6. What are the influences of external system variables (state and national guidelines)?

   _____

   _____

(continues)

Field Assignment 9–1 (continued)

7. Other concerns:

An electronic version of each field assignment is available on the CD-ROM that accompanies this text.

Sharing Knowledge

A growing body of research on student teachers focuses on shared knowledge, struggles, and stories about becoming a teacher. (Carrol, Conte, & Pan, 2000).

Field Assignment 9–2 Sharing Knowledge and Experience

Think about the times that you have shared knowledge and experiences with other teachers or when they have shared with you. List some of them here:

Think about any struggles you may have had during student teaching and list those:

Imagine telling stories about becoming a teacher to family members. Tell one of those stories here:

An electronic version of each field assignment is available on the CD-ROM that accompanies this text.

NOTICING THE CULTURE OF THE SCHOOL

In studies of first-year teachers, several variables contributed to their success: a match between their expectations and the realities of the workplace, evidence of having exerted a positive impact on their students, use of effective strategies to manage their students' behaviors, and awareness of the professional culture of the school (Kardo, Johnson, Peske, Kauffman, & Lin, 2001).

Field Assignment 9–3 Assessing Your Own Understanding of Variables Related to Successful Teaching

To assess your own understanding of the variables that can contribute to your success as a first-year teacher, complete this worksheet.

First-year worksheet

1. What are your expectations in the workplace (school)?

2. What positive impact have you had on your students?

3. What are the most effective strategies you have found to manage student behavior (guide children)?

4. What is the culture of the school? (Suggestion: Start with topics that teachers most often discuss.)

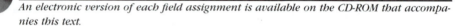

An electronic version of each field assignment is available on the CD-ROM that accompanies this text.

Other Topics to Help You Think About the Culture of the School

- Official guidelines and policies (punctuality, attendance, and so on)
- Confidentiality practices (such as children's photos, discussions in meetings)
- School safety and security
- Schoolwide guidance and discipline policies
- Procedures for IEP (individualized education program) meetings
- Professional dress (including attire for special days)
- Relationships with other professionals
  — Other teachers (such as art or music, teachers)
  — Grade-level teachers
  — Administrators
  — Learning support teachers
  — School counselor
- Approaches to curriculum and assessment
- Relationships with families
  — Policies
  — Practices
  — Communications
- Relationships with community members
  — Librarians
  — Social workers
  — Business community

Field Assignment 9–4 Considering Aspects of School Culture

List all of the aspects of culture in the school(s) you have visited or worked in.

_____
_____
_____

An electronic version of each field assignment is available on the CD-ROM that accompanies this text.

Identifying Concerns and Strategies

Deal & White (2006) have identified common concerns of two first-year teachers. Strategies and responses are listed in Figure 9–2 to address concerns that are common for first-year teachers.

Patterson, Pierce, & Aldridge (2006) also found the following difficulties as identified by first-year teachers: opening of school-year procedures, time management, administrative paperwork, dealing with special education issues, meeting the emotional needs of students, and dealing with a tremendous amount of stress. Do you have similar concerns?

Common Concerns and Frustrations of First-Year Teachers	Strategies and Responses
Time management	Revise the daily schedule.
	Establish a time for small group work while children are in centers.
	Use class transitions to teach concepts (counting, alphabet, and so on)
Social and emotional needs of students	Read or reread Dan Gartrell's book, The Power of Guidance
Social and emotional needs of adults who work with young children	Intentionally plan time for yourself to recharge and relax.
Paperwork	Enter as many forms on your computer as possible to streamline work.
Limited resources	Recruit parents to gather needed materials. Solicit contributions from buswinesses that you like.

Figure 9-2 Strategies and Responses to Common Concerns of First Year Teachers

Field Assignment 9–5 Listing Your Concerns

List concerns of first-year teachers that are similar to those listed in Figure 9–2 or others not yet discussed.

_____

_____

_____

An electronic version of each field assignment is available on the CD-ROM that accompanies this text.

Mentors and Induction Programs

Janine Certo (2005) has written about mentors and has summarized the following expectations of the mentoring process:

If you have a mentor

- expect some support (routines, procedures, materials) for getting feedback.
- expect some challenges of practices or beliefs about teaching
- experience the two-way street (that is, your mentor may receive new ideas from you)

Mary Delgado (1999, p. 28) wrote about two aspects of mentoring that are not often discussed but seem to be important. She writes, "the two most practical ways experienced teachers can help new teachers are through chance meeting in the hallways and through scheduled discussions during common preparation time."

Field Assignment 9–6 Describing Your Mentoring Experiences

Are there times when you have experienced either of these types of mentoring? If so, describe them here.

Chance Discussions	Scheduled Discussions

An electronic version of each field assignment is available on the CD-ROM that accompanies this text.

Susan Brand (1990) identified the following issues from her work with beginning preschool teachers and undergraduate students in early childhood courses:

- need for acceptance in the school or center
- anxiety about being an authority figure
- recognition of the responsibilities involved in teaching
- interest in the experience gained from the course in the context of the broader framework of their lives

---

Field Assignment 9–7 Considering Issues Related to Being a New Teacher

Can you identify with any of the issues noted by Brand? If so, which ones? Describe.

_____

_____

_____

 An electronic version of each field assignment is available on the CD-ROM that accompanies this text.

Transitions and Momentum

Based on a conversation with a principal, Feiman-Nemser (2003) found that there was a need to know and be competent about transitions and momentum. Transitions are all of those times before and after a lesson, coming into and leaving the class, and times of waiting. Teachers must be aware of transitional times of the day and plan for these in ways that support children to move from one activity to another while maintaining an encouraging learning environment. Momentum can be defined as the process of increasing motivation and interest in the topic or activity throughout a lesson. When teachers sensitively observe participation and attention from children during all types of learning activities, they can be prepared with responsive approaches to children's behaviors. Effective teachers who are aware of times when interest might be waning will ask relevant questions or have students confer with one another about a related issue.

Field Assignment 9–8 Addressing Classroom Transitions and Momentum

Consider the following questions about transitions and momentum.
How do you plan for transitions?

_____

_____

(continues)

Field Assignment 9–8 (continued)

What strategies do you have to build and maintain momentum?

_____

_____

An electronic version of each field assignment is available on the CD-ROM that accompanies this text.

Based on findings from research conducted by Ball & Cohen (1999) first-year teachers must also be able to

- think on your feet
- size up situations
- study (analyze) the effects of your practice and then use what you have learned to inform your planning and teaching

Field Assignment 9–9 Critiquing Your Own Abilities

Consider your abilities at this point and critique your own abilities using the following rubric:

Highly Skilled	Skilled	Need to Practice

Thinking on your feet:

Sizing up situations:

Analyzing your practice to inform your teaching:

An electronic version of each Field Assignment is available on the CD-ROM that accompanies this text.

Induction into the Profession

Teachers are inducted into the profession of teaching in various ways, depending on the teacher and the school setting. Sometimes induction programs are also used with mentoring. Induction may include scheduled programs with other new teachers, meetings with new and experienced teachers, reading books or other materials, and meetings with administrators.

Based on results from the New Teacher Induction Study sponsored by the National Partnership for Excellence and Accountability in Teaching, Sharon Feiman-Nemser (2003) describes some of the major components of the process of induction. She states that aspects of induction often include the following:

- A lead teacher provides guidance.
- Teams are responsible for selecting instructional materials and learning activities.
- Each child is tracked in the program.
- Parents are kept informed.
- Lead teachers stay with students until they meet each level's exit standards.

Another type of induction that became popular in Japan and is growing in awareness in the United States is known as *lesson study*. In lesson study, groups of teachers meet regularly over long periods of time to work on the design, implementation, testing, and improvement of one or several lessons. Stigler & Heibert (1999) stated that this is the linchpin of the school improvement process.

Professional growth continues throughout your career in early childhood

---

Field Assignment 9–10 Listing Induction Methods

What methods of induction have you experienced as you have moved into the early childhood teaching profession? Some methods may be planned and others unplanned. Consider this as you list as many as you can think of:

(continues)

Field Assignment 9–10 (continued)

Induction Method	Outcome for You

An electronic version of each Field Assignment is available on the CD-ROM that accompanies this text.

Conclusion

In earlier chapters of this book, you read about the NAEYC Code of Ethical Conduct and Statement of Commitment. Jalongo and Isenberg (2004) summarized the major components of this statement in a way that may be helpful to you in your interactions with children, families, other teachers, and administrators. Please reread and use it during your first years of teaching. It states that those who work with young children have an obligation to do the following:

- Appreciate childhood as a unique and valuable stage in the human life cycle

- Base their work with children on knowledge of child development

- Appreciate and support the close ties between the child and family

- Recognize that children are best understood in the context of family, culture, and society

- Respect the dignity, worth, and uniqueness of each individual (child, family member, and colleague)

- Help children and adults achieve their full potential …

Resources

Cooper, J. M. (2003). *Classroom teaching skills.* Boston, MA: Houghton Mifflin.

Delgado, M. (1999). Lifesaving 101: How a veteran teacher can help a beginner. *Educational Leadership,* (56)8.

Thompson, J. G. (2002). *First year teachers' survival kit.* Paramus, NJ: The Center For Applied Research in Education.

Thompson, M., & Thompson, J. (1991). *Learning focused strategies notebook.* Boone, NC: Learning Concepts.

References

Ball, D., & Cohen, D. (1999). *Developing practice, developing practitioners: Toward a practice-based theory of professional education.* In G. Sykes & L. Darling-Hammond (Eds.). *Teaching as the learning profession: Handbook of policy and practice* (pp. 3–32). San Francisco: Jossey-Bass.

Brand, S. F. (1990). Undergraduate and beginning preschool teachers working with young children: Educational and developmental issues. *Young Children,* 45(2).

Carrol, S. Z., Conte, A. E., Pan, A. C. (2000). Advice for student teachers. *Professional Educator,* 23(1). 1–7.

Certo, J. (2005). Support, challenge, and the two way street: Perceptions of a beginning second grade teacher and her quality mentor. *Journal of Early Childhood Education,* (26)1.

Deal, D., & White, C. S. (2006). Voices from the classroom: Literacy beliefs and practices of two novice elementary teachers. *Journal of Research in Childhood Education,* 20(4).

Delgado, M. (1999). Lifesaving 101: How a veteran teacher can help a beginner. *Educational Leadership,* 56(8).

Feiman-Nemser, Sharon. (2003). What new teachers need to learn. *Educational Leadership,* 60(8).

Giovacco-Johnson, T. (2005). I just don't feel like a teacher: Struggling to figure out the first year as an early childhood special educator. *Journal of Early Childhood Teacher Education,* 26(2).

Jalongo, M. R., & Isenberg, J. P. (2004). *Exploring your role: A practitioner's introduction to early childhood education* (2nd. Ed.). Upper Saddle, NJ: Pearson Merrill/Prentice Hall.

Kardo, S. M., Johnson, S. M., Peske, H. G., Kauffman, D., & Lin, E. (2001). Counting on colleagues: New teachers encounter the professional cultures of their schools. *Educational Administration Quarterly,* 37(20), 250–290.

Patterson, J., Pierce, C., & Aldridge, J. (2006). Beginning teachers speak to teacher educators. *Focus on Teacher Education,* 6(3). Olney, MD. Association for Childhood Education International.

Stigler, J. W., & Hiebert, J. (1999). The teaching gal: Best ideas from the world's teachers for improving education in the classroom. In Marzano, R. J. (2003). *What works in school: Translating research into action.* Alexandria, VA: Association for Supervision and Curriculum Development.

Appendix A

Standards Summary

STANDARD 1. PROMOTING CHILD DEVELOPMENT AND LEARNING

Candidates use their understanding of young children's characteristics and needs, and of multiple interacting influences on children's development and learning, to create environments that are healthy, respectful, supportive, and challenging for all children.

STANDARD 2. BUILDING FAMILY AND COMMUNITY RELATIONSHIPS

Candidates know about, understand, and value the importance and complex characteristics of children's families and communities. They use this understanding to create respectful, reciprocal relationships that support and empower families, and to involve all families in their children's development and learning.

STANDARD 3. OBSERVING, DOCUMENTING, AND ASSESSING TO SUPPORT YOUNG CHILDREN AND FAMILIES

Candidates know about and understand the goals, benefits, and uses of assessment. They know about and use systematic observations, documentation, and other effective assessment strategies in a responsible way, in partnership with families and other professionals, to positively influence children's development and learning.

STANDARD 4. TEACHING AND LEARNING

Candidates integrate their understanding of and relationships with children and families; their understanding of developmentally effective approaches to teaching and learning; and their knowledge of academic disciplines to design, implement, and evaluate experiences that promote positive development and learning for all children.

Sub-Standard 4a. Connecting with Children and Families

Candidates know, understand, and use positive relationships and supportive interactions as the foundation for their work with young children.

Sub-Standard 4b. Using Developmentally Effective Approaches

Candidates know, understand, and use a wide array of effective approaches, strategies, and tools to positively influence children's development and learning.

Sub-Standard 4c. Understanding Content Knowledge in Early Education

Candidates understand the importance of each content area in young children's learning. They know the essential concepts, inquiry tools, and structure of content areas including academic subjects and can identify resources to deepen their understanding.

Sub-Standard 4d. Building Meaningful Curriculum

Candidates use their own knowledge and other resources to design, implement, and evaluate meaningful, challenging curriculum that promotes comprehensive developmental and learning outcomes for all young children.

STANDARD 5. BECOMING A PROFESSIONAL

Candidates identify and conduct themselves as members of the early childhood profession. They know and use ethical guidelines and other professional standards related to early childhood practice. They are continuous, collaborative learners who demonstrate knowledgeable, reflective, and critical perspectives on their work, making informed decisions that integrate knowledge from a variety of sources. They are informed advocates for sound educational practices and policies.

STANDARDS

STANDARD 1. PROMOTING CHILD DEVELOPMENT AND LEARNING

Candidates use their understanding of young children's characteristics and needs, and of multiple interacting influences on children's development and learning, to create environments that are healthy, respectful, supportive, and challenging for all children.

Supporting Explanation

The early childhood field has historically been grounded in a child development knowledge base, and early childhood programs have aimed to support a broad range of positive developmental outcomes for all young children. Although the scope and emphasis of that knowledge base have changed over the years, and although early childhood professionals recognize that other sources of knowledge are also important influences on curriculum and programs for young children, early childhood practice continues to be deeply linked with a "sympathetic understanding of the young child" (Elkind 1994).

In basing their practice in child development, however, well-prepared early childhood professional candidates go beyond narrow or outdated developmental concepts. Their **knowledge and understanding of young children's characteristics and needs** encompasses multiple, interrelated areas of children's development and learning—including physical, cognitive, social, emotional, language, and aesthetic domains, play, activity, and learning processes, and motivation to learn—and is supported by coherent theoretical perspectives and by current research. Candidates also understand and apply their understanding of the many influences on young children's development and learning, and of how those influences may interact to affect development in both positive and negative ways. Candidates emphasize—both in their conceptual understanding and in their work with children—the **multiple influences on development and learning.** Those influences include the cultural and linguistic contexts for development, children's close relationships with adults and peers, economic conditions of children and families, health status and disabilities, children's individual developmental variations and learning styles, opportunities to play and learn, technology and the media, and family and community characteristics. Candidates also understand the potential influence of early childhood programs, including early intervention, on short- and long-term outcomes for children.

Candidates' competence is demonstrated in their ability to **use developmental knowledge to create healthy, respectful, supportive, and challenging learning environments** for all young children (including curriculum, interactions, teaching practices, and learning materials). Such environments reflect four critical features. First, the environments are *healthy*—that is, candidates possess the knowledge and skills needed to promote young children's physical and psychological health, safety, and sense of security. Second, the environments reflect *respect*—for each child as a feeling, thinking individual and then for each child's culture, home language, individual abilities or disabilities, family context, and community. In respectful environments, candidates model and affirm antibias perspectives on development and learning. Third, the learning environments created by early childhood teacher candidates are *supportive*—candidates demonstrate their belief in young children's ability to learn, and they show that they can use their understanding of children's development to help each child understand and make meaning from her or his experiences through play, spontaneous activity, and guided investigations. Finally, the learning environments that early childhood candidates create are appropriately *challenging*—in other words, candidates apply their knowledge of contemporary theory and research to construct learning environments that provide achievable and "stretching" experiences for all children—including children with special abilities and children with disabilities or developmental delays.

Key Elements of Standard 1

1a: Knowing and understanding young children's characteristics and needs

1b: Knowing and understanding the multiple influences on development and learning

1c: Using developmental knowledge to create healthy, respectful, supportive, and challenging learning environments

Rubrics for these key elements, outlining distinct levels of candidate performance and program evidence, are available online at www.naeyc.org.

STANDARD 2. BUILDING FAMILY AND COMMUNITY RELATIONSHIPS

Candidates know about, understand, and value the importance and complex characteristics of children's families and communities. They use this understanding to create respectful, reciprocal relationships that support and empower families, and to involve all families in their children's development and learning.

Supporting Explanation

Because young children's lives are so embedded in their families and communities, and because research indicates that successful early childhood education depends upon partnerships with families and communities, early childhood professionals need to thoroughly understand and apply their knowledge in this area.

First, well-prepared candidates possess **knowledge and understanding of family and community characteristics,** and of the many influences on families and communities. Family theory and research provide a knowledge base. Socioeconomic conditions; family structures, relationships, stresses, and supports (including the impact of having a child with special needs); home language; cultural values; ethnicity; community resources, cohesiveness, and organization—knowledge of these and other factors creates a deeper understanding of young children's lives. The knowledge is critical to candidates' ability to help children learn and develop well.

Second, candidates possess the knowledge and skills needed to **support and empower families through respectful, reciprocal relationships.** Candidates understand how to build positive relationships, taking families' preferences and goals into account and incorporating knowledge of families' languages and cultures. Candidates demonstrate respect for variations across cultures in family strengths, expectations, values, and childrearing practices. Candidates consider family members to be resources for insight into their children, as well as resources for curriculum and program development. Candidates know about and demonstrate a variety of communication skills to foster such relationships, emphasizing informal conversations while also including such approaches as exchanging e-mails and posting information and children's work on the Web, with print copies sent home for families without Web access.

In their work, early childhood teacher candidates support and empower diverse families, including those whose children have disabilities or special characteristics or learning needs; families who are facing multiple challenges in their lives; and families whose languages and cultures may differ from those of the early childhood professional. Candidates also understand that their relationships with families include assisting families in finding needed resources, such as mental health services, health care, adult education,

English language instruction, and economic assistance, that may contribute directly or indirectly to their children's positive development and learning. Well-prepared early childhood candidates are able to identify such resources and know how to connect families with services, including help with planning transitions from one educational or service system to another.

Finally, well-prepared candidates possess essential skills to **involve families and communities in many aspects of children's development and learning.** They understand and value the role of parents and other important family members as children's primary teachers. Candidates understand how to go beyond parent conferences to engage families in curriculum planning, assessing of children's learning, and planning for children's transitions to new programs. When their approaches to family involvement are not effective, candidates evaluate and modify those approaches rather than assuming that families "are just not interested."

Key Elements of Standard 2

2a: Knowing about and understanding family and community characteristics

2b: Supporting and empowering families and communities through respectful, reciprocal relationships

2c: Involving families and communities in their children's development and learning

Rubrics for these key elements, outlining distinct levels of candidate performance and program evidence, are available online at www.naeyc.org.

STANDARD 3. OBSERVING, DOCUMENTING, AND ASSESSING TO SUPPORT YOUNG CHILDREN AND FAMILIES

Candidates know about and understand the goals, benefits, and uses of assessment. They know about and use systematic observations, documentation, and other effective assessment strategies in a responsible way, in partnership with families and other professionals, to positively influence children's development and learning.

Supporting Explanation

Although definitions vary, in these standards the term "assessment" includes all methods through which early childhood professionals gain understanding of children's development and learning. Observation, documentation, and other forms of assessment are central to the practice of all early childhood professionals. Ongoing, systematic observations and other informal and formal assessments enable candidates to appreciate children's unique qualities, to develop appropriate goals, and to plan, implement, and evaluate effective curriculum. Although assessment may take many forms, early childhood candidates demonstrate its central role by embedding assessment-related activities in curriculum and in daily routines, so that assessment becomes a habitual part of professional life. Even as new professionals, they feel empowered by assessment rather than viewing assessment as a necessary evil imposed by others.

Well-prepared early childhood candidates recognize the central role that appropriate assessment plays in the design of effective programs and practices for young children. They can explain the central **goals, benefits, and uses of assessment.** In considering the goals of assessment, candidates articulate and apply the concept of "alignment"—good assessment is consistent with and connected to appropriate goals, curriculum, and teaching strategies for young children. At its best, assessment is a positive tool that supports children's development and learning, and that improves outcomes for young children and families. Positive assessment identifies the strengths of families and children; through appropriate screening and referral, assessment may also result in identifying children who may benefit from special services. Candidates are able to explain such positive uses of assessment and exemplify them in their own work, while also showing awareness of the potentially negative uses of assessment in early childhood programs and policies.

Early childhood assessment includes **observation and documentation, plus other appropriate assessment strategies.** Effective teaching of young children begins with thoughtful, appreciative, systematic observation and documentation of each child's unique qualities, strengths, and needs. Observing young children in classrooms, homes, and communities helps candidates develop a broad sense of who children are—as individuals, as group members, as family members, as members of cultural and linguistic communities. Observation gives insight into how young children develop and how they respond to opportunities and obstacles in their lives. Because spontaneous play is such a powerful window on all aspects of children's development, well-prepared candidates create opportunities to observe children in playful situations as well as in more formal learning contexts. All behavior has meaning, and well-prepared candidates demonstrate skill in reading young children's behavior cues; the skill is especially important for infants and toddlers and for children whose verbal abilities are limited. Candidates demonstrate skills in conducting systematic observations, interpreting those observations, and reflecting on their significance.

With observation and documentation as their foundation, well-prepared candidates know about a wide range of assessment tools and approaches. More than reciting a list of assessment strategies, early childhood candidates can explain the connections between specific assessment approaches and specific educational and developmental goals. They can also identify the characteristics, strengths, and limitations of specific assessment tools and strategies, including the use of technologies such as videotape and electronic record keeping. New practitioners are not assessment specialists; however, they do understand essential distinctions and definitions (e.g., *screening, diagnostic assessment, standardized testing, accountability assessment*) and are familiar with essential concepts of reliability and validity and other psychometric concepts. Their understanding helps them in selecting appropriate formal assessment measures, critiquing the limitations of inappropriate measures, and discussing assessment issues as part of interdisciplinary teams. Within the classroom or program setting, candidates demonstrate skills in using varied assessments that are appropriate to their goals and children's characteristics, with emphasis on curriculum-embedded, performance assessments.

Many young children with disabilities are included in early childhood programs, and early identification of children with developmental delays or disabilities is very important. All beginning professionals, therefore, need essential knowledge about how to collect relevant information, including appropriate uses of screening tools and play-based assessments, not only for their own planning but also to share with families and with other professionals. Well-prepared candidates are able to choose valid tools that are developmentally, culturally, and linguistically appropriate; use the tools correctly; adapt tools as needed, using assistive technology as a resource; make appropriate referrals; and interpret assessment results, with the goal of obtaining valid, useful information to inform practice and decision making.

Although assessment can be a positive tool for early childhood professionals, it has also been used in inappropriate and harmful ways. Well-prepared candidates understand and practice **responsible assessment.** Candidates understand that responsible assessment is ethically grounded and guided by sound professional standards. It is collaborative and open. Responsible assessment supports children, rather than being used to exclude them or deny them services. Candidates demonstrate understanding of appropriate, responsible assessment practices for culturally and linguistically diverse children and for children with developmental delays, disabilities, or other special characteristics. Finally, candidates demonstrate knowledge of legal and ethical issues, current educational concerns and controversies, and appropriate practices in the assessment of diverse young children.

Many aspects of effective assessment require collaboration with families and with other professionals. Such **assessment partnerships,** when undertaken with sensitivity and sound knowledge, contribute positively to understanding children's development and learning. Both family members and, as appropriate, members of interprofessional teams may be involved in assessing children's development, strengths, and needs. As new practitioners, candidates may have had limited opportunities to experience such partnerships, but they demonstrate essential knowledge and core skills in team building and in communicating with families and colleagues from other disciplines.

Key Elements of Standard 3

3a: Understanding the goals, benefits, and uses of assessment

3b: Knowing about and using observation, documentation, and other appropriate assessment tools and approaches

3c: Understanding and practicing responsible assessment

3d: Knowing about assessment partnerships with families and other professionals

Rubrics for these key elements, outlining distinct levels of candidate performance and program evidence, are available online at www.naeyc.org.

STANDARD 4. TEACHING AND LEARNING

Candidates integrate their understanding of and relationships with children and families; their understanding of developmentally effective approaches to teaching and learning; and their knowledge of academic disciplines to design, implement, and evaluate experiences that promote positive development and learning for all young children.

- ▦ Sub-Standard 4a. Connecting with children and families
- ▦ Sub-Standard 4b. Using developmentally effective approaches
- ▦ Sub-Standard 4c. Understanding content knowledge in early education
- ▦ Sub-Standard 4d. Building meaningful curriculum

Standard 4 is complex, with four Sub-Standards, because teaching and learning with young children is a complex enterprise, and its details vary depending on children's ages, characteristics, and the settings within which teaching and learning occur. Well-prepared early childhood professionals construct curriculum and program content from multiple sources. As described below, the early teaching and learning experiences that will support all children's success must be grounded in four interrelated elements: (a) positive relationships and supportive interactions; (b) a broad repertoire of appropriate, effective teaching/learning approaches; (c) essential content knowledge and familiarity with significant resources in specific academic disciplines; and (d) skills in developing, implementing, and evaluating curriculum that integrates those elements to promote positive outcomes. Especially when planning curriculum and teaching strategies for young children with developmental delays or disabilities or are learning English, well-prepared candidates know about and have the skills to collaborate with professionals from other disciplines (e.g., special education, school psychology, speech and language).

The following subsections describe each of the four sub-standards of the Teaching and Learning standard in detail.

Sub-Standard 4a. Connecting with Children and Families

Candidates know, understand, and use positive relationships and supportive interactions as the foundation for their work with young children.

Supporting Explanation

Throughout the years that children spend in educational settings, their successful learning is dependent not just on "instruction" but also on personal connections with important adults who support and facilitate their learning. It is through those connections that children develop not only academic skills but also positive learning dispositions and confidence in themselves as learners.

Infants learn about the world through their relationships with their primary caregivers. Responsiveness in caregiving creates the conditions within which very young children can explore and learn about their world. Candidates who plan to work with children of any age must have skill in creating responsive relationships, although the nature of those relationships differs as children develop. The close attachments children develop with their teachers/caregivers, the expectations and beliefs that adults have about children's capacities, and the warmth and responsiveness of adult-child interactions are powerful influences on positive developmental and educational outcomes.

Early childhood candidates demonstrate that they understand the theories and research that support the importance of relationships and high-quality interactions in early education. In their practice, they display warm, nurturing interactions with individual children and their families, communicating genuine liking for and interest in young children's activities and characteristics.

Candidates demonstrate the essential dispositions and skills to develop positive, respectful relationships with children whose cultures and languages may differ from their own, as well as with children who may have developmental delays, disabilities, or other learning challenges. In making the transition from family to a group context, very young children need continuity between the caregiving practices of family members and those used by professionals in the early childhood setting. Their feelings of safety and confidence depend on that continuity. Candidates know the cultural practices and contexts of the young children they teach, and they adapt practices to be culturally sensitive. With older children, candidates continue to emphasize cultural sensitivity while also developing culturally relevant knowledge and skills in important academic domains.

Sub-Standard 4b. Using Developmentally Effective Approaches

Candidates know, understand, and use a wide array of effective approaches, strategies, and tools to positively influence young children's development and learning.

Supporting Explanation

Early childhood professionals need appropriate, effective approaches to help young children learn and develop well. Candi-dates must ground their curriculum in a set of core approaches to teaching that are supported by research and are closely linked to the processes of early development and learning. In a sense, those approaches *are* the curriculum for infants and toddlers, although academic content can certainly be embedded in each of them. With older children, the relative weight and explicitness of subject matter or academic content become more evident in the curriculum, and yet the core approaches or strategies remain as a consistent framework.

Although this subsection describes many of those approaches, they are not merely a list from which early childhood professionals may pick at random. Well-prepared candidates' professional decisions about approaches to early childhood teaching and learning are based on understanding of children as individuals and (in most cases) as part of a group, and on alignment with important educational and developmental goals. A flexible, research-based "continuum of teaching strategies" is the best support for children's developmental and educational needs.

Well-prepared early childhood candidates understand and effectively use the following approaches, strategies, and tools to promote young children's development and learning:

Fostering oral language and communication. Early childhood candidates embed every aspect of the curriculum within the context of rich oral language and other communication strategies, using technology as needed to augment communication for children with disabilities. Both verbal and nonverbal communication create links with children from infancy onward, not only supporting close relationships but also creating the foundations for literacy and cognitive development and later academic competence.

Drawing from a continuum of teaching strategies. Well-prepared candidates display a broad range of interactive and instructional skills. They understand and use teaching approaches that span a continuum from child-initiated to adult-directed learning, and from free exploration to scaffolded support or teacher modeling. In selecting the approaches, candidates demonstrate that they are basing their selection on knowledge of individual children, on research evidence, and on understanding of appropriate, challenging teaching and learning goals.

Making the most of the environment and routines. Especially for the youngest children, the curriculum is the physical and social environment and in particular the daily routines of feeding, bathing, napping, and playtime. Candidates know the power of the environment to foster security and to support exploration, and they create physical environments and routines that offer predictability as well as opportunities for oral language development, social interaction, and investigations.

Candidates demonstrate understanding and skill in setting up all aspects of the indoor and outdoor environment to promote learning and development. Well-designed learning or activity centers can offer young children extensive opportunities to manipulate objects, build, paint, listen to stories or music, read, write, and challenge themselves. Candidates' work displays their skills in designing such centers and other features of the environment to support specific goals (including IEP and IFSP goals) and to expand children's learning. Well-prepared candidates also demonstrate skill in selecting and adapting bias-free, culturally relevant learning materials that support learning by all children, including those with developmental delays or disabilities. Daily, weekly, and longer-term schedules designed by candidates also provide evidence that candidates can apply their understanding of young children's need for balance, order, depth, variety, and challenge.

Capitalizing on incidental teaching. Because so much of young children's learning takes place informally and spontaneously, early childhood practitioners must be skilled at "incidental teaching," identifying and taking advantage of informal opportunities to build children's language, concept development, and skills. For those candidates preparing specifically to work with infants and toddlers, this will be the primary approach to teaching, but all candidates require skills in this area if they are to be effective. Depending on children's ages and program settings, candidates use diapering, meals, cleanup times, outdoor play, dressing, and other routines and transitions to support children's learning. Engaging conversations, thought-provoking questions, provision of materials, and spontaneous activities are all evident in candidates' repertoire of teaching skills.

Focusing on children's characteristics, needs, and interests. Another developmentally effective approach is to focus on children's individual characteristics, cultures, temperaments, and central developmental concerns, using families as important sources of insight. Again, such practices form the heart of teaching and learning for infants and toddlers, yet they are also effective approaches for children at the upper end of the early childhood period. And the focus on children's needs is also at the center of good practices for young children with disabilities, whose IEPs and IFSPs are based on individual and family goals. Well-prepared early childhood candidates keep the child as the center, while also paying close attention to important standards and learning outcomes, connecting new learning with children's prior knowledge and areas of individual fascination.

Linking children's language and culture to the early childhood program. Before they come to school, all children learn and develop in their own unique and highly diverse linguistic, social, and cultural context. When previous learning and development are nurtured in early education programs, the overall benefits of early education are enhanced. Recognizing and using the child's and family's primary language ensures that early childhood education adds to and does not subtract from previous experiences at home and in the community. In implementing effective approaches to teaching and learning, candidates demonstrate that they use linguistic and cultural diversity as resources, rather than seeing diversity as a deficit or problem.

Teaching through social interactions. Because so much of children's learning takes place in a social context, their peer group can be viewed as a teaching tool. When working with groups of children, candidates show competence in promoting positive social interactions and—depending on children's ages and social skills—engaging children in parallel or collaborative learning activities. Candidates understand that children who have limited social skills or who are rejected by others may have difficulty in other areas, and so candidates actively work to increase social competence in all children, treating this as an educational priority. Even as beginning teachers, they show a commitment to creating learning communities within early childhood classrooms, where children help and care for one another.

Creating support for play. All early childhood professionals must demonstrate competence in using play as a foundation for young children's learning from infancy through the primary grades. Although most children play spontaneously, well-prepared candidates can create and support environments that enrich and extend children's play, knowing when to intervene with questions, suggestions, and challenges. Especially for children with disabilities and developmental delays, candidates explicitly model and facilitate appropriate play and social interactions. Candidates create and support play experiences that reflect gender equity, respect for cultural diversity, and principles of nonviolence. Candidates demonstrate understanding of the value of play in itself, as a way for children to make sense of their experiences and to develop a wide range of skills.

Addressing children's challenging behaviors. "Classroom management" is the greatest difficulty reported by most novice practitioners. Well-prepared early childhood candidates demonstrate understanding of the multiple, underlying causes of children's challenging behaviors. Early childhood candidates demonstrate a varied repertoire of research-based guidance approaches to meet individual children's needs. Their work shows that they understand the importance of a supportive, interesting classroom environment and relationships as ways to prevent many challenging behaviors. In implementing guidance approaches, candidates aim to develop children's self-regulation and respect for others. Candidates also demonstrate knowledge and essential skills to meet the special needs of children whose behavioral difficulties are related to disabilities, family or community violence, or other stressful circumstances.

Supporting learning through technology. Rather than being merely an enrichment or add-on to the curriculum, technology has taken a central place in early childhood programs. Candidates demonstrate sound knowledge and skills in using technology as a teaching and learning tool. Appropriate technology, including computer software, digital or Web content, cameras, and other peripherals, can support and expand young children's learning, including (through assistive technology) the learning of many children with disabilities. Candidates display awareness of the benefits and potential risks of technology, as well as issues of economic and gender equity in distribution of technology resources. Candidates demonstrate knowledge about how to combine appropriate software with other teaching tools to integrate and reinforce learning.

Using integrative approaches to curriculum. Skills in developing integrated, thematic, or emergent curriculum are evident in the work of well-prepared early childhood candidates. Those skills go well beyond implementing prepackaged, superficial units of study about seasons and holidays. Depending on children's ages and developmental levels, an integrated "project approach" to teaching and learning frequently allows children to immerse themselves for extended periods in the study of a topic of high interest to an entire class or a small group. Candidates with strong subject-matter knowledge (as discussed in Sub-Standard 4c) can embed valuable content from mathematics, the arts, literacy, social studies, and other areas in such thematic studies.

Sub-Standard 4c. Understanding Content Knowledge in Early Education

Candidates understand the importance of each content area in young children's learning. They know the essential concepts, inquiry tools, and structure of content areas including academic subjects and can identify resources to deepen their understanding.

Supporting Explanation

Good early childhood curriculum does not come out of a box or a teacher-proof manual. Early childhood professionals have an especially challenging task in developing effective curriculum. As suggested in Standard 1, well-prepared candidates ground their practice in a thorough, research-based understanding of young children's *development and learning processes*. In developing curriculum, they recognize that every child constructs knowledge in personally and culturally familiar ways. In addition, in order to make curriculum powerful and accessible to all, well-prepared candidates develop curriculum that is free of biases related to ethnicity, religion, gender, or ability status—and, in fact, the curriculum actively counters such biases.

Content Areas for Early Childhood

But these tasks are only part of the challenge. Guided by standards for early learning that are effective (NAEYC & NAECS/SDE 2002), the teacher of children from birth through age 8 must also be well versed in the essentials of many academic disciplines and content areas. And because children are encountering those content areas for the first time, early childhood professionals set the foundations for later understanding and success. Well-prepared candidates choose their approaches to the task depending on the ages and developmental levels of the children they teach. With the youngest children, early childhood candidates emphasize the key experiences that will support later academic skills and understandings—with great reliance on the core approaches and strategies described in Sub-Standard 4b and with great emphasis on oral language and the development of children's background knowledge. Working with somewhat older or more skilled children, candidates also identify those aspects of each subject area that are critical to children's later academic competence. With all children, early childhood professionals support later success by modeling engagement in challenging subject matter and by building children's faith in themselves as young learners—as young mathematicians, scientists, artists, readers, writers, historians, economists, and geographers (although children may not think of themselves in such categories).

Going beyond conveying isolated facts, then, well-prepared early childhood candidates possess the kind of content knowledge that focuses on the "big ideas," methods of investigation and expression, and organization of the major academic disciplines. Thus, the early childhood professional knows not only *what* is important in each content area but also *why* it is important—how it links with earlier and later understandings both within and across areas. The following sections outline some of this essential understanding in each major discipline.

However, early childhood educators cannot be experts in everything. Because of its central place in later academic competence, the domain of language and literacy requires in-depth research-based understanding and skill. Mathematics, too, is increasingly recognized as an essential foundation. Yet because early childhood professionals must be acquainted with such a breadth of content knowledge, additional resources are needed to supplement the basic knowledge of beginning practitioners. Items in the References and Resources section of this document, especially the professional association standards documents, offer greater depth and detail in all these content areas.

Common features in candidates' work across content areas. Well-prepared candidates demonstrate certain competencies that cut across content areas or academic disciplines. Certain "basics" are common features in candidates' work, whether they are developing curriculum in language and literacy, the arts, mathematics, physical activity and physical education, science, or social studies.

Well-prepared early childhood candidates understand the importance of each content area in children's development and learning. They demonstrate essential knowledge of the developmental foundations of children's interest in, and understanding of, each content area (i.e., how children's cognitive, language, physical, social, and emotional development influence their ability to understand and benefit from curriculum in each content area—as well as how that curriculum may support development in each domain). Candidates observe and describe the early roots of children's interest and capacities in each content area, and they know how early childhood programs can build on those interests. They demonstrate the essential knowledge and skills needed to provide appropriate environments that support learning in each content area for all children, beginning in infancy (through foundational developmental experiences) and extending through the primary grades—although the nature and depth of their knowledge and skills will vary depending on which sub-periods of early childhood their program emphasizes. Candidates demonstrate basic knowledge of the research base underlying each content area and they demonstrate basic knowledge of the core concepts and standards of professional organizations in each content area, relying on sound resources for that knowledge. Finally, candidates demonstrate that they can analyze and critique early childhood curriculum experiences in terms of the relationship of the experiences to the research base and to professional standards.

Language and literacy. Early language and literacy form the basis for much later learning, and well-prepared candidates possess extensive, research-based knowledge and skill in the area, regardless of the age group or setting in which they intend to practice.

Listening, speaking, reading, and writing are integrated elements. Verbal and nonverbal communication in its diverse forms, combined with competence as a reader and writer, are essential for children's later development. Even as infants and toddlers, children are building the foundations for literacy through early experiences.

Candidates—including those who are not currently teaching linguistically diverse young children—also demonstrate knowledge of second-language acquisition and of bilingualism. They know the home language environments of the children they teach and the possible effects on children when their classroom environment does not reflect the home language. Candidates know the sociopolitical contexts of major language groups and how those may affect children's motivation to learn English. Candidates understand the benefits of bilingualism and the special needs of young English language learners (ELLs), building on the home language systems that children already have developed and assisting them to add a second language to their repertoire. For young ELLs who are learning to read, candidates use, adapt, and assess research-based literacy activities and teaching methods that build on prior knowledge and support successful transitions for those learners.

Candidates are able to articulate priorities for high-quality, meaningful language and literacy experiences in early childhood, across a developmental continuum. Across the years from infancy through third grade, those experiences should help children to, for example:

- Explore their environments and develop the conceptual, experiential, and language foundations for learning to read and write
- Develop their ability to converse at length and in depth on a topic in various settings (one-on-one with adults and peers, in small groups, etc.)
- Develop vocabulary that reflects their growing knowledge of the world around them

■ Use language, reading, and writing to strengthen their own cultural identity, as well as to participate in the shared identity of the school environment

■ Associate reading and writing with pleasure and enjoyment, as well as with skill development

■ Use a range of strategies to derive meaning from stories and texts

■ Use language, reading, and writing for various purposes

■ Use a variety of print and non-print resources

■ Develop basic concepts of print and understanding of sounds, letters, and letter-sound relationships

The arts: Music, creative movement, dance, drama, and art. Even before children can speak, they move, gesture, and respond to color, sound, and rhythm. Their joy in the "hundred languages of children" shows the value of the arts in early childhood, both as important ends in themselves and as tools for success in other areas.

Candidates are able to articulate priorities for high-quality, meaningful arts experiences in early childhood, across a developmental continuum. Depending on children's ages and other characteristics, those experiences should help children to, for example:

■ Interact musically with others

■ Express and interpret understandings of their world through structured and informal musical play

■ Sing, play, and create music

■ Respond to expressive characteristics of music—rhythm, melody, form—through speaking, singing, moving, and playing simple instruments

■ Use music to express emotions, conflicts, and needs

■ Move expressively to music of various tempos, meters, modes, genres, and cultures to express what they feel and hear

■ Understand and apply artistic media, techniques, and processes

■ Make connections between visual arts and other disciplines

Mathematics. Strong mathematical foundations are associated with later academic competence, but international comparisons have found American mathematics education to be seriously deficient. Yet for curious young children, mathematics is a powerful, exciting tool to use in making sense of their world.

Mathematics instruction should be guided by the principles and standards developed by the National Council of Teachers of Mathematics (NCTM) and by the joint position statement of NAEYC and NCTM (2002). Early childhood candidates apply the principles that guide all mathematics instruction, as well as the specific NCTM standards for preK–grade 2. The standards are based on the belief that "students learn important mathematical skills and processes with *understanding*" (NCTM 2000, ix). According to NCTM, understanding develops through interaction with materials, peers, and supportive adults in settings where students have opportunities to construct their own relationships when they first meet a new topic.

As outlined by NCTM, well-prepared candidates understand and apply the following six principles, or "themes," of mathematics instruction:

- *Equity:* high expectations and strong support for all children
- *Curriculum:* more than a collection of activities: coherent, focused on important mathematics, and well integrated across grades and developmental levels
- *Teaching:* understanding what children already know and need to learn, and challenging and supporting them to learn it well
- *Learning:* children must learn with understanding, building new mathematical knowledge from experience and prior knowledge
- *Assessment:* should support the learning of important mathematics and give useful information to teachers and children
- *Technology:* is essential in teaching and learning mathematics; a tool to enhance learning

In addition to those principles, candidates understand which concepts and skills are developmentally appropriate for preK–grade 2 children in each of five content areas—operations, algebra, geometry, measurement, data analysis, and probability—as well as in the five process areas of problem solving, reasoning and proof, connections, communication, and representation. Early childhood candidates are able to link those two sets of standards together so that the process standards are used in teaching and learning mathematical content.

Physical activity and physical education. For young children, moving and exploring what their bodies can do are essential elements of early learning. All children, with and without disabilities, set themselves physical challenges and investigate the frontiers of their physical capacities. Candidates are able to articulate priorities for high-quality, meaningful physical activity and physical education experiences in early childhood, across a developmental continuum. Depending on children's ages and other characteristics, those experiences should help children to, for example:

- Have varied, repeated experiences with functional movement and manipulation
- Demonstrate progress toward mature forms of selected physical skills
- Try new movement activities and skills

- Use feedback to improve performance
- Experience and express pleasure from participation in physical activity
- Apply rules, procedures, and safe practices
- Gain competence to provide increased enjoyment in movement

In promoting children's physical development, candidates are aware of cultural differences and gender expectations. They know when to respect children's and families' preferences regarding dress for physical activity and level of participation, and when to make adaptations to help children meet physical goals, yet support culturally sensitive practices.

Science. Although their investigations may not be systematic and their ideas and questions may not be scientifically accurate, young children's intense curiosity and love of hands-on exploration give them much in common with more mature scientists. Early childhood offers unique opportunities to explore phenomena using skills of scientific inquiry, cultivate scientific dispositions, and build a foundation for understanding core scientific concepts.

Candidates are able to articulate priorities for high-quality, meaningful science experiences in early childhood, across a developmental continuum. Focused exploration of meaningful content (for example, the growth and development of a plant over time, or investigation of the properties of water at a water table) supports early scientific understanding. Depending on children's ages and other characteristics, those experiences should help children to, for example:

- Raise questions about objects and events around them
- Explore materials, objects, and events by acting upon them and noticing what happens
- Make careful observations of objects, organisms, and events using all their senses
- Describe, compare, sort, classify, and order in terms of observable characteristics and properties
- Use a variety of simple tools to extend their observations (e.g., hand lens, measuring tools, eye dropper)
- Engage in simple investigations including making predictions, gathering and interpreting data, recognizing simple patterns, and drawing conclusions
- Record observations, explanations, and ideas through multiple forms of representation
- Work collaboratively with others, share and discuss ideas, and listen to new perspectives

Social studies. The social studies area presents special challenges to early childhood education. Because core concepts may be abstract or distant in time or space, providing many hands-on experiences is difficult yet essential for children's interest and understand-ing. Candidates are able to articulate priorities for high-quality, meaningful social studies experiences in early childhood, across a developmental continuum. Depending on children's ages and other characteristics, those experiences should help children to, for example:

Geography

- Make and use maps to locate themselves in space
- Observe the physical characteristics of the places in which they live and identify landforms, bodies of water, climate, soils, natural vegetation, and animal life of that place

History

- Use the methods of the historian, identifying questions, locating and analyzing information, and reaching conclusions
- Record and discuss the changes that occur in their lives, recalling their immediate past

Economics

- Develop awareness of the difference between wants and needs (the concept of scarcity)
- Develop interest in the economic system, understanding the contribu-tions of those who produce goods and services

Social relations/Civics

- Become a participating member of the group, giving up some individu-ality for the greater good
- Recognizing similarities among people of many cultures
- Respecting others, including those who differ in gender, ethnicity, ability, or ideas
- Learn the principles of democracy, working cooperatively with others, sharing, and voting as they solve problems

Sub-Standard 4d. Building Meaningful Curriculum

Candidates use their own knowledge and other resources to design, implement, and evaluate meaningful, challenging curriculum that promotes comprehensive developmental and learning outcomes for all young children.

Supporting Explanation

In their work with young children, candidates demonstrate that they can draw upon all the preceding tools—relationships with young children and families; appropriate, effective approaches to early childhood teaching and learning; and meaningful content in the academic disciplines—to design, implement, and evaluate curriculum for young children. The complexity of the process requires candidates, as well as experienced teachers, to go beyond their own basic knowledge to identify and use high-quality resources, including books, standards documents, Web resources, and individuals who have specialized content expertise, in developing early childhood curriculum. Curriculum planning starts with clear, appropriate goals and desired outcomes for children. Although national or state standards or desired expectations may influence curriculum in positive ways, several larger goals are also important guides:

Security and self-regulation. Appropriate, effective curriculum creates a secure base from which young children can explore and tackle challenging problems. Well-implemented curriculum also helps children become better able to manage or regulate their expressions of emotion and, over time, to cope with frustration and manage impulses effectively, rather than creating high levels of frustration and anxiety.

Problem-solving and thinking skills. Candidates who have skills in developing and implementing meaningful, challenging curriculum will also support young children's ability—and motivation—to solve problems and think well.

Academic and social competence. Because good early childhood curriculum is aligned with young children's developmental and learning styles, it supports the growth of academic and social skills.

With these goals in mind, candidates develop curriculum to include both planned and spontaneous experiences that are developmentally appropriate, meaningful, and challenging for all young children, including those with developmental delays or disabilities; that address cultural and linguistic diversities; that lead to positive learning outcomes; and that—as children become older—develop positive dispositions toward learning within each content area.

Depending on children's ages and program settings, candidates demonstrate skill in building curriculum from relationships, daily interactions, and routines (the core elements of infant/toddler curriculum); in integrating academic disciplines with other content in an emergent, interdisciplinary, or thematic curriculum; and (especially for older children) in providing focused learning opportunities within a specific content area.

Candidates demonstrate that they can implement plans in organized yet flexible ways, adapting the curriculum to meet the interests and needs of diverse children while proactively supporting their learning. They demonstrate essential skills in evaluating the curriculum in light of their own goals and of children's engagement in learning activities, and they modify curriculum in light of their own evaluation and feedback from supervisors.

Key Elements of Standard 4

4a: Knowing, understanding, and using positive relationships and supportive interactions

4b: Knowing, understanding, and using effective approaches, strategies, and tools for early education

4c: Knowing and understanding the importance, central concepts, inquiry tools, and structures of content areas or academic disciplines

4d: Using own knowledge and other resources to design, implement, and evaluate meaningful, challenging curriculum to promote positive outcomes

Rubrics for these key elements, outlining distinct levels of candidate performance and program evidence, are available online at www.naeyc.org.

Standard 5. Becoming a Professional

Candidates identify and conduct themselves as members of the early childhood profession. They know and use ethical guidelines and other professional standards related to early childhood practice. They are continuous, collaborative learners who demonstrate knowledgeable, reflective, and critical perspectives on their work, making informed decisions that integrate knowledge from a variety of sources. They are informed advocates for sound educational practices and policies.

Supporting Explanation

The early childhood field has a distinctive history, values, knowledge base, and mission. Early childhood professionals, including beginning teachers, have a strong **identification and involvement with the early childhood field,** to better serve young children and their families. Well-prepared candidates understand the nature of a profession. They know about the many connections between the early childhood field and other related disciplines and professions with which they may collaborate while serving diverse young children and families. Candidates are also aware of the broader contexts and challenges within which early childhood professionals work and might work in the future.

Because young children are at such a critical point in their development and learning, and because they are vulnerable and cannot articulate their own rights and needs, early childhood professionals have compelling responsibilities to **know about and uphold ethical guidelines and other professional standards.** The profession's code of ethical conduct guides the practice of responsible early childhood educators. Well-prepared candidates are very familiar with the NAEYC Code of Ethical Conduct and are guided by its ideals and principles. This means honoring their responsibilities to uphold high standards of confidentiality, sensitivity, and respect for children, families, and colleagues. Candidates know how to use the Code to analyze and resolve professional ethical dilemmas and are able to give defensible justifications for their resolutions of those dilemmas. Well-prepared candidates also know and obey relevant laws such as those pertaining to child abuse, the rights of children with disabilities, and school attendance. Finally, candidates are familiar with relevant professional guidelines such as national, state, or local standards for content and child outcomes; position statements about, for example, early learning standards, linguistic and cultural diversity, early childhood mathematics, technology in early childhood, and prevention of child abuse; child care licensing requirements; and other professional standards affecting early childhood practice.

Continuous, collaborative learning to inform practice is a hallmark of a professional in any field. An attitude of inquiry is evident in well-prepared candidates' writing, discussion, and actions. Whether engaging in classroom-based research, investigating ways to improve their own practices, participating in conferences, or finding resources in libraries and Internet sites, candidates demonstrate self-motivated, purposeful learning that directly influences the quality of their work with young children. Candidates—and professional preparation programs—view graduation or licensure not as the final demonstration of competence but as one milestone among many, including for-credit and not-for-credit experiences.

At its most powerful, learning is socially constructed, in interaction with others. Even as beginning teachers, early childhood candidates demonstrate involvement in collaborative learning communities with other candidates, higher education faculty, and experienced early childhood practitioners. By working together on common challenges, with lively exchanges of ideas, members of such communities benefit from one another's perspectives. Candidates also demonstrate understanding of and essential skills in interdisciplinary collaboration. Because many children with disabilities and other special needs are included in early childhood programs, every practitioner needs to understand the role of the other professionals who may be involved in young children's care and education (e.g., special educators, reading specialists, speech and hearing specialists, physical and occupational therapists, school psychologists). Candidates demonstrate that they have the essential communication skills and knowledge base to engage in interdisciplinary team meetings as informed partners and to fulfill their roles as part of IEP/IFSP teams for children with developmental delays or disabilities.

As professionals prepared in four- and five-year higher education programs, early childhood candidates' decisions and advocacy efforts are grounded in multiple sources of knowledge and multiple perspectives. Even routine decisions about what materials to use for an activity, whether to intervene in a dispute between two children, how to organize nap time, what to say about curriculum in a newsletter, or what to tell families about new video games are informed by a professional context, research-based knowledge, and values. Well-prepared candidates' practice is influenced by **knowledgeable, reflective, and critical perspectives.** In their work with young children, candidates show that they make and justify decisions on the basis of their *knowledge* of the central issues, professional values and standards, and research findings in their field.

They also show evidence of *reflective* approaches to their work, analyzing their own practices in a broader context, and using reflections to modify and improve their work with young children. Finally, well-prepared candidates display a *critical* stance, examining their own work, sources of professional knowledge, and the early childhood field with a questioning attitude. Their work demonstrates that they do not just accept a simplistic source of "truth"; instead, they recognize that while early childhood educators share the same core professional values, they do not agree on all of the field's central questions. Candidates demonstrate an understanding that through dialogue and attention to differences, early childhood professionals will continue to reach new levels of shared knowledge.

Finally, early childhood candidates demonstrate that they can engage in **informed advocacy for children and the profession.** They know about the central policy issues in the field, including professional compensation, financing of the early education system, and standards setting and assessment. They are aware of and engaged in examining ethical issues and societal concerns about program quality and provision of early childhood services and the implications of those issues for advocacy and policy change. Candidates have a basic understanding of how public policies are developed, and they demonstrate essential advocacy skills, including verbal and written communication and collaboration with others around common issues.

Key Elements of Standard 5

5a: Identifying and involving oneself with the early childhood field

5b: Knowing about and upholding ethical standards and other professional guidelines

5c: Engaging in continuous, collaborative learning to inform practice

5d: Integrating knowledgeable, reflective, and critical perspectives on early education

5e: Engaging in informed advocacy for children and the profession

Rubrics for these key elements, outlining distinct levels of candidate performance and program evidence, are available online at www.naeyc.org.

References and Resources

Publications

[Numbers in brackets denote items pertinent to one or more of the five standards; "G" denotes items of *General* usefulness.]

Adams, M. J. 1994. *Beginning to read: Thinking and learning about print.* Cambridge, MA: Bradford Books. [4]

August, D., & K. Hakuta, eds. 1998. *Educating language-minority children.* Washington, DC: National Academy Press. [1,4]

Barnett, W. S., & S. S. Boocock. 1998. *Early care and education for children in poverty: Promises, programs, and long-term results.* Albany, NY: State University of New York Press. [G]

Barnett, W. S., J. W. Young, & L. J. Schweinhart. 1998. How preschool education influences long-term cognitive development and school success. In *Early care and education for children in poverty,* eds. W. S. Barnett & S. S. Boocock, 167–84. Albany, NY: State University of New York Press. [G]

Barrera, I. 1996. Thoughts on the assessment of young children whose sociocultural background is unfamiliar to the assessor. In *New visions for the developmental assessment of infants and young children,* eds. S. J. Meisels & E. Fenichel, 69–84. Washington, DC: ZERO TO THREE/ National Center for Infants, Toddlers, and Families. [3]

Beckman, P. J. 1996. *Strategies for working with families of young children with disabilities.* Baltimore, MD: Brookes. [2]

Bentzen, W. R. 1997. *Seeing young children: A guide to observing and recording behavior.* Albany, NY: Delmar. [1]

Bergen, D., R. Reid, & L. Torelli. 2001. *Educating and caring for very young children: The infant/toddler curriculum.* New York: Teachers College Press. [4]

Berk, L. E., & A. Winsler. 1995. *Scaffolding children's learning: Vygotsky and early childhood education.* Washington, DC: NAEYC. [1]

Bodrova, E., & D. J. Leong. 1996. *Tools of the mind: The Vygotskian approach to early childhood education.* Upper Saddle River, NJ: Prentice Hall. [4]

Bredekamp, S., & C. Copple, eds. 1997. *Developmentally appropriate practice in early childhood programs.* Rev. ed. Washington, DC: NAEYC. [G]

Bredekamp, S., & T. Rosegrant, series & vol. eds. 1992. *Reaching potentials. Vol.1: Appropriate curriculum and assessment for young children.* Washington, DC: NAEYC. [3,4]

Bredekamp, S., & T. Rosegrant, series & vol. eds. 1995. *Reaching potentials. Vol. 2: Transforming early childhood curriculum and assessment.* Washington, DC: NAEYC. [3,4]

Burns, M. S., P. Griffin, & C. E. Snow, eds. 1999. *Starting out right: A guide to promoting children's reading success.* Washington, DC: National Academy Press. [4]

Campbell, F. A., C. T. Ramey, E. Pungello, J. Sparling, & S. Miller-Johnson. 2002. Early childhood education: Young adult outcomes from the Abecedarian Project. *Applied Developmental Science* 6(1): 42–57.

Campbell, F. A., R. Harms, J. J. Sparling, & C. T. Ramey. 1998. Early childhood programs and success in school: The Abecedarian study. In *Early care and education for children in poverty,* eds. W. S. Barnett & S. S. Boocock, pp. 145–66. Albany, NY: State University of New York Press. [G]

Campbell, P. S., & C. Scott-Kassner, eds. 1995. *Music in childhood, from preschool through the early grades.* Belmont, CA: Wadsworth. [4]

Chafel, J., ed. 1997. *Families and early childhood education.* Advances in Early Education and Day Care, vol. 9. Stamford, CT: JAI Press. [2]

Chang, H. N., A. Muckelroy, & D. Pulido-Tobiassen. 1996. *Looking in, looking out: Redefining child care and early education in a diverse society.* San Francisco, CA: California Tomorrow. [G]

Chang, H. N., J. O. Edwards, C. Alvarado, D. Pulido-Tobiassen, & C. L. Morgan. 1999. *Transforming curriculum, empowering faculty: Deepening teachers' understanding of race, class, culture, and language.* San Francisco, CA: California Tomorrow. [G]

Child Mental Health Foundations and Agencies Network. 2000. *A good beginning: Sending America's children to school with the social and emotional competence they need to succeed.* Bethesda, MD: National Institute of Mental Health, Office of Communications and Public Liaison. [4]

Clements, D. H. 2001. Mathematics in the preschool. *Teaching Children Mathematics* 7: 270–75. [4]

Clements, D. H., & J. Sarama. 2000. Standards for preschoolers. *Teaching Children Mathematics* 7: 38–41. [4]

Clements, D. H., J. Sarama, & A. M. DiBiase, eds. In press. *Engaging young children in mathematics: Findings of the National 2000 Conference on Standards for Preschool and Kindergarten Mathematics Education.* Hillsdale, NJ: Erlbaum. [4]

Cohen, D. H., V. Stern, & N. Balaban. 1997. *Observing and recording the behavior of young children.* 4th ed. New York: Teachers College Press. [1]

Copley, J. V. 2000. *The young child and mathematics.* Washington, DC:NAEYC. [4]

Copley, J. V., ed. 1999. *Mathematics in the early years.* Reston, VA: National Council of Teachers of Mathematics; and Washington, DC: NAEYC. [4]

Darling-Hammond, L., J. Ancess, & B. Falk. 1993. *Authentic assessment in action: Studies of schools and students at work.* New York, NY: Teachers College Press. [3]

Darling-Hammond, L., L. Einbender, F. Frelow, & J. Ley-King. 1993. *Authentic assessment in practice: A collection of portfolios, performance tasks, exhibitions, and documentation.* New York: National Center for Restructuring Education, Schools, and Teaching (NCREST). [3]

Dunst, C. J., C. M. Trivette, & A. G. Deal. 1994. *Supporting and strengthening families: Methods, strategies, and practices.* Vol. 1. Cambridge, MA: Brookline Books. [2]

Edwards, P. A., H. M. Pleasants, & S. H. Franklin. 1999. *A path to follow: Learning to listen to parents.* Portsmouth, NH: Heinemann. [2]

Elkind, D. 1994. *A sympathetic understanding of the child: Birth to sixteen,* 3d ed. Boston: Allyn & Bacon.

Epstein, J. L., M. G. Sanders, & L. A. Clark. 1999. *Preparing educators for school-family-community partnerships: Results of a national survey of colleges and universities.* Baltimore, MD: Center for Research on the Education of Students Placed at Risk. [2]

Falk, B. 2000. *The heart of the matter: Using standards and assessment to learn.* Portsmouth, NH: Heinemann. [3]

Feeney, S., & N. K. Freeman. 1999. *Ethics and the early childhood educator: Using the NAEYC code.* Washington, DC: NAEYC. [5]

Feeney, S., N. K. Freeman, & E. Moravcik. 2000. *Teaching the NAEYC code of ethical conduct.* Washington, DC: NAEYC. [5]

Fillmore, L. W., & C. E. Snow. 2000. *What teachers need to know about language.* Washington, DC: Office of Educational Research and Improvement. [4]

Forman, G., & B. Fyfe. 1998. Negotiated learning through design, documentation, and discourse. In *The hundred languages of children: The Reggio Emilia approach—Advanced reflections,* 2d ed., eds. C. Edwards, L. Gandini, & G. Forman, 239–60. Greenwich, CT: Ablex. [4]

Gandini, L., & C. P. Edwards. 2001. *Bambini: The Italian approach to infant/toddler care.* New York: Teachers College Press. [4]

Gardner, H. 1993. *Frames of mind: The theory of multiple intelligences.* New York: Basic Books. [1]

Gregory, E., ed. 1997. *One child, many worlds: Early learning in multicultural communities.* New York: Teachers College Press. [2]

Guralnick, M. J., ed. 2001. *Early childhood inclusion: Focus on change.* Baltimore, MD: Brookes. [G]

Harbin, G. L., R. A. McWilliam, & J. J. Gallagher. 2000. Services for young children with disabilities and their families. In *Handbook of early childhood intervention,* 2d ed., eds. J. P. Shonkoff & S. J. Meisels, 387–415. New York: Cambridge University Press. [G]

Hart, B., & T. R. Risley. 1995. *Meaningful differences in everyday experience of young American children.* Baltimore, MD: Brookes. [4]

Heath, S. B. 1983. *Ways with words: Language, life, and work in communities and classrooms.* New York: Cambridge University Press. [4]

Helm, J. H., S. Beneke, & K. Steinheimer. 1998. *Windows on learning: Documenting young children's work.* New York: Teachers College Press. [3]

Heubert, J. P., & R. M. Hauser. 1999. *High stakes: Testing for tracking, promotion, and graduation.* Washington, DC: National Academy Press. [3]

Hodgkinson, H. L. 1992. *A demographic look at tomorrow.* Washington, DC: Institute for Educational Leadership. [G]

Hodgkinson, H. L. 2003. *Leaving too many children behind: A demographer's view on the neglect of America's youngest children.* Washington, DC: Institute for Educational Leadership. [G]

Johnson, J., & J. B. McCracken, eds. 1994. *The early childhood career lattice: Perspectives on professional development.* Washington, DC: NAEYC. [5]

Johnson, L. J., M. J. LaMontagne, P. M. Elgas, & A. M. Bauer. 1998. *Early childhood education: Blending theory, blending practice.* Baltimore, MD: Brookes. [G]

Kaiser, B., & J. S. Rasminsky. 1999. *Meeting the challenge: Effective strategies for challenging behaviors in early childhood environments.* Ottawa, Canada: Canadian Child Care Federation. [4]

Katz, L. G., & S. C. Chard. 2000. *Engaging children's minds: The project approach.* 2d ed. Greenwich, CT: Ablex. [4]

Kohn, A. 1999. *The schools our children deserve: Moving beyond traditional classrooms and "tougher standards."* Boston, MA: Houghton Mifflin. [5]

Ladson-Billings, G. 2001. *Crossing over to Canaan: The journey of new teachers in diverse classrooms.* San Francisco: Jossey-Bass. [5]

Lally, J. R. 1995. *Caring for infants and toddlers in groups: Developmentally appropriate practice.* Arlington, VA: ZERO TO THREE/National Center for Clinical Infant Programs. [4]

Lamb, M., ed. 1999. *Parenting and child development in "nontraditional" families.* Mahwah, NJ: Erlbaum. [2]

Lee, E., D. Menkart, & M. Okazawa-Rey, eds. 1998. *Beyond heroes and holidays: A practical guide to K–12 anti-racist, multicultural education and staff development.* Washington, DC: Network of Educators on the Americas. [4]

Losardo, A., & A. Notari-Syverson. 2001. *Alternative approaches to assessing young children.* Baltimore, MD: Brookes. [3]

Lynch, E. W., & M. J. Hanson. 1998. *Developing cross-cultural competence: A guide for working with children and their families.* 2d ed. Baltimore, MD: Brookes. [1,2]

McCabe, A. 1995. *Chameleon readers: Teaching children to appreciate all kinds of good stories.* Columbus, OH: McGraw-Hill Higher Education. [4]

McCarthy, J., J. Cruz, & N. Ratcliff. 1999. *Early childhood teacher education licensure patterns and curriculum guidelines: A state by state analysis.* Washington, DC: Council for Professional Recognition. [G]

McWilliam, P. J., P. J. Winton, & E. R. Crais. 1996. *Practical strategies for family-centered intervention.* San Diego, CA: Singular Publishing Group. [2]

Mussen, P., ed. 1997. *Handbook of child psychology.* 5th ed. New York: Wiley. [1]

NAEYC. 1996a. *Guidelines for preparation of early childhood professionals.* Washington, DC: Author. [G]

NAEYC. 1996b. *Technology and young children: Ages 3 through 8.* Position Statement. Washington, DC: Author. [G]

NAEYC. 1997. *Code of ethical conduct and statement of commitment.* Position Statement. Washington, DC: Author. [G]

NAEYC. 1997. *Licensing and public regulation of early childhood programs.* Position Statement. Washington, DC: Author. [5]

NAEYC. 1998. *Accreditation criteria and procedures of the National Academy of Early Childhood Programs.* Position Statement. Washington, DC: Author. [G]

NAEYC & National Association of Early Childhood Specialists in State Departments of Education (NAECS/ SDE). 2002. *Early learning standards: Creating the conditions for success.* Joint Position Statement. Washington, DC: NAEYC. [G]

NAEYC & National Council of Teachers of Mathematics (NCTM). 2002. *Early childhood mathematics: Promoting good beginnings.* Joint Position Statement. Washington, DC: NAEYC. [4]

National Commission on Teaching and America's Future. 1996. *What matters most: Teaching for America's future.* New York: Author. [G]

National Council of Teachers of Mathematics (NCTM). 2000. *Principles and standards for school mathematics.* Reston, VA: Author. [4]

National Institute of Child Health and Human Development. 2000. *Report of the National Reading Panel. Teaching children to read: An evidence-based assessment of the scientific research literature on reading and its implications for reading instruction.* NIH Publication No. 00-4769. Washington, DC: U.S. Government Printing Office. [4]

National Institute on Early Childhood Development and Education, U.S. Department of Education. 2000. *New teachers for a new century: The future of early childhood professional preparation.* Jessup, MD: U.S. Department of Education, ED Publishing. [G]

National Research Council. 1998. *Preventing reading difficulties in young children,* eds. C. E. Snow, M. S. Burns, & P. Griffin. Committee on the Prevention of Reading Difficulties in Young Children, Commission on Behavioral and Social Sciences and Education. Washington, DC: National Academy Press. [4]

National Research Council. 1999. *How people learn: Brain, mind, experience, and school,* eds. J. D. Bransford, A. L. Brown, & R. R. Cocking. Committee on Developments in the Science of Learning, Commission on Behavioral and Social Sciences and Education. Washington, DC: National Academy Press. [G]

National Research Council. 2001a. *Adding it up: Helping children learn mathematics,* eds. J. Kilpatrick, J. Swafford, & B. Findell. Mathematics Learning Study Committee, Center for Education, Division of Behavioral and Social Sciences and Education. Washington, DC: National Academy Press. [4]

National Research Council. 2001b. *Eager to learn: Educating our preschoolers,* eds. B. T. Bowman, M. S. Donovan, & M. S. Burns. Committee on Early Childhood Pedagogy, Commission on Behavioral and Social Sciences and Education. Washington, DC: National Academy Press. [G]

National Research Council and Institute of Medicine. 2000. *From neurons to neighborhoods: The science of early childhood development,* eds. J. P. Shonkoff & D. A. Phillips. Board on Children, Youth, and Families, Commission on Behavioral and Social Sciences and Education. Washington, DC: National Academy Press. [G]

Neelly, L. P. 2001. Developmentally appropriate music practice: Children learn what they live. *Young Children* 56 (3): 32–43. [4]

Neuman, S. B., & D. K. Dickinson. 2001. *Handbook of early literacy research.* New York: Guilford. [4]

Neuman, S. B., C. Copple, & S. Bredekamp. 1999. *Learning to read and write: Developmentally appropriate practices for young children.* Washington, DC: NAEYC. [4]

New Standards/Speaking and Listening Committee. 2001. *Speaking and listening for preschool through third grade.* Washington, DC: National Center on Education and the Economy. [4]

Peisner-Feinberg, E. S., M. R. Burchinal, R. M. Clifford, M. L. Culkin, C. Howes, S. L. Kagan, N. Yazejian, P. Byler, J. Rustici, & J. Zelazo. 1999. *The children of the Cost, Quality, and Outcomes Study go to school.* Chapel Hill: University of North Carolina at Chapel Hill, Frank Porter Graham Child Development Center. [G]

Reynolds, A. J., J. A. Temple, D. L. Robertson, & E. A. Mann. 2001. Long-term effects of an early childhood intervention on educational achievement and juvenile arrest: A 15-year follow-up of low-income children in public schools. *Journal of the American Medical Association* 285 (18): 2339–46. [G]

Rosin, P., A. D. Whitehead, L. I. Tuchman, G. S. Jesien, A. L. Begun, & L. Irwin. 1996. *Partnerships in family-centered care: A guide to collaborative early intervention.* Baltimore, MD: Brookes. [2]

Sandall, S., M. McLean, & B. Smith. 2000. *DEC recommended practices in early intervention/early childhood special education.* Longmont, CO: Sopris West Educational Services. [G]

Seefeldt, C. 1995. Transforming curriculum in social studies. In *Reaching potentials. Vol. 2: Transforming early childhood curriculum and assessment,* eds. S. Bredekamp & T. Rosegrant, 145–66. Washington, DC: NAEYC. [4]

Seefeldt, C. 2001. *Social studies for the preschool/primary child.* 6th ed. Upper Saddle River, NJ: Prentice Hall/ Merrill. [4]

Seefeldt, C., & A. Galper. 2000. *Active experiences for active children: Social studies.* Upper Saddle River, NJ: Prentice Hall/Merrill. [4]

Shartrand, A. M., H. B. Weiss, H. M. Kreider, & M. E. Lopez. 1997. *New skills for new schools.* Washington, DC: U.S. Department of Education. [2]

Shore, R. 1997. *Rethinking the brain: New insights into early development.* New York: Families and Work Institute. [G]

Sims, W. L. ed.; J. Cassidy, A. Freshwater, & C. D. Mack, assoc. eds. 1995. *Strategies for teaching: Prekindergarten music.* Reston, VA: National Association for Music Education (MENC). [4]

Snell, M. E., & R. Janney. 2000. *Teachers' guides to inclusive practices: Collaborative teaming.* Baltimore, MD: Brookes. [G]

Stauffer, S. L., & J. Davidson, eds. 1996. *Strategies for teaching: K-4 general music.* Reston, VA: National Association for Music Education (MENC). [4]

Tabors, P. O. 1997. *One child, two languages: A guide for preschool educators of children learning English as a second language.* Baltimore, MD: Brookes. [4]

Tabors, P. O. 1998. What early childhood educators need to know: Developing effective programs for linguistically and culturally diverse children and families. *Young Children* 53 (6): 20–26. [1,4]

Tabors, P. O., & C. E. Snow. 2001. Young bilingual children and early literacy development. In *Handbook of early literacy research,* eds. S. B. Neuman & D. K. Dickinson, 159–78. New York: Guilford. [4]

Teaching Children Mathematics. 2001. Focus issue: Mathematics and culture, 7 (6). [4]

Tertell, E. A., S. M. Klein, & J. L. Jewett, eds. 1998. *When teachers reflect: Journeys toward effective, inclusive practice.* Washington, DC: NAEYC. [5]

Turnbull, A. P., & H. R. Turnbull. 1997. *Families, professionals, and exceptionality: A special partnership.* 3d ed. Columbus, OH: Merrill. [2]

Van Scoter, J., E. Ellis, & J. Railsback. 2001. *Technology in early childhood education: Finding a balance.* Portland, OR: Northwest Regional Education Laboratory. [4]

Von Blackensee, L. 1999. *Technology tools for young learners.* Larchmont, NY: Eye on Education. [4]

Vygotsky, L. S. 1978. *Mind in society: The development of higher psychological processes.* Cambridge, MA: Harvard University Press. [1]

Whitebook, M., C. Howes, & D. Phillips. 1998. *Worthy work, unlivable wages: The National Child Care Staffing Study, 1988–97.* Washington, DC: National Center for the Early Childhood Work Force. [5].

Winton, P. J., J. McCollum, & C. Catlett, eds. 1997. *Reforming personnel preparation in early intervention: Issues, models, and practical strategies.* Baltimore, MD: Brookes. [G]

Wolery, M., & J. S. Wilbers, eds. 1994. *Including children with special needs in early childhood programs.* Washington, DC: NAEYC. [G]

Wozniak, R. H., & K. W. Fischer, eds. 1993. Development in context: Acting and thinking in specific environments, 3–44. Mahwah, NJ: Erlbaum. [1]

Yelland, N. J., ed. 2000. *Promoting meaningful learning: Innovations in educating early childhood professionals.* Washington, DC: NAEYC. [5]

Websites

American Associate Degree Early Childhood Educators, www.accessece.org

American Association of Colleges for Teacher Education, www.aacte.org

American Alliance for Health, Physical Education, Recreation, and Dance, www.aahperd.org

Center for the Improvement of Early Reading Achievement, www.ciera.org

CEO Forum on Education and Technology, Self-Assessment for Teacher Preparation, www.ceoforum.org

Children and Computers, www.childrenandcomputers.com

Council for Exceptional Children, www.cec.sped.org

Division for Early Childhood, www.dec-sped.org

ERIC Clearinghouse on Assessment and Evaluation, http://ericae.net

International Reading Association, www.reading.org

MENC: National Association for Music Education, www.menc.org

MuSICA: Music and Science Information Computer Archive, www.musica.uci.edu

National Association for Bilingual Education, www.nabe.org

National Association for Early Childhood Teacher Educators, www.naecte.org

National Association for the Education of Young Children, www.naeyc.org

National Center for Research on Evaluation, Standards, and Student Testing, http://cresst96.cse.ucla.edu

National Center on Education and the Economy, www.ncee.org

National Clearinghouse for English Language Acquisition and Language Instruction Educational Programs, www.ncela.gwu.edu

National Council of Teachers of Mathematics, www.nctm.org

National Early Childhood Technical Assistance Center, www.nectac.org

National Education Goals Panel, www.negp.gov

National Educational Technology Standards Projects, http://cnets.iste.org

National Geographic Society, National Standards for Geography, www.nationalgeographic.com/xpeditions/ standards/

National Institute for Early Education Research, http://nieer.org/

Program for Infant/Toddler Caregivers, www.pitc.org

Technology & Young Children (NAEYC Technology & Young Children Interest Forum), http:// techandyoungchildren.org/index.shtml

ZERO TO THREE, www.zerotothree.org

Appendix B

Code of Ethical Conduct and Statement of Commitment

A position statement of the National Association for the Education of Young Children

Revised April 2005 © The National Association for the Education of Young Children, Washington, D.C.

Preamble

NAEYC recognizes that those who work with young children face many daily decisions that have moral and ethical implications. The NAEYC Code of Ethical Conduct offers guidelines for responsible behavior and sets forth a common basis for resolving the principal ethical dilemmas encountered in early childhood care and education. The Statement of Commitment is not part of the Code but is a personal acknowledgement of an individual's willingness to embrace the distinctive values and moral obligations of the field of early childhood care and education. The primary focus of the Code is on daily practice with children and their families in programs for children from birth through 8 years of age, such as infant/toddler programs, preschool and prekindergarten programs, child care centers, hospital and child life settings, family child care homes, kindergartens, and primary classrooms. When the issues involve young children, then these provisions also apply to specialists who do not work directly with children, including program administrators, parent educators, early childhood adult educators, and officials with responsibility for program monitoring and licensing. (Note: See also the "Code of Ethical Conduct: Supplement for Early Childhood Adult Educators.")

Core Values

Standards of ethical behavior in early childhood care and education are based on commitment to the following core values that are deeply rooted in the history of the field of early childhood care and education. We have made a commitment to:

■ Appreciate childhood as a unique and valuable stage of the human life cycle

■ Base our work on knowledge of how children develop and learn

■ Appreciate and support the bond between the child and family

■ Recognize that children are best understood and supported in the context of family, culture,* community, and society

■ Respect the dignity, worth, and uniqueness of each individual (child, family member, and colleague)

■ Respect diversity in children, families, and colleagues

■ Recognize that children and adults achieve their full potential in the context of relationships that are based on trust and respect

Culture includes ethnicity, racial identity, economic level, family structure, language, and religious and political beliefs, which profoundly influence each child's development and relationship to the world.

Conceptual Framework

The Code sets forth a framework of professional responsibilities in four sections. Each section addresses an area of professional relationships: (1) with children, (2) with families, (3) among colleagues, and (4) with the community and society. Each section includes an introduction to the primary responsibilities of the early childhood practitioner in that context. The introduction is followed by (1) a set of ideals that reflect exemplary professional practice and (2) a set of principles describing practices that are required, prohibited, or permitted.

The **ideals** reflect the aspirations of practitioners. The **principles** guide conduct and assist practitioners in resolving ethical dilemmas.* Both ideals and principles are intended to direct practitioners to those questions which, when responsibly answered, can provide the basis for conscientious decision making. While the Code provides specific direction for addressing some ethical dilemmas, many others will require the practitioner to combine the guidance of the Code with professional judgment. The ideals and principles in this Code present a shared framework of professional responsibility that affirms our commitment to the core values of our field. The Code publicly acknowledges the responsibilities that we in the field have assumed and in so doing supports ethical behavior in our work. Practitioners who face situations with ethical dimensions are urged to seek guidance in the applicable parts of this Code and in the spirit that informs the whole. Often, "the right answer"—the best ethical course of action to take—is not obvious. There may be no readily apparent, positive way to handle a situation. When one important value contradicts another, we face an ethical dilemma. When we face a dilemma, it is our professional responsibility to consult the Code and all relevant parties to find the most ethical resolution.

*There is not necessarily a corresponding principle for each ideal.

SECTION I

Ethical Responsibilities to Children

Childhood is a unique and valuable stage in the human life cycle. Our paramount responsibility is to provide care and education in settings that are safe, healthy, nurturing, and responsive for each child. We are committed to supporting children's development and learning; respecting individual differences; and helping children learn to live, play, and work cooperatively. We are also committed to promoting children's self-awareness, competence, self-worth, resiliency, and physical well-being.

Ideals

I-1.1—To be familiar with the knowledge base of early childhood care and education and to stay informed through continuing education and training.

I-1.2—To base program practices upon current knowledge and research in the field of early childhood education, child development, and related disciplines, as well as on particular knowledge of each child.

I-1.3—To recognize and respect the unique qualities, abilities, and potential of each child.

I-1.4—To appreciate the vulnerability of children and their dependence on adults.

I-1.5—To create and maintain safe and healthy settings that foster children's social, emotional, cognitive, and physical development and that respect their dignity and their contributions.

I-1.6—To use assessment instruments and strategies that are appropriate for the children to be assessed, that are used only for the purposes for which they were designed, and that have the potential to benefit children.

I-1.7—To use assessment information to understand and support children's development and learning, to support instruction, and to identify children who may need additional services.

I-1.8—To support the right of each child to play and learn in an inclusive environment that meets the needs of children with and without disabilities.

I-1.9—To advocate for and ensure that all children, including those with special needs, have access to the support services needed to be successful.

I-1.10—To ensure that each child's culture, language, ethnicity, and family structure are recognized and valued in the program.

I-1.11—To provide all children with experiences in a language that they know, as well as support children in maintaining the use of their home language and in learning English.

I-1.12—To work with families to provide a safe and smooth transition as children and families move from one program to the next.

Principles

P-1.1—**Above all, we shall not harm children. We shall not participate in practices that are emotionally damaging, physically harmful, disrespectful, degrading, dangerous, exploitative, or intimidating to children.** *This principle has precedence over all others in this Code.*

P-1.2—We shall care for and educate children in positive emotional and social environments that are cognitively stimulating and that support each child's culture, language, ethnicity, and family structure.

P-1.3—We shall not participate in practices that discriminate against children by denying benefits, giving special advantages, or excluding them from programs or activities on the basis of their sex, race, national origin, religious beliefs, medical condition, disability, or the marital status/family structure, sexual orientation, or religious beliefs or other affiliations of their families. (Aspects of this principle do not apply in programs that have a lawful mandate to provide services to a particular population of children.)

P-1.4—We shall involve all those with relevant knowledge (including families and staff) in decisions concerning a child, as appropriate, ensuring confidentiality of sensitive information.

P-1.5—We shall use appropriate assessment systems, which include multiple sources of information, to provide information on children's learning and development.

P-1.6—We shall strive to ensure that decisions such as those related to enrollment, retention, or assignment to special education services, will be based on multiple sources of information and will never be based on a single assessment, such as a test score or a single observation.

P-1.7—We shall strive to build individual relationships with each child; make individualized adaptations in teaching strategies, learning environments, and curricula; and consult with the family so that each child benefits from the program. If after such efforts have been exhausted, the current placement does not meet a child's needs, or the child is seriously jeopardizing the ability of other children to benefit from the program, we shall collaborate with the child's family and appropriate specialists to determine the additional services needed and/or the placement option(s) most likely to ensure the child's success. (Aspects of this principle may not apply in programs that have a lawful mandate to provide services to a particular population of children.)

P-1.8—We shall be familiar with the risk factors for and symptoms of child abuse and neglect, including physical, sexual, verbal, and emotional abuse and physical, emotional, educational, and medical neglect. We shall know and follow state laws and community procedures that protect children against abuse and neglect.

P-1.9—When we have reasonable cause to suspect child abuse or neglect, we shall report it to the appropriate community agency and follow up to ensure that appropriate action has been taken. When appropriate, parents or guardians will be informed that the referral will be or has been made.

P-1.10—When another person tells us of his or her suspicion that a child is being abused or neglected, we shall assist that person in taking appropriate action in order to protect the child.

P-1.11—When we become aware of a practice or situation that endangers the health, safety, or well-being of children, we have an ethical responsibility to protect children or inform parents and/or others who can.

 SECTION II

Ethical Responsibilities to Families

Families* are of primary importance in children's development. Because the family and the early childhood practitioner have a common interest in the child's well-being, we acknowledge a primary responsibility to bring about communication, cooperation, and collaboration between the home and early childhood program in ways that enhance the child's development.

* The term *family* may include those adults, besides parents, with the responsibility of being involved in educating, nurturing, and advocating for the child.

Ideals

I-2.1—To be familiar with the knowledge base related to working effectively with families and to stay informed through continuing education and training.

I-2.2—To develop relationships of mutual trust and create partnerships with the families we serve.

I-2.3—To welcome all family members and encourage them to participate in the program.

I-2.4—To listen to families, acknowledge and build upon their strengths and competencies, and learn from families as we support them in their task of nurturing children.

I-2.5—To respect the dignity and preferences of each family and to make an effort to learn about its structure, culture, language, customs, and beliefs.

I-2.6—To acknowledge families' childrearing values and their right to make decisions for their children.

I-2.7—To share information about each child's education and development with families and to help them understand and appreciate the current knowledge base of the early childhood profession.

I-2.8—To help family members enhance their understanding of their children and support the continuing development of their skills as parents.

I-2.9—To participate in building support networks for families by providing them with opportunities to interact with program staff, other families, community resources, and professional services.

Principles

P-2.1—We shall not deny family members access to their child's classroom or program setting unless access is denied by court order or other legal restriction.

P-2.2—We shall inform families of program philosophy, policies, curriculum, assessment system, and personnel qualifications, and explain why we teach as we do—which should be in accordance with our ethical responsibilities to children (see Section I).

P-2.3—We shall inform families of and, when appropriate, involve them in policy decisions.

P-2.4—We shall involve the family in significant decisions affecting their child.

P-2.5—We shall make every effort to communicate effectively with all families in a language that they understand. We shall use community resources for translation and interpretation when we do not have sufficient resources in our own programs.

P-2.6—As families share information with us about their children and families, we shall consider this information to plan and implement the program.

P-2-7—We shall inform families about the nature and purpose of the program's child assessments and how data about their child will be used.

P-2.8—We shall treat child assessment information confidentially and share this information only when there is a legitimate need for it.

P-2.9—We shall inform the family of injuries and incidents involving their child, of risks such as exposures to communicable diseases that might result in infection, and of occurrences that might result in emotional stress.

P-2.10—Families shall be fully informed of any proposed research projects involving their children and shall have the opportunity to give or withhold consent without penalty. We shall not permit or participate in research that could in any way hinder the education, development, or well-being of children.

P-2.11—We shall not engage in or support exploitation of families. We shall not use our relationship with a family for private advantage or personal gain, or enter into relationships with family members that might impair our effectiveness working with their children.

P-2.12—We shall develop written policies for the protection of confidentiality and the disclosure of children's records. These policy documents shall be made available to all program personnel and families. Disclosure of children's records beyond family members, program personnel, and consultants having an obligation of confidentiality shall require familial consent (except in cases of abuse or neglect).

P-2.13—We shall maintain confidentiality and shall respect the family's right to privacy, refraining from disclosure of confidential information and intrusion into family life. However, when we have reason to believe that a child's welfare is at risk, it is permissible to share confidential information with agencies, as well as with individuals who have legal responsibility for intervening in the child's interest.

P-2.14—In cases where family members are in conflict with one another, we shall work openly, sharing our observations of the child, to help all parties involved make informed decisions. We shall refrain from becoming an advocate for one party.

P-2.15—We shall be familiar with and appropriately refer families to community resources and professional support services. After a referral has been made, we shall follow up to ensure that services have been appropriately provided.

SECTION III

Ethical Responsibilities to Colleagues

In a caring, cooperative workplace, human dignity is respected, professional satisfaction is promoted, and positive relationships are developed and sustained. Based upon our core values, our primary responsibility to colleagues is to establish and maintain settings and relationships that support productive work and meet professional needs. The same ideals that apply to children also apply as we interact with adults in the workplace.

A—Responsibilities to Co-workers
Ideals

I-3A.1—To establish and maintain relationships of respect, trust, confidentiality, collaboration, and cooperation with co-workers.

I-3A.2—To share resources with co-workers, collaborating to ensure that the best possible early childhood care and education program is provided.

I-3A.3—To support co-workers in meeting their professional needs and in their professional development.

I-3A.4—To accord co-workers due recognition of professional achievement.

Principles

P-3A.1—We shall recognize the contributions of colleagues to our program and not participate in practices that diminish their reputations or impair their effectiveness in working with children and families.

P-3A.2—When we have concerns about the professional behavior of a co-worker, we shall first let that person know of our concern in a way that shows respect for personal dignity and for the diversity to be found among staff members, and then attempt to resolve the matter collegially and in a confidential manner.

P-3A.3—We shall exercise care in expressing views regarding the personal attributes or professional conduct of co-workers. Statements should be based on firsthand knowledge, not hearsay, and relevant to the interests of children and programs.

P-3A.4—We shall not participate in practices that discriminate against a co-worker because of sex, race, national origin, religious beliefs or other affiliations, age, marital status/family structure, disability, or sexual orientation.

B—Responsibilities to Employers

Ideals

I-3B.1—To assist the program in providing the highest quality of service.

I-3B.2—To do nothing that diminishes the reputation of the program in which we work unless it is violating laws and regulations designed to protect children or is violating the provisions of this Code.

Principles

P-3B.1—We shall follow all program policies. When we do not agree with program policies, we shall attempt to effect change through constructive action within the organization.

P-3B.2—We shall speak or act on behalf of an organization only when authorized. We shall take care to acknowledge when we are speaking for the organization and when we are expressing a personal judgment.

P-3B.3—We shall not violate laws or regulations designed to protect children and shall take appropriate action consistent with this Code when aware of such violations.

P-3B.4—If we have concerns about a colleague's behavior, and children's well-being is not at risk, we may address the concern with that individual. If children are at risk or the situation does not improve after it has been brought to the colleague's attention, we shall report the colleague's unethical or incompetent behavior to an appropriate authority.

P-3B.5—When we have a concern about circumstances or conditions that impact the quality of care and education within the program, we shall inform the program's administration or, when necessary, other appropriate authorities.

C—Responsibilities to Employees

Ideals

I-3C.1—To promote safe and healthy working conditions and policies that foster mutual respect, cooperation, collaboration, competence, well-being, confidentiality, and self esteem in staff members.

I-3C.2—To create and maintain a climate of trust and candor that will enable staff to speak and act in the best interests of children, families, and the field of early childhood care and education.

I-3C.3—To strive to secure adequate and equitable compensation (salary and benefits) for those who work with or on behalf of young children.

I-3C.4—To encourage and support continual development of employees in becoming more skilled and knowledgeable practitioners.

Principles

P-3C.1—In decisions concerning children and programs, we shall draw upon the education, training, experience, and expertise of staff members.

P-3C.2—We shall provide staff members with safe and supportive working conditions that honor confidences and permit them to carry out their responsibilities through fair performance evaluation, written grievance procedures, constructive feedback, and opportunities for continuing professional development and advancement.

P-3C.3—We shall develop and maintain comprehensive written personnel policies that define program standards. These policies shall be given to new staff members and shall be available and easily accessible for review by all staff members.

P-3C.4—We shall inform employees whose performance does not meet program expectations of areas of concern and, when possible, assist in improving their performance.

P-3C.5—We shall conduct employee dismissals for just cause, in accordance with all applicable laws and regulations. We shall inform employees who are dismissed of the reasons for their termination. When a dismissal is for cause, justification must be based on evidence of inadequate or inappropriate behavior that is accurately documented, current, and available for the employee to review.

P-3C.6—In making evaluations and recommendations, we shall make judgments based on fact and relevant to the interests of children and programs.

P-3C.7—We shall make hiring, retention, termination, and promotion decisions based solely on a person's competence, record of accomplishment, ability to carry out the responsibilities of the position, and professional preparation specific to the developmental levels of children in his/her care.

P-3.C.8—We shall not make hiring, retention, termination, and promotion decisions based on an individual's sex, race, national origin, religious beliefs or other affiliations, age, marital status/family structure, disability, or sexual orientation. We shall be familiar with and observe laws and regulations that pertain to employment discrimination. (Aspects of this principle do not apply to programs that have a lawful mandate to determine eligibility based on one or more of the criteria identified above.)

P-3C.9—We shall maintain confidentiality in dealing with issues related to an employee's job performance and shall respect an employee's right to privacy regarding personal issues.

SECTION IV

Ethical Responsibilities to Community and Society

Early childhood programs operate within the context of their immediate community made up of families and other institutions concerned with children's welfare. Our responsibilities to the community are to provide programs that meet the diverse needs of families, to cooperate with agencies and professions that share the responsibility for children, to assist families in gaining access to those agencies and allied professionals, and to assist in the development of community programs that are needed but not currently available. As individuals, we acknowledge our responsibility to provide the best possible programs of care and education for children and to conduct ourselves with honesty and integrity. Because of our specialized expertise in early childhood development and education and because the larger society shares responsibility for the welfare and protection of young children, we acknowledge a collective obligation to advocate for the best interests of children within early childhood programs and in the larger community and to serve as a voice for young children everywhere. The ideals and principles in this section are presented to distinguish between those that pertain to the work of the individual early childhood educator and those that more typically are engaged in collectively on behalf of the best interests of children—with the understanding that individual early childhood educators have a shared responsibility for addressing the ideals and principles that are identified as "collective."

Ideal (Individual)

1-4.1—To provide the community with high-quality early childhood care and education programs and services.

Ideals (Collective)

I-4.2—To promote cooperation among professionals and agencies and interdisciplinary collaboration among professions concerned with addressing issues in the health, education, and well-being of young children, their families, and their early childhood educators.

I-4.3—To work through education, research, and advocacy toward an environmentally safe world in which all children receive health care, food, and shelter; are nurtured; and live free from violence in their home and their communities.

I-4.4—To work through education, research, and advocacy toward a society in which all young children have access to high-quality early care and education programs.

I-4.5—To work to ensure that appropriate assessment systems, which include multiple sources of information, are used for purposes that benefit children.

I-4.6—To promote knowledge and understanding of young children and their needs. To work toward greater societal acknowledgment of children's rights and greater social acceptance of responsibility for the well-being of all children.

I-4.7—To support policies and laws that promote the well-being of children and families, and to work to change those that impair their well-being. To participate in developing policies and laws that are needed, and to cooperate with other individuals and groups in these efforts.

I-4.8—To further the professional development of the field of early childhood care and education and to strengthen its commitment to realizing its core values as reflected in this Code.

Principles (Individual)

P-4.1—We shall communicate openly and truthfully about the nature and extent of services that we provide.

P-4.2—We shall apply for, accept, and work in positions for which we are personally well-suited and professionally qualified. We shall not offer services that we do not have the competence, qualifications, or resources to provide.

P-4.3—We shall carefully check references and shall not hire or recommend for employment any person whose competence, qualifications, or character makes him or her unsuited for the position.

P-4.4—We shall be objective and accurate in reporting the knowledge upon which we base our program practices.

P-4.5—We shall be knowledgeable about the appropriate use of assessment strategies and instruments and interpret results accurately to families.

P-4.6—We shall be familiar with laws and regulations that serve to protect the children in our programs and be vigilant in ensuring that these laws and regulations are followed.

P-4.7—When we become aware of a practice or situation that endangers the health, safety, or well-being of children, we have an ethical responsibility to protect children or inform parents and/or others who can.

P-4.8—We shall not participate in practices that are in violation of laws and regulations that protect the children in our programs.

P-4.9—When we have evidence that an early childhood program is violating laws or regulations protecting children, we shall report the violation to appropriate authorities who can be expected to remedy the situation.

P-4.10—When a program violates or requires its employees to violate this Code, it is permissible, after fair assessment of the evidence, to disclose the identity of that program.

Principles (Collective)

P-4.11—When policies are enacted for purposes that do not benefit children, we have a collective responsibility to work to change these practices.

P-4-12—When we have evidence that an agency that provides services intended to ensure children's well-being is failing to meet its obligations, we acknowledge a collective ethical responsibility to report the problem to appropriate authorities or to the public. We shall be vigilant in our follow-up until the situation is resolved.

P-4.13—When a child protection agency fails to provide adequate protection for abused or neglected children, we acknowledge a collective ethical responsibility to work toward the improvement of these services.

NAEYC has taken reasonable measures to develop the Code in a fair, reasonable, open, unbiased, and objective manner, based on currently available data. However, further research or developments may change the current state of knowledge. Neither NAEYC nor its officers, directors, members, employees, or agents will be liable for any loss, damage, or claim with respect to any liabilities, including direct, special, indirect, or consequential damages incurred in connection with the Code or reliance on the information presented.

Statement of Commitment*

As an individual who works with young children, I commit myself to furthering the values of early childhood education as they are reflected in the ideals and principles of the NAEYC Code of Ethical Conduct. To the best of my ability I will

- Never harm children
- Ensure that programs for young children are based on current knowledge and research of child development and early childhood education.
- Respect and support families in their task of nurturing children.
- Respect colleagues in early childhood care and education and support them in maintaining the NAEYC Code of Ethical Conduct.
- Serve as an advocate for children, their families, and their teachers in community and society.
- Stay informed of and maintain high standards of professional conduct.

■   Engage in an ongoing process of self-reflection, realizing that personal characteristics, biases, and beliefs have an impact on children and families.

■   Be open to new ideas and be willing to learn from the suggestions of others.

■   Continue to learn, grow, and contribute as a professional.

■   Honor the ideals and principles of the NAEYC Code of Ethical Conduct.

*This Statement of Commitment is not part of the Code but is a personal acknowledgement of the individual's willingness to embrace the distinctive values and moral obligations of the field of early childhood care and education. It is recognition of the moral obligations that lead to an individual becoming part of the profession.

Glossary of Terms Related to Ethics

Code of Ethics. Defines the core values of the field and provides guidance for what professionals should do when they encounter conflicting obligations or responsibilities in their work.

Values. Qualities or principles that individuals believe to be desirable or worthwhile and that they prize for themselves, for others, and for the world in which they live.

Core Values. Commitments held by a profession that are consciously and knowingly embraced by its practitioners because they make a contribution to society. There is a difference between personal values and the core values of a profession.

Morality. Peoples' views of what is good, right, and proper; their beliefs about their obligations; and their ideas about how they should behave.

Ethics. The study of right and wrong, or duty and obligation, that involves critical reflection on morality and the ability to make choices between values and the examination of the moral dimensions of relationships.

Professional Ethics. The moral commitments of a profession that involve moral reflection that extends and enhances the personal morality practitioners bring to their work, that concern actions of right and wrong in the workplace, and that help individuals resolve moral dilemmas they encounter in their work.

Ethical Responsibilities. Behaviors that one must or must not engage in. Ethical responsibilities are clear-cut and are spelled out in the Code of Ethical Conduct (for example, early childhood educators should never share confidential information about a child or family with a person who has no legitimate need for knowing).

Ethical Dilemma. A moral conflict that involves determining appropriate conduct when an individual faces conflicting professional values and responsibilities.

Sources for Glossary Terms and Definitions

Feeney, S., & N. Freeman. 1999. *Ethics and the early childhood educator: Using the NAEYC code*. Washington, DC: NAEYC.

Kidder, R. M. 1995. *How good people make tough choices: Resolving the dilemmas of ethical living*. New York: Fireside.

Kipnis, K. 1987. How to discuss professional ethics. *Young Children* 42(4): 26–30.

Developmentally Appropriate Practice in Early Childhood Programs Serving Children from Birth through Age 8

A position statement of the National Association for the Education of Young Children

Adopted July 1996

This statement defines and describes principles of developmentally appropriate practice in early childhood programs for administrators, teachers, parents, policy-makers, and others who make decisions about the care and education of young children. An early childhood program is any group program in a center, school, or other facility that serves children from birth through age 8. Early childhood programs include child care centers, family child care homes, private and public preschools, kindergartens, and primary-grade schools.

The early childhood profession is responsible for establishing and promoting standards of high-quality, professional practice in early childhood programs. These standards must reflect current knowledge and shared beliefs about what constitutes high-quality, developmentally appropriate early childhood education in the context within which services are delivered.

This position paper is organized into several components, which include the following:

1. a description of the current context in which early childhood programs operate;

2. a description of the rationale and need for NAEYC's position statement;

3. a statement of NAEYC's commitment to children;

4. the statement of the position and definition of *developmentally appropriate practice*;

5. a summary of the principles of child development and learning and the theoretical perspectives that inform decisions about early childhood practice;

6. guidelines for making decisions about developmentally appropriate practices that address the following integrated components of early childhood practice: creating a caring community of learners, teaching to enhance children's learning and development, constructing appropriate curriculum, assessing children's learning and development, and establishing reciprocal relationships with families;

7. a challenge to the field to move from *either/or* to *both/and* thinking; and

8. recommendations for policies necessary to ensure developmentally appropriate practices for all children.

This statement is designed to be used in conjunction with NAEYC's "Criteria for High Quality Early Childhood Programs," the standards for accreditation by the National Academy of Early Childhood Programs (NAEYC 1991), and with "Guidelines for Appropriate Curriculum Content and Assessment in Programs Serving Children Ages 3 through 8" (NAEYC & NAECS/SDE 1992; Bredekamp & Rosegrant 1992, 1995).

THE CURRENT CONTEXT OF EARLY CHILDHOOD PROGRAMS

The early childhood knowledge base has expanded considerably in recent years, affirming some of the profession's cherished beliefs about good practice and challenging others. In addition to gaining new knowledge, early childhood programs have experienced several important changes in recent years. The number of programs continues to increase not only in response to the growing demand for out-of-home child care but also in recognition of the critical importance of educational experiences during the early years (Willer et al. 1991; NCES 1993). For example, in the late 1980s Head Start embarked on the largest expansion in its history, continuing this expansion into the 1990s with significant new services for families with infants and toddlers. The National Education Goals Panel established as an objective of Goal 1 that by the year 2000 all children will have access to high-quality, developmentally appropriate preschool programs (NEGP 1991). Welfare reform portends a greatly increased demand for child care services for even the youngest children from very-low-income families.

Some characteristics of early childhood programs have also changed in recent years. Increasingly, programs serve children and families from diverse cultural and linguistic backgrounds, requiring that all programs demonstrate understanding of and responsiveness to cultural and linguistic diversity. Because culture and language are critical components of children's development, practices cannot be developmentally appropriate unless they are responsive to cultural and linguistic diversity.

The Americans with Disabilities Act and the Individuals with Disabilities Education Act now require that all early childhood programs make reasonable accommodations to provide access for children with disabilities or developmental delays (DEC/CEC & NAEYC 1993). This legal right reflects the growing consensus that young children with disabilities are best served in the same community settings where their typically developing peers are found (DEC/CEC 1994).

The trend toward full inclusion of children with disabilities must be reflected in descriptions of recommended practices, and considerable work has been done toward converging the perspectives of early childhood and early childhood special education (Carta et al. 1991; Mallory 1992, 1994; Wolery, Strain, & Bailey 1992; Bredekamp 1993b; DEC Task Force 1993; Mallory & New 1994b; Wolery & Wilbers 1994).

Other important program characteristics include age of children and length of program day. Children are now enrolled in programs at younger ages, many from infancy. The length of the program day for all ages of children has been extended in response to the need for extended hours of care for employed families. Similarly, program sponsorship has become more diverse. The public schools in the majority of states now provide prekindergarten programs, some for children as young as 3, and many offer before- and after-school child care (Mitchell, Seligson, & Marx 1989; Seppanen, Kaplan deVries, & Seligson 1993; Adams & Sandfort 1994).

Corporate America has become a more visible sponsor of child care programs, with several key corporations leading the way in promoting high quality (for example, IBM, AT&T, and the American Business Collaboration). Family child care homes have become an increasingly visible sector of the child care community, with greater emphasis on professional development and the National Association for Family Child Care taking the lead in establishing an accreditation system for high-quality family child care (Hollestelle 1993; Cohen & Modigliani 1994; Galinsky et al. 1994). Many different settings in this country provide services to young children, and it is legitimate—even beneficial—for these settings to vary in certain ways. However, since it is vital to meet children's learning and developmental needs wherever they are served, high standards of quality should apply to all settings.

The context in which early childhood programs operate today is also characterized by ongoing debates about how best to teach young children and discussions about what sort of practice is most likely to contribute to their development and learning. Perhaps the most important contribution of NAEYC's 1987 position statement on developmentally appropriate practice (Bredekamp 1987) was that it created an opportunity for increased conversation within and outside the early childhood field about practices. In revising the position statement, NAEYC's goal is not only to improve the quality of current early childhood practice but also to continue to encourage the kind of questioning and debate among early childhood professionals that are necessary for the continued growth of professional knowledge in the field. A related goal is to express NAEYC's position more clearly so that energy is not wasted in unproductive debate about apparent rather than real differences of opinion.

 ## RATIONALE FOR THE POSITION STATEMENT

The increased demand for early childhood education services is partly due to the increased recognition of the crucial importance of experiences during the earliest years of life. Children's experiences during early childhood not only influence their later functioning in school but can have effects throughout life. For example, current research demonstrates the early and lasting effects of children's environments and experiences on brain development and cognition (Chugani, Phelps, & Mazziotta 1987; Caine & Caine 1991; Kuhl 1994). Studies show that, "From infancy through about age 10, brain cells not only form most of the connections they will maintain throughout life but during this time they retain their greatest malleability" (Dana Alliance for Brain Initiatives 1996, 7).

Positive, supportive relationships, important during the earliest years of life, appear essential not only for cognitive development but also for healthy emotional development and social attachment (Bowlby 1969; Stern 1985). The preschool years are an optimum time for development of fundamental motor skills (Gallahue 1993), language development (Dyson & Genishi 1993), and other key foundational aspects of development that have lifelong implications.

Recognition of the importance of the early years has heightened interest and support for early childhood education programs. A number of studies demonstrating long-term, positive consequences of participation in high-quality early childhood programs for children from low-income families influenced the expansion of Head Start and public school prekindergarten (Lazar & Darlington 1982; Lee, Brooks-Gunn, & Schuur 1988; Schweinhart, Barnes, & Weikart 1993; Campbell & Ramey 1995). Several decades of research clearly demonstrate that high-quality, developmentally appropriate early childhood programs produce short- and long-term positive effects on children's cognitive and social development (Barnett 1995).

From a thorough review of the research on the long-term effects of early childhood education programs, Barnett concludes that "across all studies, the findings were relatively uniform and constitute overwhelming evidence that early childhood care and education can produce sizeable improvements in school success" (1995, 40). Children from low-income families who partici- pated in high-quality preschool programs were significantly less likely to have been assigned to special education, retained in grade, engaged in crime, or to have dropped out of school. The longitudinal studies, in general, suggest positive consequences for programs that used an approach consistent with principles of developmentally appropriate practice (Lazar & Darlington 1982; Berreuta-Clement et al. 1984; Miller & Bizzell 1984; Schweinhart, Weikart, & Larner 1986; Schweinhart, Barnes, & Weikart 1993; Frede 1995; Schweinhart & Weikart 1996).

Research on the long-term effects of early childhood programs indicates that children who attend good-quality child care programs, even at very young ages, demonstrate positive outcomes, and children who attend poor-quality programs show negative effects (Vandell & Powers 1983; Phillips, McCartney, & Scarr 1987; Fields et al. 1988; Vandell, Henderson, & Wilson 1988; Arnett 1989; Vandell & Corasanti 1990; Burchinal et al. 1996). Specifically, children who experience high-quality, stable child care engage in more complex play, demonstrate more secure attachments to adults and other children, and score higher on measures of thinking ability and language development. High- quality child care can predict academic success, adjustment to school, and reduced behavioral problems for children in first grade (Howes 1988).

While the potential positive effects of high-quality child care are well doc- umented, several large-scale evaluations of child care find that high-quality experiences are not the norm (Whitebook, Howes, & Phillips 1989; Howes, Phillips, & Whitebook 1992; Layzer, Goodson, & Moss 1993; Galinsky et al. 1994; Cost, Quality, & Child Outcomes Study Team 1995). Each of these stud- ies, which included observations of child care and preschool quality in several states, found that good quality that supports children's health and social and cognitive development is being provided in only about 15% of programs.

Of even greater concern was the large percentage of classrooms and family child care homes that were rated "barely adequate" or "inadequate" for quality. From 12 to 20% of the children were in settings that were con- sidered dangerous to their health and safety and harmful to their social and cognitive development. An alarming number of infants and toddlers (35 to 40%) were found to be in unsafe settings (Cost, Quality, & Child Outcomes Study Team 1995).

Experiences during the earliest years of formal schooling are also formative. Studies demonstrate that children's success or failure during the first years of school often predicts the course of later schooling (Alexander & Entwisle 1988; Slavin, Karweit, & Madden 1989). A growing body of research indicates that more developmentally appropriate teaching in preschool and kindergarten predicts greater success in the early grades (Frede & Barnett 1992; Marcon 1992; Charlesworth et al. 1993).

As with preschool and child care, the observed quality of children's early schooling is uneven (Durkin 1987, 1990; Hiebert & Papierz 1990; Bryant, Clifford, & Peisner 1991; Carnegie Task Force 1996). For instance, in a state-wide observational study of kindergarten classrooms, Durkin (1987) found that despite assessment results indicating considerable individual variation in children's literacy skills, which would call for various teaching strategies as well as individual and small-group work, teachers relied on one instructional strategy—whole-group, phonics instruction—and judged children who did not learn well with this one method as unready for first grade. Currently, too many children—especially children from low-income families and some minority groups—experience school failure, are retained in grade, get assigned to special education, and eventually drop out of school (Natriello, McDill, & Pallas 1990; Legters & Slavin 1992).

Results such as these indicate that while early childhood programs have the potential for producing positive and lasting effects on children, this potential will not be achieved unless more attention is paid to ensuring that all programs meet the highest standards of quality. As the number and type of early childhood programs increase, the need increases for a shared vision and agreed-upon standards of professional practice.

 NAEYC'S COMMITMENT TO CHILDREN

It is important to acknowledge at the outset the core values that undergird all of NAEYC's work. As stated in NAEYC's *Code of Ethical Conduct,* standards of professional practice in early childhood programs are based on commitment to certain fundamental values that are deeply rooted in the history of the early childhood field:

- appreciating childhood as a unique and valuable stage of the human life cycle [and valuing the quality of children's lives in the present, not just as preparation for the future];

- basing our work with children on knowledge of child development [and learning];

- appreciating and supporting the close ties between the child and family;

- recognizing that children are best understood in the context of family, culture, and society;

- respecting the dignity, worth, and uniqueness of each individual (child, family member, and colleague); and

- helping children and adults achieve their full potential in the context of relationships that are based on trust, respect, and positive regard. (Feeney & Kipnis 1992, 3)

 ## STATEMENT OF THE POSITION

Based on an enduring commitment to act on behalf of children, NAEYC's mission is to promote high-quality, developmentally appropriate programs for all children and their families. Because we define developmentally appropriate programs as programs that contribute to children's development, we must articulate our goals for children's development. The principles of practice advocated in this position statement are based on a set of goals for children: what we want for them, both in their present lives and as they develop to adulthood, and what personal characteristics should be fostered because these contribute to a peaceful, prosperous, and democratic society.

As we approach the 21st century, enormous changes are taking place in daily life and work. At the same time, certain human capacities will undoubtedly remain important elements in individual and societal well-being—no matter what economic or technological changes take place. With a recognition of both the continuities in human existence and the rapid changes in our world, broad agreement is emerging (e.g., Resnick 1996) that when today's children become adults they will need the ability to

- communicate well, respect others and engage with them to work through differences of opinion, and function well as members of a team;

- analyze situations, make reasoned judgments, and solve new problems as they emerge;

- access information through various modes, including spoken and written language, and intelligently employ complex tools and technologies as they are developed; and

- continue to learn new approaches, skills, and knowledge as conditions and needs change.

Clearly, people in the decades ahead will need, more than ever, fully developed literacy and numeracy skills, and these abilities are key goals of the educational process. In science, social studies (which includes history and geography), music and the visual arts, physical education and health, children need to acquire a body of knowledge and skills, as identified by those in the various disciplines (e.g., Bredekamp & Rosegrant 1995).

Besides acquiring a body of knowledge and skills, children must develop positive dispositions and attitudes. They need to understand that effort is necessary for achievement, for example, and they need to have curiosity and confidence in themselves as learners. Moreover, to live in a highly pluralistic society and world, young people need to develop a positive self-identity and a tolerance for others whose perspective and experience may be different from their own.

Beyond the shared goals of the early childhood field, every program for young children should establish its own goals in collaboration with families. All early childhood programs will not have identical goals; priorities may vary in some respects because programs serve a diversity of children and families. Such differences notwithstanding, NAEYC believes that all high-quality, developmentally appropriate programs will have certain attributes in common. A high-quality early childhood program is one that provides a safe and nurturing environment that promotes the physical, social, emotional, aesthetic, intellectual, and language development of each child while being sensitive to the needs and preferences of families.

Many factors influence the quality of an early childhood program, including (but not limited to) the extent to which knowledge about how children develop and learn is applied in program practices. Developmentally appropriate programs are based on what is known about how children develop and learn; such programs promote the development and enhance the learning of each individual child served.

Developmentally appropriate practices result from the process of professionals making decisions about the well-being and education of children based on at least three important kinds of information or knowledge:

1. *what is known about child development and learning*—knowledge of age-related human characteristics that permits general predictions within an age range about what activities, materials, interactions, or experiences will be safe, healthy, interesting, achievable, and also challenging to children;

2. *what is known about the strengths, interests, and needs of each individual child in the group* to be able to adapt for and be responsive to inevitable individual variation; and

3. *knowledge of the social and cultural contexts in which children live* to ensure that learning experiences are meaningful, relevant, and respectful for the participating children and their families.

Furthermore, each of these dimensions of knowledge—human development and learning, individual characteristics and experiences, and social and cultural contexts—is dynamic and changing, requiring that early childhood teachers remain learners throughout their careers.

An example illustrates the interrelatedness of these three dimensions of the decisionmaking process. Children all over the world acquire language at approximately the same period of the life span and in similar ways (Fernald

1992). But tremendous individual variation exists in the rate and pattern of language acquisition (Fenson et al. 1994). Also, children acquire the language or languages of the culture in which they live (Kuhl 1994). Thus, to adequately support a developmental task such as language acquisition, the teacher must draw on at least all three interrelated dimensions of knowledge to determine a developmentally appropriate strategy or intervention.

Principles of child development and learning that inform developmentally appropriate practice

Taken together, these core values define NAEYC's basic commitment to children and underlie its position on developmentally appropriate practice.

Developmentally appropriate practice is based on knowledge about how children develop and learn. As Katz states, "In a developmental approach to curriculum design, ... [decisions] about what should be learned and how it would best be learned depend on what we know of the learner's developmental status and our understanding of the relationships between early experience and subsequent development" (1995, 109). To guide their decisions about practice, all early childhood teachers need to understand the developmental changes that typically occur in the years from birth through age 8 and beyond, variations in development that may occur, and how best to support children's learning and development during these years.

A complete discussion of the knowledge base that informs early childhood practice is beyond the scope of this document (see, for example, Seefeldt 1992; Sroufe, Cooper, & DeHart 1992; Kostelnik, Soderman, & Whiren 1993; Spodek 1993; Berk 1996). Because development and learning are so complex, no one theory is sufficient to explain these phenomena. However, a broad-based review of the literature on early childhood education generates a set of principles to inform early childhood practice. *Principles* are generalizations that are sufficiently reliable that they should be taken into account when making decisions (Katz & Chard 1989; Katz 1995). Following is a list of empirically based principles of child development and learning that inform and guide decisions about developmentally appropriate practice.

1. Domains of children's development—physical, social, emotional, and cognitive—are closely related. Development in one domain influences and is influenced by development in other domains.

Development in one domain can limit or facilitate development in others (Sroufe, Cooper, & DeHart 1992; Kostelnik, Soderman, & Whiren 1993). For example, when babies begin to crawl or walk, their ability to explore the world expands, and their mobility, in turn, affects their cognitive development. Likewise, children's language skill affects their ability to establish social relationships with adults and other children, just as their skill in social interaction can support or impede their language development.

Because developmental domains are interrelated, educators should be aware of and use these interrelationships to organize children's learning experiences in ways that help children develop optimally in all areas and that make meaningful connections across domains.

Recognition of the connections across developmental domains is also useful for curriculum planning with the various age groups represented in the early childhood period. Curriculum with infants and toddlers is almost solely driven by the need to support their healthy development in all domains. During the primary grades, curriculum planning attempts to help children develop conceptual understandings that apply across related subject-matter disciplines.

2. Development occurs in a relatively orderly sequence, with later abilities, skills, and knowledge building on those already acquired.

Human development research indicates that relatively stable, predictable sequences of growth and change occur in children during the first nine years of life (Piaget 1952; Erikson 1963; Dyson & Genishi 1993; Gallahue 1993; Case & Okamoto 1996). Predictable changes occur in all domains of development—physical, emotional, social, language, and cognitive—although the ways that these changes are manifest and the meaning attached to them may vary in different cultural contexts. Knowledge of typical development of children within the age span served by the program provides a general framework to guide how teachers prepare the learning environment and plan realistic curriculum goals and objectives and appropriate experiences.

3. Development proceeds at varying rates from child to child as well as unevenly within different areas of each child's functioning.

Individual variation has at least two dimensions: the inevitable variability around the average or normative course of development and the uniqueness of each person as an individual (Sroufe, Cooper, & DeHart 1992). Each child is a unique person with an individual pattern and timing of growth, as well as individual personality, temperament, learning style, and experiential and family background. All children have their own strengths, needs, and interests; for some children, special learning and developmental needs or abilities are identified. Given the enormous variation among children of the same chronological age, a child's age must be recognized as only a crude index of developmental maturity.

Recognition that individual variation is not only to be expected but also valued requires that decisions about curriculum and adults' interactions with children be as individualized as possible. Emphasis on individual appropriateness is not the same as "individualism." Rather, this recognition requires that children be considered not solely as members of an age group, expected to perform to a predetermined norm and without adaptation to individual variation of any kind. Having high expectations for all children is important, but rigid expectations of group norms do not reflect what is known about real differences in individual development and learning during the early years. Group-norm expectancy can be especially harmful for children with special learning and developmental needs (NEGP 1991; Mallory 1992; Wolery, Strain, & Bailey 1992).

4. Early experiences have both cumulative and delayed effects on individual children's development; optimal periods exist for certain types of development and learning.

Children's early experiences, either positive or negative, are cumulative in the sense that if an experience occurs occasionally, it may have minimal effects. If positive or negative experiences occur frequently, however, they can have powerful, lasting, even "snowballing," effects (Katz & Chard 1989; Kostelnik, Soderman, & Whiren 1993; Wieder & Greenspan 1993). For example, a child's social experiences with other children in the preschool years help him develop social skills and confidence that enable him to make friends in the early school years, and these experiences further enhance the child's social competence. Conversely, children who fail to develop minimal social competence and are neglected or rejected by peers are at significant risk to drop out of school, become delinquent, and experience mental health problems in adulthood (Asher, Hymel, & Renshaw 1984; Parker & Asher 1987).

Similar patterns can be observed in babies whose cries and other attempts at communication are regularly responded to, thus enhancing their own sense of efficacy and increasing communicative competence. Likewise, when children have or do not have early literacy experiences, such as being read to regularly, their later success in learning to read is affected accordingly. Perhaps most convincing is the growing body of research demonstrating that social and sensorimotor experiences during the first three years directly affect neurological development of the brain, with important and lasting implications for children's capacity to learn (Dana Alliance for Brain Initiatives 1996).

Early experiences can also have delayed effects, either positive or negative, on subsequent development. For instance, some evidence suggests that reliance on extrinsic rewards (such as candy or money) to shape children's behavior, a strategy that can be very effective in the short term, under certain circumstances lessens children's intrinsic motivation to engage in the rewarded behavior in the long term (Dweck 1986; Kohn 1993). For example, paying children to read books may over time undermine their desire to read for their own enjoyment and edification.

At certain points in the life span, some kinds of learning and development occur most efficiently. For example, the first three years of life appear to be an optimal period for verbal language development (Kuhl 1994). Although delays in language development due to physical or environmental deficits can be ameliorated later on, such intervention usually requires considerable effort. Similarly, the preschool years appear to be optimum for fundamental motor development (that is, fundamental motor skills are more easily and efficiently acquired at this age) (Gallahue 1995). Children who have many opportunities and adult support to practice large-motor skills (running, jumping, hopping, skipping) during this period have the cumulative benefit of being better able to acquire more sophisticated, complex motor skills (balancing on a beam or riding a two-wheel bike) in subsequent years. On the other hand, children whose early motor experiences are severely limited may struggle to acquire physical competence and may also experience delayed effects when attempting to participate in sports or personal fitness activities later in life.

5. Development proceeds in predictable directions toward greater complexity, organization, and internalization.

Learning during early childhood proceeds from behavioral knowledge to symbolic or representational knowledge (Bruner 1983). For example, children learn to navigate their homes and other familiar settings long before they can understand the words *left* and *right* or read a map of the house. Developmentally appropriate programs provide opportunities for children to broaden and deepen their behavioral knowledge by providing a variety of firsthand experiences and by helping children acquire symbolic knowledge through representing their experiences in a variety of media, such as drawing, painting, construction of models, dramatic play, verbal and written descriptions (Katz 1995).

Even very young children are able to use various media to represent their understanding of concepts. Furthermore, through representation of their knowledge, the knowledge itself is enhanced (Edwards, Gandini, & Forman 1993; Malaguzzi 1993; Forman 1994). Representational modes and media also vary with the age of the child. For instance, most learning for infants and toddlers is sensory and motoric, but by age 2 children use one object to stand for another in play (a block for a phone or a spoon for a guitar).

6. Development and learning occur in and are influenced by multiple social and cultural contexts.

Bronfenbrenner (1979, 1989, 1993) provides an ecological model for understanding human development. He explains that children's development is best understood within the sociocultural context of the family, educational setting, community, and broader society. These various contexts are interrelated, and all have an impact on the developing child. For example, even a child in a loving, supportive family within a strong, healthy community is affected by the biases of the larger society, such as racism or sexism, and may show the effects of negative stereotyping and discrimination.

We define *culture* as the customary beliefs and patterns of and for behavior, both explicit and implicit, that are passed on to future generations by the society they live in and/or by a social, religious, or ethnic group within it.

Because culture is often discussed in the context of diversity or multicultural-ism, people fail to recognize the powerful role that culture plays in influenc-ing the development of *all* children. Every culture structures and interprets children's behavior and development (Edwards & Gandini 1989; Tobin, Wu, & Davidson 1989; Rogoff et al. 1993). As Bowman states, "Rules of development are the same for all children, but social contexts shape children's develop-ment into different configurations" (1994, 220). Early childhood teachers need to understand the influence of sociocultural contexts on learning, recognize children's developing competence, and accept a variety of ways for chil-dren to express their developmental achievements (Vygotsky 1978; Wertsch 1985; Forman, Minick, & Stone 1993; New 1993, 1994; Bowman & Stott 1994; Mallory & New 1994a; Phillips 1994; Bruner 1996; Wardle 1996).

Teachers should learn about the culture of the majority of the children they serve if that culture differs from their own. However, recognizing that development and learning are influenced by social and cultural contexts does not require teachers to understand all the nuances of every cultural group they may encounter in their practice; this would be an impossible task. Rather, this fundamental recognition sensitizes teachers to the need to acknowledge how their own cultural experience shapes their perspective and to realize that multiple perspectives, in addition to their own, must be considered in decisions about children's development and learning.

Children are capable of learning to function in more than one cultural context simultaneously. However, if teachers set low expectations for chil-dren based on their home culture and language, children cannot develop and learn optimally. Education should be an additive process. For example, children whose primary language is not English should be able to learn English without being forced to give up their home language (NAEYC 1996a). Likewise, children who speak only English benefit from learning another language. The goal is that all children learn to function well in the society as a whole and move comfortably among groups of people who come from both similar and dissimilar backgrounds.

7. Children are active learners, drawing on direct physical and social experience as well as culturally transmitted knowledge to con-struct their own understandings of the world around them.

Children contribute to their own development and learning as they strive to make meaning out of their daily experiences in the home, the early child-hood program, and the community. Principles of developmentally appropri-ate practice are based on several prominent theories that view intellectual development from a constructivist, interactive perspective (Dewey 1916; Piaget 1952; Vygotsky 1978; DeVries & Kohlberg 1990; Rogoff 1990; Gardner 1991; Kamii & Ewing 1996).

From birth, children are actively engaged in constructing their own under-standings from their experiences, and these understandings are mediated by and clearly linked to the sociocultural context. Young children actively learn from observing and participating with other children and adults, including parents and teachers. Children need to form their own hypotheses and keep trying them out through social interaction, physical manipulation, and their own thought processes—observing what happens, reflecting on their findings, asking questions, and formulating answers. When objects, events, and other people challenge the working model that the child has mentally constructed, the child is forced to adjust the model or alter the mental structures to account for the new information. Throughout early childhood, the child in processing new experiences continually reshapes, expands, and reorganizes mental structures (Piaget 1952; Vygotsky 1978; Case & Okamoto 1996). When teachers and other adults use various strategies to encourage children to reflect on their experiences by planning beforehand and "revisiting" afterward, the knowledge and understanding gained from the experience is deepened (Copple, Sigel, & Saunders 1984; Edwards, Gandini, & Forman 1993; Stremmel & Fu 1993; Hohmann & Weikart 1995).

In the statement of this principle, the term "physical and social experience" is used in the broadest sense to include children's exposure to physical knowledge, learned through firsthand experience of using objects (observing that a ball thrown in the air falls down), and social knowledge, including the vast body of culturally acquired and transmitted knowledge that children need to function in the world. For example, children progressively construct their own understanding of various symbols, but the symbols they use (such as the alphabet or numerical system) are the ones used within their culture and transmitted to them by adults.

In recent years, discussions of cognitive development have at times become polarized (see Seifert 1993). Piaget's theory stressed that development of certain cognitive structures was a necessary prerequisite to learning (i.e., development precedes learning), while other research has demonstrated that instruction in specific concepts or strategies can facilitate development of more mature cognitive structures (learning precedes development) (Vygotsky 1978; Gelman & Baillargeon 1983). Current attempts to resolve this apparent dichotomy (Seifert 1993; Sameroff & McDonough 1994; Case & Okamoto 1996) acknowledge that essentially both theoretical perspectives are correct in explaining aspects of cognitive development during early childhood. Strategic teaching, of course, can enhance children's learning. Yet, direct instruction may be totally ineffective; it fails when it is not attuned to the cognitive capacities and knowledge of the child at that point in development.

8. Development and learning result from interaction of biological maturation and the environment, which includes both the physical and social worlds that children live in.

The simplest way to express this principle is that human beings are products of both heredity and environment and these forces are interrelated. Behaviorists focus on the environmental influences that determine learning, while maturationists emphasize the unfolding of predetermined, hereditary characteristics. Each perspective is true to some extent, and yet neither perspective is sufficient to explain learning or development. More often today, development is viewed as the result of an interactive, transactional process between the growing, changing individual and his or her experiences in the social and physical worlds (Scarr & McCartney 1983; Plomin 1994a, b). For example, a child's genetic makeup may predict healthy growth, but inadequate nutrition in the early years of life may keep this potential from being fulfilled. Or a severe disability, whether inherited or environmentally caused, may be ameliorated through systematic, appropriate intervention. Likewise, a child's inherited temperament—whether a predisposition to be wary or outgoing—shapes and is shaped by how other children and adults communicate with that child.

9. **Play is an important vehicle for children's social, emotional, and cognitive development, as well as a reflection of their development.**

Understanding that children are active constructors of knowledge and that development and learning are the result of interactive processes, early childhood teachers recognize that children's play is a highly supportive context for these developing processes (Piaget 1952; Fein 1981; Bergen 1988; Smilansky & Shefatya 1990; Fromberg 1992; Berk & Winsler 1995). Play gives children opportunities to understand the world, interact with others in social ways, express and control emotions, and develop their symbolic capabilities. Children's play gives adults insights into children's development and opportunities to support the development of new strategies. Vygotsky (1978) believed that play leads development, with written language growing out of oral language through the vehicle of symbolic play that promotes the development of symbolic representation abilities. Play provides a context for children to practice newly acquired skills and also to function on the edge of their developing capacities to take on new social roles, attempt novel or challenging tasks, and solve complex problems that they would not (or could not) otherwise do (Mallory & New 1994b).

Research demonstrates the importance of sociodramatic play as a tool for learning curriculum content with 3- through 6-year-old children. When teachers provide a thematic organization for play; offer appropriate props, space, and time; and become involved in the play by extending and elaborating on children's ideas, children's language and literacy skills can be enhanced (Levy, Schaefer, & Phelps 1986; Schrader 1989, 1990; Morrow 1990; Pramling 1991; Levy, Wolfgang, & Koorland 1992).

In addition to supporting cognitive development, play serves important functions in children's physical, emotional, and social development (Herron & Sutton-Smith 1971). Children express and represent their ideas, thoughts, and feelings when engaged in symbolic play. During play a child can learn to deal with emotions, to interact with others, to resolve conflicts, and to gain a sense of competence—all in the safety that only play affords. Through play, children also can develop their imaginations and creativity. Therefore, child-initiated, teacher-supported play is an essential component of developmentally appropriate practice (Fein & Rivkin 1986).

10. Development advances when children have opportunities to practice newly acquired skills as well as when they experience a challenge just beyond the level of their present mastery.

Research demonstrates that children need to be able to successfully negotiate learning tasks most of the time if they are to maintain motivation and persistence (Lary 1990; Brophy 1992). Confronted by repeated failure, most children will simply stop trying. So most of the time, teachers should give young children tasks that with effort they can accomplish and present them with content that is accessible at their level of understanding. At the same time, children continually gravitate to situations and stimuli that give them the chance to work at their "growing edge" (Berk & Winsler 1995; Bodrova & Leong 1996). Moreover, in a task just beyond the child's independent reach, the adult and more-competent peers contribute significantly to development by providing the supportive "scaffolding" that allows the child to take the next step.

Development and learning are dynamic processes requiring that adults understand the continuum, observe children closely to match curriculum and teaching to children's emerging competencies, needs, and interests, and then help children move forward by targeting educational experiences to the edge of children's changing capacities so as to challenge but not frustrate them. Human beings, especially children, are highly motivated to understand what they almost, but not quite, comprehend and to master what they can almost, but not quite, do (White 1965; Vygotsky 1978). The principle of learning is that children can do things first in a supportive context and then later independently and in a variety of contexts. Rogoff (1990) describes the process of adult-assisted learning as "guided participation" to emphasize that children actively collaborate with others to move to more complex levels of understanding and skill.

11. Children demonstrate different modes of knowing and learning and different ways of representing what they know.

For some time, learning theorists and developmental psychologists have recognized that human beings come to understand the world in many ways and that individuals tend to have preferred or stronger modes of learning. Studies of differences in learning modalities have contrasted visual, auditory, or tactile learners. Other work has identified learners as field-dependent or independent (Witkin 1962). Gardner (1983) expanded on this concept by theorizing that human beings possess at least seven "intelligences." In addition to having the ones traditionally emphasized in schools, linguistic and logical-mathematical, individuals are more or less proficient in at least these other areas: musical, spatial, bodily-kinesthetic, intrapersonal, and interpersonal.

Malaguzzi (1993) used the metaphor of "100 languages" to describe the diverse modalities through which children come to understand the world and represent their knowledge. The processes of representing their understanding can with the assistance of teachers help children deepen, improve, and expand their understanding (Copple, Sigel, & Saunders 1984; Forman 1994; Katz 1995). The principle of diverse modalities implies that teachers should provide not only opportunities for individual children to use their preferred modes of learning to capitalize on their strengths (Hale-Benson 1986) but also opportunities to help children develop in the modes or intelligences in which they may not be as strong.

12. **Children develop and learn best in the context of a community where they are safe and valued, their physical needs are met, and they feel psychologically secure.**

Maslow (1954) conceptualized a hierarchy of needs in which learning was not considered possible unless physical and psychological needs for safety and security were first met. Because children's physical health and safety too often are threatened today, programs for young children must not only provide adequate health, safety, and nutrition but may also need to ensure more comprehensive services, such as physical, dental, and mental health and social services (NASBE 1991; U.S. Department of Health & Human Services 1996). In addition, children's development in all areas is influenced by their ability to establish and maintain a limited number of positive, consistent primary relationships with adults and other children (Bowlby 1969; Stern 1985; Garbarino et al. 1992). These primary relationships begin in the family but extend over time to include children's teachers and members of the community; therefore, practices that are developmentally appropriate address children's physical, social, and emotional needs as well as their intellectual development.

GUIDELINES FOR DECISIONS ABOUT DEVELOPMENTALLY APPROPRIATE PRACTICE

A linear listing of principles of child development and learning, such as the above, cannot do justice to the complexity of the phenomena that it attempts to describe and explain. Just as all domains of development and learning are interrelated, so, too, there are relationships among the principles. Similarly, the following guidelines for practice do not match up one-to-one with the principles. Instead, early childhood professionals draw on all these fundamental ideas (as well as many others) when making decisions about their practice.

An understanding of the nature of development and learning during the early childhood years, from birth through age 8, generates guidelines that inform the practices of early childhood educators. Developmentally appropriate practice requires that teachers integrate the many dimensions of their knowledge base. They must know about child development and the implications of this knowledge for how to teach, the content of the curriculum—what to teach and when—how to assess what children have learned, and how to adapt curriculum and instruction to children's individual strengths, needs, and interests. Further, they must know the particular children they teach and their families and be knowledgeable as well about the social and cultural context.

The following guidelines address five interrelated dimensions of early childhood professional practice: creating a caring community of learners, teaching to enhance development and learning, constructing appropriate curriculum, assessing children's development and learning, and establishing reciprocal relationships with families. (The word *teacher* is used to refer to any adult responsible for a group of children in any early childhood program, including infant/toddler caregivers, family child care providers, and specialists in other disciplines who fulfill the role of teacher.)

Examples of appropriate and inappropriate practice in relation to each of these dimensions are given for infants and toddlers (Part 3, pp. 72–90), children 3 through 5 (Part 4, pp. 123–35), and children 6 through 8 (Part 5, pp. 161–78). In the references at the end of each part, readers will be able to find fuller discussion of the points summarized here and strategies for implementation.

1. CREATING A CARING COMMUNITY OF LEARNERS

Developmentally appropriate practices occur within a context that supports the development of relationships between adults and children, among children, among teachers, and between teachers and families. Such a community reflects what is known about the social construction of knowledge and the importance of establishing a caring, inclusive community in which all children can develop and learn.

A. The early childhood setting functions as a community of learners in which all participants consider and contribute to each other's well-being and learning.

B. Consistent, positive relationships with a limited number of adults and other children are a fundamental determinant of healthy human development and provide the context for children to learn about themselves and their world and also how to develop positive, constructive relationships with other people. The early childhood classroom is a community in which each child is valued. Children learn to respect and acknowledge differences in abilities and talents and to value each person for his or her strengths.

C. Social relationships are an important context for learning. Each child has strengths or interests that contribute to the overall functioning of the group. When children have opportunities to play together, work on projects in small groups, and talk with other children and adults, their own development and learning are enhanced. Interacting with other children in small groups provides a context for children to operate on the edge of their developing capacities. The learning environment enables children to construct understanding through interactions with adults and other children.

D. The learning environment is designed to protect children's health and safety and is supportive of children's physiological needs for activity, sensory stimulation, fresh air, rest, and nourishment. The program provides a balance of rest and active movement for children throughout the program day. Outdoor experiences are provided for children of all ages. The program protects children's psychological safety; that is, children feel secure, relaxed, and comfortable rather than disengaged, frightened, worried, or stressed.

E. Children experience an organized environment and an orderly routine that provides an overall structure in which learning takes place; the environment is dynamic and changing but predictable and comprehensible from a child's point of view. The learning environment provides a variety of materials and opportunities for children to have firsthand, meaningful experiences.

2. TEACHING TO ENHANCE DEVELOPMENT AND LEARNING

Adults are responsible for ensuring children's healthy development and learning. From birth, relationships with adults are critical determinants of children's healthy social and emotional development and serve as well as mediators of language and intellectual development. At the same time, children are active constructors of their own understanding, who benefit from initiating and regulating their own learning activities and interacting with peers. Therefore, early childhood teachers strive to achieve an optimal balance between children's self-initiated learning and adult guidance or support.

Teachers accept responsibility for actively supporting children's development and provide occasions for children to acquire important knowledge and skills. Teachers use their knowledge of child development and learning to identify the range of activities, materials, and learning experiences that are appropriate for a group or individual child. This knowledge is used in conjunction with knowledge of the context and understanding about individual children's growth patterns, strengths, needs, interests, and experiences to design the curriculum and learning environment and guide teachers' interactions with children. The following guidelines describe aspects of the teachers' role in making decisions about practice:

A. Teachers respect, value, and accept children and treat them with dignity at all times.

B. Teachers make it a priority to know each child well.

(1) Teachers establish positive, personal relationships with children to foster the child's development and keep informed about the child's needs and potentials. Teachers listen to children and adapt their responses to children's differing needs, interests, styles, and abilities.

(2) Teachers continually observe children's spontaneous play and interaction with the physical environment and with other children to learn about their interests, abilities, and developmental progress. On the basis of this information, teachers plan experiences that enhance children's learning and development.

(3) Understanding that children develop and learn in the context of their families and communities, teachers establish relationships with families that increase their knowledge of children's lives outside the classroom and their awareness of the perspectives and priorities of those individuals most significant in the child's life.

(4) Teachers are alert to signs of undue stress and traumatic events in children's lives and aware of effective strategies to reduce stress and support the development of resilience.

(5) Teachers are responsible at all times for all children under their supervision and plan for children's increasing development of self-regulation abilities.

C. Teachers create an intellectually engaging, responsive environment to promote each child's learning and development.

(1) Teachers use their knowledge about children in general and the particular children in the group as well as their familiarity with what children need to learn and develop in each curriculum area to organize the environment and plan curriculum and teaching strategies.

(2) Teachers provide children with a rich variety of experiences, projects, materials, problems, and ideas to explore and investigate, ensuring that these are worthy of children's attention.

(3) Teachers provide children with opportunities to make meaningful choices and time to explore through active involvement. Teachers offer children the choice to participate in a small-group or a solitary activity, assist and guide children who are not yet able to use and enjoy child-choice activity periods, and provide opportunities for practice of skills as a self-chosen activity.

(4) Teachers organize the daily and weekly schedule and allocate time so as to provide children with extended blocks of time in which to engage in play, projects, and/or study in integrated curriculum.

D. Teachers make plans to enable children to attain key curriculum goals across various disciplines, such as language arts, mathematics, social studies, science, art, music, physical education, and health (see "Constructing appropriate curriculum," pp. 20–21).

(1) Teachers incorporate a wide variety of experiences, materials and equipment, and teaching strategies in constructing curriculum to accommodate a broad range of children's individual differences in prior experiences, maturation rates, styles of learning, needs, and interests.

(2) Teachers bring each child's home culture and language into the shared culture of the school so that the unique contributions of each group are recognized and valued by others.

(3) Teachers are prepared to meet identified special needs of individual children, including children with disabilities and those who exhibit unusual interests and skills. Teachers use all the strategies identified here, consult with appropriate specialists, and see that the child gets the specialized services he or she requires.

E. Teachers foster children's collaboration with peers on interesting, important enterprises.

(1) Teachers promote children's productive collaboration without taking over to the extent that children lose interest.

(2) Teachers use a variety of ways of flexibly grouping children for the purposes of instruction, supporting collaboration among children, and building a sense of community. At various times, children have opportunities to work individually, in small groups, and with the whole group.

F. Teachers develop, refine, and use a wide repertoire of teaching strategies to enhance children's learning and development.

(1) To help children develop their initiative, teachers encourage them to choose and plan their own learning activities.

(2) Teachers pose problems, ask questions, and make comments and suggestions that stimulate children's thinking and extend their learning.

(3) Teachers extend the range of children's interests and the scope of their thought through presenting novel experiences and introducing stimulating ideas, problems, experiences, or hypotheses.

(4) To sustain an individual child's effort or engagement in purposeful activities, teachers select from a range of strategies, including but not limited to modeling, demonstrating specific skills, and providing information, focused attention, physical proximity, verbal encouragement, reinforcement and other behavioral procedures, as well as additional structure and modification of equipment or schedules as needed.

(5) Teachers coach and/or directly guide children in the acquisition of specific skills as needed.

(6) Teachers calibrate the complexity and challenge of activities to suit children's level of skill and knowledge, increasing the challenge as children gain competence and understanding.

(7) Teachers provide cues and other forms of "scaffolding" that enable the child to succeed in a task that is just beyond his or her ability to complete alone.

(8) To strengthen children's sense of competence and confidence as learners, motivation to persist, and willingness to take risks, teachers provide experiences for children to be genuinely successful and to be challenged.

(9) To enhance children's conceptual understanding, teachers use various strategies that encourage children to reflect on and "revisit" their learning experiences.

G. Teachers facilitate the development of responsibility and self-regulation in children.

(1) Teachers set clear, consistent, and fair limits for children's behavior and hold children accountable to standards of acceptable behavior. To the extent that children are able, teachers engage them in developing rules and procedures for behavior of class members.

(2) Teachers redirect children to more acceptable behavior or activity or use children's mistakes as learning opportunities, patiently reminding children of rules and their rationale as needed.

(3) Teachers listen and acknowledge children's feelings and frustrations, respond with respect, guide children to resolve conflicts, and model skills that help children to solve their own problems.

3. CONSTRUCTING APPROPRIATE CURRICULUM

The content of the early childhood curriculum is determined by many factors, including the subject matter of the disciplines, social or cultural values, and parental input. In developmentally appropriate programs, decisions about curriculum content also take into consideration the age and experience of the learners. Achieving success for all children depends, among other essentials, on providing a challenging, interesting, developmentally appropriate curriculum. NAEYC does not endorse specific curricula. However, one purpose of these guidelines is as a framework for making decisions about developing curriculum or selecting a curriculum model. Teachers who use a validated curriculum model benefit from the evidence of its effectiveness and the accumulated wisdom and experience of others.

In some respects, the curriculum strategies of many teachers today do not demand enough of children and in other ways demand too much of the wrong thing. On the one hand, narrowing the curriculum to those basic skills that can be easily measured on multiple-choice tests diminishes the intellectual challenge for many children. Such intellectually impoverished curriculum underestimates the true competence of children, which has been demonstrated to be much higher than is often assumed (Gelman & Baillargeon 1983; Gelman & Meck 1983; Edwards, Gandini, & Forman 1993; Resnick 1996). Watered-down, oversimplified curriculum leaves many children unchallenged, bored, uninterested, or unmotivated. In such situations, children's experiences are marked by a great many missed opportunities for learning.

On the other hand, curriculum expectations in the early years of schooling sometimes are not appropriate for the age groups served. When next-grade expectations of mastery of basic skills are routinely pushed down to the previous grade and whole group and teacher-led instruction is the dominant teaching strategy, children who cannot sit still and attend to teacher lectures or who are bored and unchallenged or frustrated by doing workbook pages for long periods of time are mislabeled as immature, disruptive, or unready for school (Shepard & Smith 1988). Constructing appropriate curriculum requires attention to at least the following guidelines for practice:

A. Developmentally appropriate curriculum provides for all areas of a child's development: physical, emotional, social, linguistic, aesthetic, and cognitive.

B. Curriculum includes a broad range of content across disciplines that is socially relevant, intellectually engaging, and personally meaningful to children.

C. Curriculum builds upon what children already know and are able to do (activating prior knowledge) to consolidate their learning and to foster their acquisition of new concepts and skills.

D. Effective curriculum plans frequently integrate across traditional subject-matter divisions to help children make meaningful connections and provide opportunities for rich conceptual development; focusing on one subject is also a valid strategy at times.

E. Curriculum promotes the development of knowledge and understanding, processes and skills, as well as the dispositions to use and apply skills and to go on learning.

F. Curriculum content has intellectual integrity, reflecting the key concepts and tools of inquiry of recognized disciplines in ways that are accessible and achievable for young children, ages 3 through 8 (e.g., Bredekamp & Rosegrant 1992, 1995). Children directly participate in study of the disciplines, for instance, by conducting scientific experiments, writing, performing, solving mathematical problems, collecting and analyzing data, collecting oral history, and performing other roles of experts in the disciplines.

G. Curriculum provides opportunities to support children's home culture and language while also developing all children's abilities to participate in the shared culture of the program and the community.

H. Curriculum goals are realistic and attainable for most children in the designated age range for which they are designed.

I. When used, technology is physically and philosophically integrated in the classroom curriculum and teaching. (See "NAEYC Position Statement: Technology and Young Children—Ages Three through Eight" [NAEYC 1996b].)

4. ASSESSING CHILDREN'S LEARNING AND DEVELOPMENT

Assessment of individual children's development and learning is essential for planning and implementing appropriate curriculum. In developmentally appropriate programs, assessment and curriculum are integrated, with teachers continually engaging in observational assessment for the purpose of improving teaching and learning.

Accurate assessment of young children is difficult because their development and learning are rapid, uneven, episodic, and embedded within specific cultural and linguistic contexts. Too often, inaccurate and inappropriate assessment measures have been used to label, track, or otherwise harm young children. Developmentally appropriate assessment practices are based on the following guidelines:

A. Assessment of young children's progress and achievements is ongoing, strategic, and purposeful. The results of assessment are used to benefit children—in adapting curriculum and teaching to meet the developmental and learning needs of children, communicating with the child's family, and evaluating the program's effectiveness for the purpose of improving the program.

B. The content of assessments reflects progress toward important learning and developmental goals. The program has a systematic plan for collecting and using assessment information that is integrated with curriculum planning.

C. The methods of assessment are appropriate to the age and experiences of young children. Therefore, assessment of young children relies heavily on the results of observations of children's development, descriptive data, collections of representative work by children, and demonstrated performance during authentic, not contrived, activities. Input from families as well as children's evaluations of their own work are part of the overall assessment strategy.

D. Assessments are tailored to a specific purpose and used only for the purpose for which they have been demonstrated to produce reliable, valid information.

E. Decisions that have a major impact on children, such as enrollment or placement, are never made on the basis of a single developmental assessment or screening device but are based on multiple sources of relevant information, particularly observations by teachers and parents.

F. To identify children who have special learning or developmental needs and to plan appropriate curriculum and teaching for them, developmental assessments and observations are used.

G. Assessment recognizes individual variation in learners and allows for differences in styles and rates of learning. Assessment takes into consideration such factors as the child's facility in English, stage of language acquisition, and whether the child has had the time and opportunity to develop proficiency in his or her home language as well as in English.

H. Assessment legitimately addresses not only what children can do independently but what they can do with assistance from other children or adults. Teachers study children as individuals as well as in relationship to groups by documenting group projects and other collaborative work.

(For a more complete discussion of principles of appropriate assessment, see the position statement *Guidelines for Appropriate Curriculum Content and Assessment for Children Ages 3 through 8* [NAEYC & NAECS/SDE 1992]; see also Shepard 1994.)

5. ESTABLISHING RECIPROCAL RELATIONSHIPS WITH FAMILIES

Developmentally appropriate practices derive from deep knowledge of individual children and the context within which they develop and learn. The younger the child, the more necessary it is for professionals to acquire this knowledge through relationships with children's families. The traditional approach to families has been a parent education orientation in which the professionals see themselves as knowing what is best for children and view parents as needing to be educated. There is also the limited view of parent involvement that sees PTA membership as the primary goal. These approaches do not adequately convey the complexity of the partnership between teachers and parents that is a fundamental element of good practice (Powell 1994).

When the parent education approach is criticized in favor of a more family-centered approach, this shift may be misunderstood to mean that parents dictate all program content and professionals abdicate responsibility, doing whatever parents want regardless of whether professionals agree that it is in children's best interest. Either of these extremes oversimplifies the importance of relationships with families and fails to provide the kind of environment in which parents and professionals work together to achieve shared goals for children; such programs with this focus are characterized by at least the following guidelines for practice:

A. Reciprocal relationships between teachers and families require mutual respect, cooperation, shared responsibility, and negotiation of conflicts toward achievement of shared goals.

B. Early childhood teachers work in collaborative partnerships with families, establishing and maintaining regular, frequent two-way communication with children's parents.

C. Parents are welcome in the program and participate in decisions about their children's care and education. Parents observe and participate and serve in decisionmaking roles in the program.

D. Teachers acknowledge parents' choices and goals for children and respond with sensitivity and respect to parents' preferences and concerns without abdicating professional responsibility to children.

E. Teachers and parents share their knowledge of the child and understanding of children's development and learning as part of day-to-day communication and planned conferences. Teachers support families in ways that maximally promote family decisionmaking capabilities and competence.

F. To ensure more accurate and complete information, the program involves families in assessing and planning for individual children.

G. The program links families with a range of services, based on identified resources, priorities, and concerns.

H. Teachers, parents, programs, social service and health agencies, and consultants who may have educational responsibility for the child at different times should, with family participation, share developmental information about children as they pass from one level or program to another.

 ## MOVING FROM EITHER/OR TO BOTH/AND THINKING IN EARLY CHILDHOOD PRACTICE

Some critical reactions to NAEYC's (1987) position statement on developmentally appropriate practice reflect a recurring tendency in the American discourse on education: the polarizing into *either/or* choices of many questions that are more fruitfully seen as *both/ands*. For example, heated debates have broken out about whether children in the early grades should receive whole-language or phonics instruction, when, in fact, the two approaches are quite compatible and most effective in combination.

It is true that there are practices that are clearly inappropriate for early childhood professionals—use of physical punishment or disparaging verbal comments about children, discriminating against children or their families, and many other examples that could be cited (see Parts 3, 4, and 5 for examples relevant to different age groups). However, most questions about practice require more complex responses. It is not that children need food **or** water; they need both.

To illustrate the many ways that early childhood practice draws on *both/and* thinking and to convey some of the complexity and interrelationship among the principles that guide our practice, we offer the following statements as **examples:**

■ Children construct their own understanding of concepts, **and** they benefit from instruction by more competent peers and adults.

■ Children benefit from opportunities to see connections across disciplines through integration of curriculum **and** from opportunities to engage in in-depth study within a content area.

■ Children benefit from predictable structure and orderly routine in the learning environment **and** from the teacher's flexibility and spontaneity in responding to their emerging ideas, needs, and interests.

■ Children benefit from opportunities to make meaningful choices about what they will do and learn **and** from having a clear understanding of the boundaries within which choices are permissible.

■ Children benefit from situations that challenge them to work at the edge of their developing capacities **and** from ample opportunities to practice newly acquired skills and to acquire the disposition to persist.

■ Children benefit from opportunities to collaborate with their peers and acquire a sense of being part of a community **and** from being treated as individuals with their own strengths, interests, and needs.

■ Children need to develop a positive sense of their own self-identity **and** respect for other people whose perspectives and experiences may be different from their own.

■ Children have enormous capacities to learn and almost boundless curiosity about the world, **and** they have recognized, age-related limits on their cognitive and linguistic capacities.

■ Children benefit from engaging in self-initiated, spontaneous play **and** from teacher-planned and -structured activities, projects, and experiences.

The above list is not exhaustive. Many more examples could be cited to convey the interrelationships among the principles of child development and learning or among the guidelines for early childhood practice.

POLICIES ESSENTIAL FOR ACHIEVING DEVELOPMENTALLY APPROPRIATE EARLY CHILDHOOD PROGRAMS

Early childhood professionals working in diverse situations with varying levels of funding and resources are responsible for implementing practices that are developmentally appropriate for the children they serve. Regardless of the resources available, professionals have an ethical responsibility to practice, to the best of their ability, according to the standards of their profession. Nevertheless, the kinds of practices advocated in this position statement are more likely to be implemented within an infrastructure of supportive policies and resources. NAEYC strongly recommends that policymaking groups at the state and local levels consider the following when implementing early childhood programs:

1. A comprehensive professional preparation and development system is in place to ensure that early childhood programs are staffed with qualified personnel (NAEYC 1994).

   ■ A system exists for early childhood professionals to acquire the knowledge and practical skills needed to practice through college-level specialized preparation in early childhood education/child development.

▓ Teachers in early childhood programs are encouraged and supported to obtain and maintain, through study and participation in inservice training, current knowledge of child development and learning and its application to early childhood practice.

▓ Specialists in early childhood special education are available to provide assistance and consultation in meeting the individual needs of children in the program.

▓ In addition to management and supervision skills, administrators of early childhood programs have appropriate professional qualifications, including training specific to the education and development of young children, and they provide teachers time and opportunities to work collaboratively with colleagues and parents.

2. Funding is provided to ensure adequate staffing of early childhood programs and fair staff compensation that promotes continuity of relationships among adults and children (Willer 1990).

▓ Funding is adequate to limit the size of the groups and provide sufficient numbers of adults to ensure individualized and appropriate care and education. Even the most well-qualified teacher cannot individualize instruction and adequately supervise too large a group of young children. An acceptable adult-child ratio for 4- and 5-year-olds is two adults with no more than 20 children (Ruopp et al. 1979; Francis & Self 1982; Howes 1983; Taylor & Taylor 1989; Howes, Phillips, & Whitebook 1992; Cost, Quality, & Child Outcomes Study Team 1995; Howes, Smith, & Galinsky 1995). Younger children require much smaller groups. Group size and ratio of children to adults should increase gradually through the primary grades, but one teacher with no more than 18 children or two adults with no more than 25 children is optimum (Nye et al. 1992; Nye, Boyd-Zaharias, & Fulton 1994). Inclusion of children with disabilities may necessitate additional adults or smaller group size to ensure that all children's needs are met.

▓ Programs offer staff salaries and benefits commensurate with the skills and qualifications required for specific roles to ensure the provision of quality services and the effective recruitment and retention of qualified, competent staff. (See *Compensation Guidelines for Early Childhood Professionals* [NAEYC 1993].)

▓ Decisions related to how programs are staffed and how children are grouped result in increased opportunities for children to experience continuity of relationships with teachers and other children. Such strategies include but are not limited to multiage grouping and multiyear teacher-child relationships (Katz, Evangelou, & Hartman 1990; Zero to Three 1995; Burke 1996).

3. Resources and expertise are available to provide safe, stimulating learning environments with a sufficient number and variety of appropriate materials and equipment for the age group served (Bronson 1995; Kendrick, Kaufmann, & Messenger 1995).

4. Adequate systems for regulating and monitoring the quality of early childhood programs are in place (see position on licensing [NAEYC 1987]; accreditation criteria and procedures [NAEYC 1991]).

5. Community resources are available and used to support the comprehensive needs of children and families (Kagan 1991; NASBE 1991; Kagan et al. 1995; NCSL 1995).

6. When individual children do not make expected learning progress, neither grade retention nor social promotion are used; instead, initiatives such as more focused time, individualized instruction, tutoring, or other individual strategies are used to accelerate children's learning (Shepard & Smith 1989; Ross et al. 1995).

7. Early childhood programs use multiple indicators of progress in all development domains to evaluate the effect of the program on children's development and learning and regularly report children's progress to parents. Group-administered, standardized, multiple-choice achievement tests are not used before third grade, preferably before fourth grade. When such tests are used to demonstrate public accountability, a sampling method is used (see Shepard 1994).

References

Adams, G., & J. Sandfort. 1994. *First steps, promising futures: State prekindergarten initiatives in the early 1990s.* Washington, DC: Children's Defense Fund.

Alexander, K. L., & D. R. Entwisle. 1988. *Achievement in the first 2 years of school: Patterns and processes.* Monographs of the Society for Research in Child Development, vol. 53, no. 2, serial no. 218. Ann Arbor: University of Michigan.

Arnett, J. 1989. Caregivers in day-care centers: Does training matter? *Journal of Applied Developmental Psychology* 10 (4): 541–52.

Asher, S., S. Hymel, & P. Renshaw. 1984. Loneliness in children. *Child Development* 55: 1456–64.

Barnett, W. S. 1995. Long-term effects of early childhood programs on cognitive and school outcomes. *The Future of Children* 5 (3): 25–50.

Bergen, D. 1988. *Play as a medium for learning and development.* Portsmouth, NH: Heinemann.

Berk, L. E. 1996. *Infants and children: Prenatal through middle childhood.* 2d ed. Needham Heights, MA: Allyn & Bacon.

Berk, L., & A. Winsler. 1995. *Scaffolding children's learning: Vygotsky and early childhood education.* Washington, DC: NAEYC.

Berruetta-Clement, J. R., L. J. Schweinhart, W. S. Barnett, A. S. Epstein, & D. P. Weikart. 1984. *Changed lives: The effects of the Perry Preschool Program on youths through age 19.* Monographs of the High/Scope Educational Research Foundation, no. 8. Ypsilanti, MI: High/Scope Press.

Bodrova, E., & D. Leong. 1996. *Tools of the mind: The Vygotskian approach to early childhood education.* Englewood Cliffs, NJ: Merrill/Prentice Hall.

Bowlby, J. 1969. *Attachment and loss: Vol. 1. Attachment.* New York: Basic.

Bowman, B. 1994. The challenge of diversity. *Phi Delta Kappan* 76 (3): 218–25.

Bowman, B., & F. Stott. 1994. Understanding development in a cultural context: The challenge for teachers. In *Diversity and developmentally appropriate practices: Challenges for early childhood education,* eds. B. Mallory & R. New, 119–34. New York: Teachers College Press.

Bredekamp, S., ed. 1987. *Developmentally appropriate practice in early childhood programs serving children from birth through age 8.* Exp. ed. Washington, DC: NAEYC.

Bredekamp, S. 1993a. Reflections on Reggio Emilia. *Young Children* 49 (1): 13–17.

Bredekamp, S. 1993b. The relationship between early childhood education and early childhood special education: Healthy marriage or family feud? *Topics in Early Childhood Special Education* 13 (3): 258–73.

Bredekamp, S., & T. Rosegrant, eds. 1992. *Reaching potentials: Appropriate curriculum and assessment for young children, volume 1.* Washington, DC: NAEYC.

Bredekamp, S., & T. Rosegrant, eds. 1995. *Reaching potentials: Transforming early childhood curriculum and assessment, volume 2.* Washington, DC: NAEYC.

Bronfenbrenner, U. 1979. *The ecology of human development: Experiments by nature and design.* Cambridge, MA: Harvard University Press.

Bronfenbrenner, U. 1989. Ecological systems theory. In *Annals of child development,* Vol. 6, ed. R. Vasta, 187–251. Greenwich, CT: JAI Press.

Bronfenbrenner, U. 1993. The ecology of cognitive development: Research models and fugitive findings. In *Development in context,* eds. R. H. Wozniak & K. W. Fischer, 3–44. Hillsdale, NJ: Erlbaum.

Bronson, M. B. 1995. *The right stuff for children birth to 8: Selecting play materials to support development.* Washington, DC: NAEYC.

Brophy, J. 1992. Probing the subtleties of subject matter teaching. *Educational Leadership* 49 (7): 4–8.

Bruner, J. S. 1983. *Child's talk: Learning to use language.* New York: Norton.

Bruner, J. S. 1996. *The culture of education.* Cambridge, MA: Harvard University Press.

Bryant, D. M., R. Clifford, & E. S. Peisner. 1991. Best practices for beginners: Developmental appropriateness in kindergarten. *American Educational Research Journal* 28 (4): 783–803.

Burchinal, M., J. Robert, L. Nabo, & D. Bryant. 1996. Quality of center child care and infant cognitive and language development. *Child Development* 67 (2): 606–20.

Burke, D. 1996. Multi-year teacher/student relationships are a long-overdue arrangement. *Phi Delta Kappan* 77 (5): 360–61.

Caine, R., & G. Caine. 1991. *Making connections: Teaching and the human brain.* New York: Addison-Wesley.

Campbell, F., & C. Ramey. 1995. Cognitive and school outcomes for high-risk African-American students at middle adolescence: Positive effects of early intervention. *American Educational Research Journal* 32 (4): 743–72.

Carnegie Task Force on Learning in the Primary Grades. 1996. *Years of promise: A comprehensive learning strategy for America's children*. New York: Carnegie Corporation of New York.

Carta, J., I. Schwartz, J. Atwater, & S. McConnell. 1991. Developmentally appropriate practice: Appraising its usefulness for young children with disabilities. *Topics in Early Childhood Special Education* 11 (1): 1–20.

Case, R., & Y. Okamoto. 1996. *The role of central conceptual structures in the development of children's thought*. Monographs of the Society of Research in Child Development, vol. 61, no. 2, serial no. 246. Chicago: University of Chicago Press.

Charlesworth, R., C. H. Hart, D. C. Burts, & M. DeWolf. 1993. The LSU studies: Building a research base for developmentally appropriate practice. In *Perspectives on developmentally appropriate practice,* vol. 5 of *Advances in early education and day care,* ed. S. Reifel, 3–28. Greenwich, CT: JAI Press.

Chugani, H., M. E. Phelps, & J. C. Mazziotta. 1987. Positron emission tomography study of human brain functional development. *Annals of Neurology* 22 (4): 495.

Cohen, N., & K. Modigliani. 1994. The family-to-family project: Developing family child care providers. In *The early childhood career lattice: Perspectives on professional development,* eds. J. Johnson & J. B. McCracken, 106–10. Washington, DC: NAEYC.

Copple, C., I. E. Sigel, & R. Saunders. 1984. *Educating the young thinker: Classroom strategies for cognitive growth*. Hillsdale, NJ: Erlbaum.

Cost, Quality, & Child Outcomes Study Team. 1995. *Cost, quality, and child outcomes in child care centers, public report*. 2d ed. Denver: Economics Department, University of Colorado at Denver.

Dana Alliance for Brain Initiatives. 1996. *Delivering results: A progress report on brain research*. Washington, DC: Author.

DEC/CEC (Division for Early Childhood of the Council for Exceptional Children). 1994. Position on inclusion. *Young Children* 49 (5): 78.

DEC (Division for Early Childhood) Task Force on Recommended Practices. 1993. *DEC recommended practices: Indicators of quality in programs for infants and young children with special needs and their families*. Reston, VA: Council for Exceptional Children.

DEC/CEC & NAEYC (Division for Early Childhood of the Council for Exceptional Children & the National Association for the Education of Young Children). 1993. *Understanding the ADA—The Americans with Disabilities Act: Information for early childhood programs*. Pittsburgh, PA, & Washington, DC: Authors.

DeVries, R., & W. Kohlberg. 1990. *Constructivist early education: Overview and comparison with other programs*. Washington, DC: NAEYC.

Dewey, J. 1916. *Democracy and education: An introduction to the philosophy of education*. New York: Macmillan.

Durkin, D. 1987. A classroom-observation study of reading instruction in kindergarten. *Early Childhood Research Quarterly* 2 (3): 275–300.

Durkin, D. 1990. Reading instruction in kindergarten: A look at some issues through the lens of new basal reader materials. *Early Children Research Quarterly* 5 (3): 299–316.

Dweck, C. 1986. Motivational processes affecting learning. *American Psychologist* 41: 1030–48.

Dyson, A. H., & C. Genishi. 1993. Visions of children as language users: Language and language education in early childhood. In *Handbook of research on the education of young children,* ed. B. Spodek, 122–36. New York: Macmillan.

Edwards, C. P., & L. Gandini. 1989. Teachers' expectations about the timing of developmental skills: A cross-cultural study. *Young Children* 44 (4): 15–19.

Edwards, C., L. Gandini, & G. Forman, eds. 1993. *The hundred languages of children: The Reggio Emilia approach to early childhood education.* Norwood, NJ: Ablex.

Erikson, E. 1963. *Childhood and society.* New York: Norton.

Feeney, S., & K. Kipnis. 1992. *Code of ethical conduct & statement of commitment.* Washington, DC: NAEYC.

Fein, G. 1981. Pretend play: An integrative review. *Child Development* 52: 1095–118.

Fein, G., & M. Rivkin, eds. 1986. *The young child at play: Reviews of research.* Washington, DC: NAEYC.

Fenson, L., P. Dale, J. S. Reznick, E. Bates, D. Thal, & S. Pethick. 1994. *Variability in early communicative development.* Monographs of the Society for Research in Child Development, vol. 59, no. 2, serial no. 242. Chicago: University of Chicago Press.

Fernald, A. 1992. Human maternal vocalizations to infants as biologically relevant signals: An evolutionary perspective. In *The adapted mind: Evolutionary psychology and the generation of culture,* eds. J. H. Barkow, L. Cosmides, & J. Tooby, 391–428. New York: Oxford University Press.

Fields, T., W. Masi, S. Goldstein, S. Perry, & S. Parl. 1988. Infant day care facilities preschool social behavior. *Early Childhood Research Quarterly* 3 (4): 341–59.

Forman, G. 1994. Different media, different languages. In *Reflections on the Reggio Emilia approach,* eds. L. Katz & B. Cesarone, 37–46. Urbana, IL: ERIC Clearinghouse on EECE.

Forman, E. A., N. Minick, & C. A. Stone. 1993. *Contexts for learning: Sociocultural dynamics in children's development.* New York: Oxford University Press.

Francis, P., & P. Self. 1982. Imitative responsiveness of young children in day care and home settings: The importance of the child to caregiver ratio. *Child Study Journal* 12: 119–26

Frede, E. 1995. The role of program quality in producing early childhood program benefits. *The Future of Children,* 5 (3): 115–132.

Frede, E., & W. S. Barnett. 1992. Developmentally appropriate public school preschool: A study of implementation of the High/Scope curriculum and its effects on disadvantaged children's skills at first grade. *Early Childhood Research Quarterly* 7 (4): 483–99.

Fromberg, D. 1992. Play. In *The early childhood curriculum: A review of current research,* 2d ed., ed. C. Seefeldt, 35–74. New York: Teachers College Press.

Galinsky, E., C. Howes, S. Kontos, & M. Shinn. 1994. *The study of children in family child care and relative care: Highlights of findings.* New York: Families and Work Institute.

Gallahue, D. 1993. Motor development and movement skill acquisition in early childhood education. In *Handbook of research on the education of young children,* ed. B. Spodek, 24–41. New York: Macmillan.

Gallahue, D. 1995. Transforming physical education curriculum. In *Reaching potentials: Transforming early childhood curriculum and assessment, volume 2,* eds. S. Bredekamp & T. Rosegrant, 125–44. Washington, DC: NAEYC.

Garbarino, J., N. Dubrow, K. Kostelny, & C. Pardo. 1992. *Children in danger: Coping with the consequences of community violence.* San Francisco: Jossey-Bass.

Gardner, H. 1983. *Frames of mind: The theory of multiple intelligences.* New York: Basic.

Gardner, H. 1991. *The unschooled mind: How children think and how schools should teach.* New York: Basic.

Gelman, R., & R. Baillargeon. 1983. A review of some Piagetian concepts. In *Handbook of Child Psychology,* vol. 3, ed. P. H. Mussen, 167–230. New York: Wiley.

Gelman, R., & E. Meck. 1983. Preschoolers' counting: Principles before skill. *Cognition* 13: 343–59.

Hale-Benson, J. 1986. *Black children: Their roots, cultures, and learning styles.* Rev. ed. Baltimore: Johns Hopkins University Press.

Herron, R., & B. Sutton-Smith. 1971. *Child's play.* New York: Wiley.

Hiebert, E. H., & J. M. Papierz. 1990. The emergent literacy construct and kindergarten and readiness books of basal reading series. *Early childhood Research Quarterly* 5 (3): 317–34.

Hohmann, M., & D. Weikart. 1995. *Educating young children: Active learning practices for preschool and child care programs.* Ypsilanti, MI: High/Scope Educational Research Foundation.

Hollestelle, K. 1993. At the core: Entrepreneurial skills for family child care providers. In *The early childhood career lattice: Perspectives on professional development,* eds. J. Johnson & J. B. McCracken, 63–65. Washington, DC: NAEYC.

Howes, C. 1983. Caregiver behavior in center and family day care. *Journal of Applied Developmental Psychology* 4: 96–107. Howes, C. 1988. Relations between early child care and schooling. *Developmental Psychology* 24 (1): 53–57.

Howes, C., D. A. Phillips, M. Whitebook. 1992. Thresholds of quality: Implications for the social development of children in center-based child care. *Child Development* 63 (2): 449–60.

Howes, C., E. Smith, & E. Galinsky. 1995. *The Florida child care quality improvement study.* New York: Families and Work Institute.

Kagan, S. L. 1991. *United we stand: Collaboration for child care and early educaion services.* New York: Teachers College Press.

Kagan, S., S. Goffin, S. Golub, & E. Pritchard. 1995. *Toward systematic reform: Service integration for young children and their families.* Falls Church, VA: National Center for Service Integration.

Kamii, C., & J. K. Ewing. 1996. Basing teaching on Piaget's constructivism. *Childhood Education* 72 (5): 260–64.

Katz, L. 1995. *Talks with teachers of young children: A collection.* Norwood, NJ: Ablex.

Katz, L., & S. Chard. 1989. *Engaging children minds: The project approach.* Norwood, NJ: Ablex.

Katz, L., D. Evangelou, & J. Hartman. 1990. *The case for mixed-age grouping in early education.* Washington, DC: NAEYC.

Kendrick, A., R. Kaufmann, & K. Messenger, eds. 1995. *Healthy young children: A manual for programs.* Washington, DC: NAEYC.

Kohn, A. 1993. *Punished by rewards.* Boston: Houghton Mifflin. Kostelnik, M.,
A. Soderman, & A. Whiren. 1993. *Developmentally appropriate programs in early
childhood education.* New York: Macmillan.

Kuhl, P. 1994. Learning and representation in speech and language. *Current
Opinion in Neurobiology* 4: 812–22.

Lary, R. T. 1990. Successful students. *Education Issues* 3 (2): 11–17.

Layzer, J. I., B. D. Goodson, & M. Moss. 1993. *Life in preschool: Volume one of an
observational study of early childhood programs for disadvantaged four-year-
olds.* Cambridge, MA: Abt Association.

Lazar, I., & R. Darlington. 1982. *Lasting effects of early education: A report from
the consortium for longitudinal studies.* Monographs of the Society for Research
in Child Development, vol. 47, nos. 2-3, serial no. 195. Chicago: University of
Chicago Press.

Lee, V. E., J. Brooks-Gunn, & E. Schuur. 1988. Does Head Start work? A 1-year
follow-up comparison of disadvantaged children attending Head Start, no preschool, and other preschool programs. *Developmental Psychology* 24 (2):
210–22.

Legters, N., & R. E. Slavin. 1992. Elementary students at risk: A status report. Paper
commissioned by the Carnegie Corporation of New York for meeting on ele-
mentary-school reform. 1–2 June.

Levy, A. K., L. Schaefer, & P. C. Phelps. 1986. Increasing preschool effectiveness:
Enhancing the language abilities of 3- and 4-year-old children through planned
sociodramatic play. *Early Childhood Research Quarterly* 1 (2): 133–40.

Levy, A. K., C. H. Wolfgang, & M. A. Koorland. 1992. Sociodramatic play as a method
for enhancing the language performance of kindergarten age students. *Early
Childhood Research Quarterly* 7 (2): 245–62.

Malaguzzi, L. 1993. History, ideas, and basic philosophy. In *The hundred languages
of children: The Reggio Emilia approach to early childhood education,* eds.
C. Edwards, L. Gandini, & G. Forman, 41–89. Norwood, NJ: Ablex.

Mallory, B. 1992. Is it always appropriate to be developmental? Convergent models
for early intervention practice. *Topics in Early Childhood Special Education* 11
(4): 1–12.

Mallory, B. 1994. Inclusive policy, practice, and theory for young children with
developmental differences. In *Diversity and developmentally appropriate practices: Challenges for early childhood education,* eds. B. Mallory & R. New,
44–61. New York: Teachers College Press.

Mallory, B. L., & R. S. New. 1994a. *Diversity and developmentally appropriate practices: Challenges for early childhood education.* New York: Teachers College
Press.

Mallory, B. L., & R. S. New. 1994b. Social constructivist theory and principles of
inclusion: Challenges for early childhood special education. *Journal of Special
Education* 28 (3): 322–37.

Marcon, R. A. 1992. Differential effects of three preschool models on inner-city
4-year-olds. *Early Childhood Research Quarterly* 7 (4): 517–30.

Maslow, A. 1954. *Motivation and personality.* New York: Harper & Row.

Miller, L. B., & R. P. Bizzell. 1984. Long-term effects of four preschool programs:
Ninth and tenth-grade results. *Child Development* 55 (4): 1570–87.

Mitchell, A., M. Seligson, & F. Marx. 1989. *Early childhood programs and the public
schools.* Dover, MA: Auburn House.

Morrow, L. M. 1990. Preparing the classroom environment to promote literacy during play. *Early Childhood Research Quarterly* 5 (4): 537–54.

NAEYC. 1987. *NAEYC position statement on licensing and other forms of regulation of early childhood programs in centers and family day care.* Washington, DC: Author.

NAEYC. 1991. *Accreditation criteria and procedures of the National Academy of Early Childhood Programs.* Rev. ed. Washington, DC: Author.

NAEYC. 1993. *Compensation guidelines for early childhood professionals.* Washington, DC: Author.

NAEYC. 1994. NAEYC position statement: A conceptual framework for early childhood professional development, adopted November 1993. *Young Children* 49 (3): 68–77.

NAEYC. 1996a. NAEYC position statement: Responding to linguistic and cultural diversity—Recommendations for effective early childhood education. *Young Children* 51 (2): 4–12.

NAEYC. 1996b. NAEYC position statement: Technology and young children—Ages three through eight. *Young Children* 51 (6): 11–16.

NAEYC & NAECS/SDE (National Association of Early Childhood Specialists in State Departments of Education). 1992. Guidelines for appropriate curriculum content and assessment in programs serving children ages 3 through 8. In *Reaching potentials: Appropriate curriculum and assessment for young children, volume 1,* eds. S. Bredekamp & T. Rosegrant, 9–27. Washington, DC: NAEYC.

NASBE (National Association of State Boards of Education). 1991. *Caring communities: Supporting young children and families.* Alexandria, VA: Author.

Natriello, G., E. McDill, & A. Pallas. 1990. *Schooling disadvantaged children: Racing against catastrophe.* New York: Teachers College Press.

NCES (National Center for Education Statistics). 1993. *The condition of education, 1993.* Washington, DC: U.S. Department of Education.

NCSL (National Conference of State Legislatures). 1995. *Early childhood care and education: An investment that works.* Denver: Author.

NEGP (National Education Goals Panel). 1991. *National education goals report: Building a nation of learners.* Washington, DC: Author.

New, R. 1993. Cultural variations on developmentally appropriate practice: Challenges to theory and practice. In *The hundred languages of children: The Reggio Emilia approach to early childhood education,* eds C. Edwards, L. Gandini, & G. Forman, 215–32. Norwood, NJ: Ablex.

New, R. 1994. Culture, child development, and developmentally appropriate practices: Teachers as collaborative researchers. In *Diversity and developmentally appropriate practices: Challenges for early childhood education,* eds. B. Mallory & R. New, 65–83. New York: Teachers College Press.

Nye, B. A., J. Boyd-Zaharias, & B. D. Fulton. 1994. *The lasting benefits study: A continuing analysis of the effect of small class size in kindergarten through third grade on student achievement test scores in subsequent grade levels—seventh grade (1992–93), technical report.* Nashville: Center of Excellence for Research in Basic Skills, Tennessee State University.

Nye, B. A., J. Boyd-Zaharias, B. D. Fulton, & M. P. Wallenhorst. 1992. Smaller classes really are better. *The American School Board Journal* 179 (5): 31–33.

Parker, J. G., & S. R. Asher. 1987. Peer relations and later personal adjustment: Are low-accepted children at risk? *Psychology Bulletin* 102 (3): 357–89.

Phillips, C. B. 1994. The movement of African-American children through socio-cultural contexts: A case of conflict resolution. In *Diversity and developmentally appropriate practices: Challenges for early childhood education,* eds. B. Mallory & R. New, 137–54. New York: Teachers College Press.

Phillips, D. A., K. McCartney, & S. Scarr. 1987. Child care quality and children's social development. *Developmental Psychology* 23 (4): 537–43.

Piaget, J. 1952. *The origins of intelligence in children.* New York: International Universities Press.

Plomin, R. 1994a. *Genetics and experience: The interplay between nature and nurture.* Thousand Oaks, CA: Sage.

Plomin, R. 1994b. Nature, nurture, and social development. *Social Development* 3: 37–53.

Powell, D. 1994. Parents, pluralism, and the NAEYC statement on developmentally appropriate practice. In *Diversity and developmentally appropriate practices: Challenges for early childhood education,* eds. B. Mallory & R. New, 166–82. New York: Teachers College Press.

Pramling, I. 1991. Learning about "the shop": An approach to learning in preschool. *Early Children Research Quarterly* 6 (2): 151–66.

Resnick, L. 1996. Schooling and the workplace: What relationship? In *Preparing youth for the 21st century,* 21–27. Washington, DC: Aspen Institute.

Rogoff, B. 1990. *Apprenticeship in thinking: Cognitive development in social context.* New York: Oxford University Press.

Rogoff, B., J. Mistry, A. Goncu, & C. Mosier. 1993. *Guided participation in cultural activity by toddlers and caregivers.* Monographs of the Society for Research in Child Development, vol. 58, no. 8, serial no. 236. Chicago: University of Chicago Press.

Ross, S. M., L. J. Smith, J. Casey, & R. E. Slavin. 1995. Increasing the academic success of disadvantaged children: An examination of alternative early intervention programs. *American Educational Research Journal* 32 (4): 773–800.

Ruopp, R., J. Travers, F. Glantz, & C. Coelen. 1979. *Children at the center: Final report of the National Day Care Study.* Cambridge, MA: ABT Associates.

Sameroff, A., & S. McDonough. 1994. Educational implications of developmental transitions: Revisiting the 5- to 7-year shift. *Phi Delta Kappan* 76 (3): 188–93.

Scarr, S., & K. McCartney. 1983. How people make their own environments: A theory of genotype—environment effects. *Child Development* 54: 425–35.

Schrader, C. T. 1989. Written language use within the context of young children's symbolic play. *Early Childhood Research Quarterly* 4 (2): 225–44.

Schrader, C. T. 1990. Symbolic play as a curricular tool for early literacy development. *Early Childhood Research Quarterly* 5 (1): 79–103.

Schweinhart, L. J., & D. P. Weikart. 1996. *Lasting differences: The High/Scope preschool curriculum comparison study through age 23.* Monographs of the High/Scope Educational Research Foundation, no 12. Ypsilanti, MI: High/Scope Press.

Schweinhart, L. J., H. V. Barnes, & D. P. Weikart. 1993. *Significant benefits: The High/Scope Perry Preschool Study through age 27.* Monographs of the High/Scope Educational Research Foundation, no. 10, Ypsilanti, MI: High/Scope Press.

Schweinhart, L. J., D. P. Weikart, & M. B. Larner. 1986. Child-initiated activities in early childhood programs may help prevent delinquency. *Early Childhood Research Quarterly* 1 (3): 303–12.

Seefeldt, C., ed. 1992. *The early childhood curriculum: A review of current research.* 2d ed. New York: Teachers College Press.

Seifert, K. 1993. Cognitive development and early childhood education. In *Handbook of research on the education of young children,* ed. B. Spodek, 9–23. New York: Macmillan.

Seppanen, P. S., D. Kaplan deVries, & M. Seligson. 1993. *National study of before and after school programs.* Portsmouth, NH: RMC Research Corp.

Shepard, L. 1994. The challenges of assessing young children appropriately. *Phi Delta Kappan* 76 (3): 206–13.

Shepard, L. A., & M. L. Smith. 1988. Escalating academic demand in kindergarten: Some nonsolutions. *Elementary School Journal* 89 (2): 135–46.

Shepard, L. A., & M. L. Smith. 1989. *Flunking grades: Research and policies on retention.* Bristol, PA: Taylor & Francis.

Slavin, R., N. Karweit, & N. Madden, eds. 1989. *Effective programs for students at-risk.* Boston: Allyn & Bacon.

Smilansky, S., & L. Shefatya. 1990. *Facilitating play: A medium for promoting cognitive, socioemotional, and academic development in young children.* Gaithersburg, MD: Psychosocial & Educational Publications.

Spodek, B., ed. 1993. *Handbook of research on the education of young children.* New York: Macmillan.

Sroufe, L. A., R. G. Cooper, & G. B. DeHart. 1992. *Child development: Its nature and course.* 2d ed. New York: Knopf.

Stern, D. 1985. *The psychological world of the human infant.* New York: Basic.

Stremmel, A. J., & V. R. Fu. 1993. Teaching in the zone of proximal development: Implications for responsive teaching practice. *Child and Youth Care Forum* 22 (5): 337–50.

Taylor, J. M., & W. S. Taylor. 1989. *Communicable diseases and young children in group settings.* Boston: Little, Brown.

Tobin, J., D. Wu, & D. Davidson. 1989. *Preschool in three cultures.* New Haven, CT: Yale University Press.

U.S. Department of Health & Human Services. 1996. *Head Start performance standards.* Washington, DC: Author.

Vandell, D. L., & M. A. Corasanti. 1990. Variations in early child care: Do they predict subsequent social, emotional, and cognitive differences? *Early Childhood Research Quarterly* 5 (4): 555–72.

Vandell, D. L., & C. D. Powers. 1983. Day care quality and children's freeplay activities. *American Journal of Orthopsychiatry* 53 (4): 493–500.

Vandell, D. L., V. K. Henderson, & K. S. Wilson. 1988. A longitudinal study of children with day-care experiences of varying quality. *Child Development* 59 (5): 1286–92.

Vygotsky, L. 1978. *Mind in society: The development of higher psychological processes.* Cambridge, MA: Harvard University Press.

Wardle, F. 1996. Proposal: An anti-bias and ecological model for multicultural education. *Childhood Education* 72 (3): 152–56.

Wertsch, J. 1985. *Culture, communication, and cognition: Vygotskian perspectives.* New York: Cambridge University Press.

White, S. H. 1965. Evidence for a hierarchical arrangement of learning processes. In *Advances in child development and behavior,* eds. L. P. Lipsitt & C. C. Spiker, 187–220. New York: Academic Press.

Whitebook, M., C. Howes, & D. Phillips. 1989. *The national child care staffing study: Who cares? Child care teachers and the quality of care in America.* Final report. Oakland, CA: Child Care Employee Project.

Wieder, S., & S. I. Greenspan. 1993. The emotional basis of learning. In *Handbook of research on the education of young children,* ed. B. Spodek, 77–104. New York: Macmillan.

Willer, B. 1990. *Reaching the full cost of quality in early childhood programs.* Washington, DC: NAEYC.

Willer, B., S. L. Hofferth, E. E. Kisker, P. Divine-Hawkins, E. Farquhar, & F. B. Glantz. 1991. *The demand and supply of child care in* 1990. Washington, DC: NAEYC.

Witkin, H. 1962. *Psychological differentiation: Studies of development.* New York: Wiley.

Wolery, M., & J. Wilbers, eds. 1994. *Including children with special needs in early childhood programs.* Washington, DC: NAEYC.

Wolery, M., P. Strain, & D. Bailey. 1992. Reaching potentials of children with special needs. In *Reaching Potentials: Appropriate curriculum and assessment for young children, volume 1,* eds. S. Bredekamp & T. Rosegrant, 92–111. Washington, DC: NAEYC.

Zero to Three: The National Center. 1995. *Caring for infants and toddlers in groups: Developmentally appropriate practice.* Arlington, VA: Author.

Appendix  D

Principles and Standards for School Mathematics

Overview: Standards for Prekindergarten–Grade 2

Number and Operations Standard for Grades Prekindergarten-2

	EXPECTATIONS
Instructional programs from pre-kindergarten through grade 12 school enable all students to—	In prekindergarten through grade 2, all students should—
Understand numbers, ways of representing numbers, relationships among numbers, and number systems	• count with, understand, and recognize "how many" in sets of objects; • use multiple models to develop initial understandings of place value and the base-ten number systems; • develop understanding of the relative position and magnitude of whole numbers and of ordinal and cardinal numbers and their connections; • develop a sense of whole numbers and represent and use them in flexible ways, including relating, composing, and decomposing numbers; • connect number words and numerals to the quantities they represent, using various physical models and representations; • understand and represent commonly used fractions, such as 1/4, 1/3, and 1/2.

Instructional programs from pre-kindergarten through grade 12 school enable all students to—	In prekindergarten through grade 2, all students should—
Understand meanings of operations and how they relate to one another	• understand various meanings of addition and subtraction of whole numbers and the relationship between the two operations; • understand the effects of adding and subtracting whole numbers; • understand situations that entail multiplication and division, such as equal groupings of objects and sharing equally.
Compute fluently and make reasonable estimates	• develop and use strategies for whole-number computations, with a focus on addition and subtraction; • develop fluency with basic number combinations for addition and subtraction; • use a variety of methods and tools to compute, including objects, mental computation, estimation, paper and pencil, and calculators.

Algebra Standard for Grades Prekindergarten–2

	EXPECTATIONS
Instructional programs for pre-kindergarten through grade 12 should enable all students to—	In prekindergarten through grade 2, all students should—
Understand patterns, relations, and functions	• sort, classify, and order by size, number, and other properties; • recognize, describe, and extend patterns such as sequences of sounds and shapes or simple numeric patterns and translate from one representation to another; • analyze how both repeating and growing patterns are generated.
Represent and analyze mathematical situations and structures using algebraic symbols	• illustrate general principles and properties of operations, such as commutativity, using specific numbers; • use concrete, pictorial, and verbal representations to develop an understanding of invented and conventional symbolic notations.

Instructional programs for pre-kindergarten through grade 12 should enable all students to—	In prekindergarten through grade 2, all students should—
Use mathematical models to represent and understand quantitative relationships	• model situations that involve the addition and subtraction of whole numbers, using objects, pictures, and symbols.
Analyze change in various contexts	• describe qualitative change, such as a student's growing taller; • describe quantitative change, such as a student's growing two inches in one year.

Measurement Standard for Grades Prekindergarten–2

EXPECTATIONS

Instructional programs from pre-kindergarten through grade 12 should enable all students to—	In prekindergarten through grade 2, all students should—
Understand measurable attributes of objects and the units, systems, and process of measurements	• recognize the attributes of length, volume, weight, area, and time; • compare and order objects according to these attributes; • understand how to measure using nonstandard and standard units; • select an appropriate unit and tool for the attribute being measured.
Apply appropriate techniques, tools, and formulas to determine measurements	• measure with multiple copies of units of the same size, such a paper clips laid end to end; • use repetition of a single unit to measure something larger than the unit, for instance, measuring the length of a room with a single meterstick; • use tools to measure; • develop common referents for measure to make comparisons and estimates.

Data Analysis and Probability Standard for Grades Prekindergarten–2

	EXPECTATIONS
Instructional programs from pre-kindergarten through grade 12 should enable all students to—	**In prekindergarten through grade 2, all students should—**
Formulate questions that can be addressed with data and collect, organize, and display relevant data to answer them	• pose questions and gather data about themselves and their surroundings; • sort and classify objects according to their attributes and organize data about the objects; • represent data using concrete objects, pictures, and graphs.
Select and use appropriate statistical methods to analyze data	• describe parts of the data and the set of data as a whole to determine what the data show.
Develop and evaluate inferences and predications that are based on data	• discuss events related to students' experiences as likely or unlikely
Understand and apply basic concepts of probability	

Index

Italic page numbers indicate material in figures or tables.